# How Industries Evolve

*Principles for Achieving and Sustaining Superior Performance*

## Anita M. McGahan

HARVARD BUSINESS SCHOOL PRESS

*Boston, Massachusetts*

Copyright 2004 Harvard Business School Publishing Corporation

All rights reserved

Printed in the United States of America

08 07 06 05 04     5 4 3 2 1

**Library of Congress Cataloging-in-Publication Data**

McGahan, Anita M. (Anita Marie)
How industries evolve : principles for achieving and sustaining superior
performance / Anita M. McGahan.
p. cm.
Includes bibliographical references.
ISBN 1-57851-840-7 (hardcover : alk. paper)
1. Organizational change. 2. Industries—Technological
innovations—Economic aspects. 3. Strategic planning. 4. Industrial
organization. 5. Organizational effectiveness. I. Title.
HD58.8.M3445 2004
658.4'012—dc22
2004011378

The paper used in this publication meets the requirements of the
American National Standard for Permanence of Paper for Publications
and Documents in Libraries and Archives Z39.48-1992.

*With gratitude to*
*Jenny Mansbridge*

# Contents

# Preface

THIS BOOK IS WRITTEN for executives who sense that their industry offers untapped opportunities and who are frustrated with their organization's track record on innovation. The substance of the book is a set of integrated tools for aligning strategy with the course of industry change to achieve and sustain superior performance. Consultants and investment analysts will find the book's diagnostic tools useful for evaluating the potential of a firm's strategy to deliver outstanding financial returns.

The ideas are grounded in a series of ten detailed statistical studies and more than twenty-five case studies that identified patterns in the performance of a broad cross-section of firms participating in a wide variety of industries across the economy.[1] The research was conducted over a period of ten years at the Harvard Business School, Stanford University, and Boston University.

The statistical and case research developed simultaneously in an iterative process with refinements in the precise questions under investigation. The statistical studies explored more than 700 industries for the magnitude and persistence of industry effects on business performance, which was measured both by profitability and investor returns. Emerging questions about industry evolution were tested against available theory and ultimately were used to develop hypotheses about how industries evolve. For example, the results of several of the statistical studies led to the hypothesis that architectural change in an industry could take more than one form, depending on whether the assets in the business could be redeployed into other businesses.

The hypotheses were tested and refined in case studies, which were written to explore the managerial problems confronting executives in different situations. Many of the cases are available through Harvard Business School Publishing and are used at leading business schools in

M.B.A. classes on industry structure, industry change, and competitive advantage. This book synthesizes the deductive findings of the statistical studies with the inductive findings of the case investigations. The result is a set of frameworks, supported by statistical regularities, that deals with the issues raised by the case research.

I have many colleagues to thank. Professor Michael E. Porter of the Harvard Business School and I collaborated on many of the statistical studies that are the antecedents of this book. I began to think systematically about industry structure nearly twenty years ago in Porter's path-breaking course, which was unique in business education because it built theory from observations about reality and because it offered grounded frameworks for analyzing competition.[2] I continue to benefit from Porter's broad and detailed ideas about the nature of competition through his Institute for Strategy and Competitiveness at Harvard, and am deeply grateful for our collaboration.

Thanks to Professor Richard Caves of Harvard's Economics Department and Business School. Caves's ideas on industrial structure, conduct, and performance were seminal in the fields of both industrial economics and management strategy, and have had an important influence on the development of the ideas put forth here.

The approach of this book was influenced by my experience at the Harvard Business School while teaching a course in 1999 called "Business History Foundations" under the leadership of Professor Thomas McCraw. The course introduced students to the challenges of business leadership through case discussions on pioneering companies in the United States, Japan, Germany, and the United Kingdom. Signature characteristics of the course that have permeated this book are a long view on industry evolution, a comparative methodology, and an emphasis on the institutions that shape the context for business decisions.

In the autumn of 2000, the London Business School's *Business Strategy Review* published "How Industries Evolve," an article in which I focused on the implications of industry evolution for corporate performance. I am grateful to editors Patrick Barwise and Mary Campbell and to the *Review* for the chance to air an early version of the ideas that are the foundation of this book.

Thanks to Hollis Heimbouch of the Harvard Business School Press, who has edited the book, and special thanks to Regina Maruca and Suzanne Rotondo for extensive developmental editing on every chapter. Their involvement was essential to this project. I am grateful to

Ann English, Ken Hatten, Charles Riordan, Kim Vaeth, and Brian Waldman for providing detailed comments on major sections of the book. Additional thanks to Rotondo for persuading me to take on the project in the first place. I thank several anonymous reviewers for their comments and suggestions.

Thanks to Research Associates Dale Coxe, Cedric Escalle, Manuela Hoehn-Weiss, Julia Kou, John McGuire, Suzanne Purdy, Charles Riordan, and Geoffrey Verter for excellent assistance in developing case studies, researching specific examples, proofreading, and copy editing. Thanks also to Marcy Barnes-Henrie, Melinda Merino, Zeenat Potia, Astrid Sandoval, Brian Surette, and Gayle Treadwell of HBS Press for their goodwill, support, and editorial expertise. Sowmyanarayan Sampath and Abby Levendusky, M.B.A. candidates at Boston University, and Ilgaz Arikan and Manuela Hoehn-Weiss, instructors at Boston University, provided extensive support in gathering the data for the exhibits and in verifying examples. Thanks as well to friends from southern Chile for their encouragement as I wrote the first draft of part I while on a boat in the Andes, and to colleagues at New York University who hosted my visit in the spring of 2003 as the manuscript underwent revision.

Thanks to Nicholas Argyres, Joel A.C. Baum, Jeffrey L. Furman, Pankaj Ghemawat, Brian S. Silverman, and Belen Villalonga for their thoughtful collaboration and long-standing friendship. Thanks to many colleagues who supported this book and the studies that preceded it, especially Rafael Amit, George Baker, Severin Borenstein, Stephen Bradley, Adam Brandenburger, Iain Cockburn, Barbara Feinberg, Paul Geroski, Kathleen Gilroy, Ken Hatten, John Henderson, Rebecca Henderson, Nalin Kulatilaka, Michael Lawson, Louis Lataif, John McArthur, Tom McCraw, Warren McFarlan, Will Mitchell, David Mowery, Richard Nelson, Jackson Nickerson, Jim Post, Jan Rivkin, Richard Rosenbloom, Michael Ryall, Arthur Schleifer, Al Silk, Richard Tedlow, Sushil Vachani, N. Venkatraman, Sidney Winter, Sarah Woolverton, and Michael Yoshino. I thank students in the course entitled "How Industries Evolve" at Boston University, which was taught when this book was in draft in 2002 and 2003. Thanks also to the Systems Research Center, BUILDE, and the Dean's office at Boston University for financial resources.

I am grateful to my friends and family for their patience and support.

# I

## Introduction and Overview

M OST EXECUTIVES THINK CAREFULLY about the future and are committed to the long-term health of their organizations. They see their personal interests as fully aligned with those of the companies that they are leading. They take risks by investing in projects that create new options and, if necessary, reorganize their firms to exploit these options.

For executives with this perspective, a central challenge is to distinguish the true opportunities that arise from industry change from those that are transient. Consultants, conferences, market research, and the business press all provide important information on trends, and yet developing a strategy for addressing them remains difficult. As a result, many organizations have changed direction so frequently that performance has suffered. Impatient investors have threatened to remove executives from office out of frustration with investments that become obsolete before they pay off. At the operating level, employees become exhausted and cynical as a result of repeated calls for change followed by the abandonment of the urgent initiatives.

The central purpose of this book is to help you achieve and sustain superior performance in your organization by adhering to two principles. The first is to avoid the unnecessary risks and costs that arise from a strategy that breaks the rules of industry change. The goal is to make sure that the strategy you envision for a business can succeed given the specific conditions in your industry today and in the future. The second principle involves recognizing and then capitalizing on the lasting opportunities for developing advantage in your business that arise from industry change. The challenge here is to see the implications of structural change before your competitors see them, and to use your existing strengths to achieve an enduring competitive advantage.

With a strategy grounded in knowledge about the specific evolutionary path of an industry, the kinds of questions that executives regularly confront become easier to answer. The following list identifies just some of these questions:

- *When do new technologies carry the potential to transform the industry structure? When will they be absorbed into the current structure?* The energy sector continues to be confronted with a range of new technologies for generating electricity. Will the same companies that dominate the industry today dominate after new technologies develop?

- *How can the organization promote innovation without dissipating resources unnecessarily?* Many companies sponsor a range of small entrepreneurial ventures from corporate headquarters in the hope that one or more will pay off. When is small-scale corporate venturing enough to keep a company at the forefront of industry evolution? When is small-scale venturing too expensive to be worthwhile?

- *When is the market ready to accept new kinds of products? When are buyers likely to be more interested in current products?* Honda and Toyota have introduced hybrid automobiles powered in part by electricity. When is an invention ahead of its time? How long will it be until hybrids really take off and cut significantly into sales of conventional small cars?

- *When can a company rely on feedback from its existing buyers in making important strategic decisions?* Procter & Gamble became famous for using focus groups to refine new products before introducing them into the marketplace. The company conducted extensive research on such familiar items as soap, laundry detergent, and toothpaste, and used the information to make new-product decisions that became legendarily successful. When is market research reliable? When are new products too different for market research to yield good information?

- *When does a firm have to rush new products into the marketplace to secure competitive position, and when does it have the time to refine new products before introducing them?* Many companies got into trouble during the dot-com boom by scrambling to win buyer attention, even at the cost of compromising product quality. The rush for first-mover advantage was so pervasive that some companies launched Web sites before they had the capability to fill orders. When can a company afford to wait, and when does it have to match the competition? How can executives evaluate whether a rush among competitors has staying power?

- *How can an organization successfully defend against competitor initiatives that threaten to distract buyers? When can a company use alliances or acquisitions to preempt competitive challenges? How can a company defend itself economically?* Many smaller biotechnology companies intend to develop breakthrough drugs, enter the lucrative pharmaceutical industry, and threaten the positions of established pharmaceutical leaders. The biotech companies that have succeeded, however, have tended to market their products (at least for a time) through partnerships with traditional leaders, such as Merck, GlaxoSmithKline, and Pfizer. Have the alliances been economical for the pharmaceutical leaders? Do the alliances give the larger partners competitive advantages over nonintegrated rivals? Are the partnerships sufficient for protecting established firms against new entrants? Are they blunting the abilities of the biotech firms to enter the pharmaceutical industry?

- *When can a firm transform itself through innovation in a separate division?* Are there circumstances in which a firm can transform itself by adopting innovations that originate in a small division within the organization? When are separate divisions likely to fail as engines of innovation? Are there specific circumstances where firms can profitably avoid the hard work of integrating a separate division into the mainstream of the company's activities?

- *When should a company leader take charge of innovation initiatives, and when should a company allow a newcomer with a fresh perspective to lead innovation?* Charles Schwab led his organization's launch of online trading products in the late 1990s. But it took Lou Gerstner, an outsider with no specialized expertise in computing, to lead the transformation of IBM during the same decade. When is continuity of leadership central to the transformation

of a company, and when does an outsider bring the perspective
necessary to drive change?

- *When is it most appropriate for a firm to tolerate low or negative profitability in the hope of improving profits?* Amazon.com announced
  its first quarterly profit early in 2002 (for the last quarter of
  2001), four-and-a-half years after IPO investors fell in love
  with the idea that the bookseller's early losses would be followed by a spectacular profit stream. Many other start-ups
  running on the same premise have long since gone out of business. When is it reasonable to expect that short-term losses
  will be followed by fast growth in earnings?

The best answers to these questions depend on how the industry
structure is changing in a specific situation. By understanding the trajectory of industry change, you can make faster decisions, avoid distractions, and ultimately improve the firm's returns on investment.

The ideas in this book reflect years of statistical research and case
studies on industries in nearly all sectors of the economy. Because the
underlying research is empirical rather than theoretical or historical,
the findings are based on careful observation of what has actually
happened in practice over time. In some parts of the book, you'll see
how these observations are consistent with a range of theoretical and
historical explanations for *why* the reported patterns emerge. The
basic approach involves focusing on the implications of multifaceted
change rather than on a single, isolated driver of change in a complex
situation.

The case studies at the heart of the research show that a failure to
achieve better performance almost always occurs because of a gap between the understanding that innovation drives performance and an
understanding that only some forms of innovation work within an industry context. While this book will not deliver recipes for how to innovate, it is designed to fill the gap by providing frameworks and tools
for evaluating whether your strategy follows the broad rules for how
change takes hold in the industry environment.

The title, *How Industries Evolve*, is intended to convey the idea that
truly transformational change takes time—usually decades—and unfolds
in stages.[1] You can identify the implications of change far in advance if
you are willing to take a long view. If you don't focus on the long trajectory of industry change, you may be forced to take unnecessary risks by

reacting quickly during unanticipated periods of transition. Evidence shows that great companies have lost ground needlessly when their executives were caught off guard by major change and moved too aggressively. A better course of action is to understand the *nature* of industry change so that you can prepare for the inevitable challenges and opportunities that arise. Preparation allows you to avoid quick, unconsidered action when the stakes are high.

## An Antidote to Innovation Fatigue

Innovation fatigue is what happens when an organization constantly strives to get ahead of the competition and then struggles to generate performance that meets the standard set in prior years. It typically occurs when executives scramble in response to each opportunity because they lack the perspective to separate truly important developments from temporary distractions. By crafting a strategy that adheres to the rules of industry change and reflects long-term opportunity in the environment, the organization can channel its efforts to maintain distinctiveness and avoid head-to-head competitive battles that lead to poor performance.

The word "innovation" is used in this book to refer to any investment made by a company that has a deferred payoff, including, for example, expenditures on training programs, infrastructure development, or skunk works.[2] In many organizations, executives have become discouraged about innovation because they have not achieved an acceptable return on their investments, especially over the last decade. Many of the recent disappointments have occurred because innovation involves risk; the environment and the organization's internal structure may change before the payoff occurs. The opportunity is also in the risk, however. Innovation drives the longevity and long-term profitability of any organization. Without ongoing innovation, a company fails to track its buyers' needs, it suppliers' capabilities, and the standards for competing effectively—a recipe for disaster over the long run.

There are two fundamental ways that innovation can benefit a firm: an improved chance of survival and better profitability.[3] Survival depends on innovation that can keep a company operationally effective in the face of threats to its activities and assets. When investment and strategy are divorced, efforts to innovate are left flailing. The firm may overspend on fruitless initiatives and executives may become cynical about the potential payoff of innovation. In the end, the company incurs unnecessary costs and alienates buyers, which puts its survival at stake.

Better profitability in the future depends on innovating in ways that capitalize on the company's strategy—its source of uniqueness. Another way of saying this is that investment can deliver superior performance over the competition in the future only if the company uses the investment to generate greater future revenues or to lower future costs (or both, which is possible only under specialized conditions). The irony is that a company *cannot* profitably sustain itself without ongoing innovation that is integrated into the strategy (see box 1-1 for a discussion of the risks of growth as a primary objective).

Industry evolution is important because it defines the broadest set of investment opportunities that will ultimately lead to superior profitability. While a company may face other opportunities to improve performance—perhaps through better organizational processes or enhanced features on established products—the truly significant, long-term opportunities arise from environmental change.

Consider the fate of Apple Computer and of Kmart, two organizations with strategies that were not aligned with evolution in their core industries during the early 2000s. Before it developed the iPod, Apple's principal industry was the manufacture of computing hardware and software. Despite its new-product development in this business (particularly with the iMac), the company's prospects continued to be hampered by its proprietary operating system. Ongoing concerns about system pricing, the firm's retail outlets, and the availability of application software reflected a lack of alignment with the rules of industry change. Apple's opportunities in the computing hardware industry involved capitalizing on its established sources of uniqueness while taking advantage of major changes in the environment, such as the movement toward open-source code and aggressive inventory-management practices. Becoming a viable alternative to giants such as Dell Computer, Hewlett-Packard, and Microsoft required figuring out ways to meet emerging buyer needs and to build scale in unprecedented ways. At the same time, the company also found ways to exploit its resources—especially its brand capital and expertise at industrial design—through the introduction of new products like the iPod into related businesses on different evolutionary trajectories.

## box 1-1   Growth, Survival, and Profitability

The approach in this book emphasizes that there are two components to performance: survival and profitability. Where does growth fit into the equation?

Growth is a worthwhile objective, but only when its benefits—measured in terms of improved survival or better profitability—outweigh its costs. Too many companies pursue growth for its own sake without considering whether growth will generate a return on investment either in the short or long run.

In a broad sense, the appropriateness of a growth objective depends in a sensitive way on both the evolutionary trajectory and the stage of change in the industry of a particular business unit. For example, consider an industry in the shakeout stage of a life cycle. In this situation, a moderate rate of growth (of the right kind) is essential to both survival and profitability. But once the industry reaches the decline stage, additional growth is not likely to generate enough of a return to cover its costs.

In other situations, the consequences of an inappropriate commitment to growth can be grave. When the industry is undergoing an Architectural change (which will be defined precisely in chapter 2), a growth objective may be tantamount to taking the perspective that the industry will support business as usual over the long run. This perspective, if it persists, is almost certain to enhance the firm's commitment to an industry without the potential to generate reasonable returns over the long run.

In the end, growth itself should be a subsidiary goal that is adopted when it is necessary for survival or is tied tightly to realistic objectives for profitability over time. For example, growth is essential to survival when a company must achieve the minimum level of scale or scope necessary to compete effectively as an industry goes through shakeout—a situation that arises only under specialized circumstances. Growth may be integral to profitability when the company is striving to achieve an advantaged competitive position, or when it is taking advantage of particular changes in industry structure. In each of these cases, the challenge is to link growth to the primary objectives of survival and profitability so that the executive team responsible for implementing the strategy knows how to assess accurately whether the growth generates a return over time that exceeds its costs.

Kmart's problems during the early years of the twenty-first century were more daunting than those confronting Apple. The company filed for bankruptcy protection in January of 2002 in an effort to reorganize and become more efficient in the face of formidable competition from Wal-Mart. The rules of industry change in discount retailing revolved around massive efficiencies that were accessible only by building an interlocking system of activities in distribution, store operations, purchasing, human resource policies, marketing, and many other activities. Achieving competitive parity required that Kmart make up for lost ground in operational effectiveness, a task made all the more difficult because Wal-Mart, the industry's standard-bearer, made itself a moving target through continuous improvement.

The frameworks in this book are designed to support you in developing a strategy that integrates insights about innovation and industry evolution. They can help executives in companies that face problems like those confronting Kmart and Apple to see where opportunity really lies, and to chart a path for making the organization effective in exploiting it. By connecting efforts to innovate directly with the prospect of a payoff in the future, a company can improve the odds of success and reduce the fatigue that results from disappointing financial results and from scrambling to make each decision independently.

## The Approach

The frameworks of this book for assessing industry evolution are described extensively in chapters 2 and 3, and chapter 4 offers techniques for analyzing a particular industry. The fundamental concept is that industries each follow one of four evolutionary trajectories: "Progressive," "Creative," "Intermediating," and "Radical."[4] Figure 1-1 provides an introduction to the differences among each of the four trajectories.

Progressive change, which is the most common type of industry evolution, involves incremental innovation through basic blocking and tackling to enhance operational effectiveness. The discount retailing industry is evolving Progressively as companies grow steadily through geographic expansion and improve profits through process enhancements in distribution, information technology, and store operations.

Creative change, the least common type of change, occurs when relationships between the industry and its buyers are stable, but there's

FIGURE 1-1

# Introduction to the Four Industry Trajectories

### Progressive

Examples: Discount retailing, long-haul trucking, commercial airlines

Rules of change include:

- Constant market testing before full-scale commitment
- Competitive benchmarking and openness about accomplishments
- Building capabilities incrementally over time rather than through the acquisition of assets

Opportunities for innovation involve:

- Building a system that dominates a geographic or product market
- Tightly linking activities

### Creative

Examples: Pharmaceuticals, motion-picture production, oil and gas exploration

Rules of change include:

- Committing resources to high-potential projects without reliable market information
- Developing a system for bringing successful projects to market
- Abandoning failing projects

Opportunities for innovation involve:

- Creating breakthrough asset-development projects
- Developing efficient and effective systems for delivering projects to market

### Intermediating

Examples: Investment brokerage, fine-arts auctions, automobile dealerships

Rules of change include:

- Adapting to new ways of transacting with customers and suppliers
- Scaling back commitments to fixed infrastructure
- Finding ways to redeploy assets out of the business into more profitable uses

Opportunities for innovation involve:

- Focusing early on a core group of loyal customers
- Engaging in partnerships and alliances with rivals, customers, or suppliers
- Forward or backward integrating into a customer's or supplier's business

### Radical

Examples: Overnight letter delivery, landline telephone manufacturing, typewriter manufacturing

Rules of change include:

- Carefully identifying profitable activities and scaling back unprofitable activities
- Avoiding the commitment of long-lived assets into the business

Opportunities for innovation involve:

- Assessing the timing of change accurately and retaining a profitable position as long as possible
- Developing efficiencies by replacing fixed assets with variable activities

rapid turnover in the resources necessary to survive and to sustain leadership in the industry. Think of the oil and gas exploration or film production businesses, in which companies engage in large multiyear projects to create new assets. New investments occur as old oil stocks become depleted and as moviegoers lose interest in last year's film library.

Intermediating change, which is less common than Progressive change but more common than Creative or Radical change, occurs when the relationships at the heart of the industry structure are jeopardized while old resources retain some of their value. Intermediation usually involves widespread shifts in market boundaries such as those currently under way in many wholesale electricity markets, where new trading mechanisms allow generators to sell their services to a much broader range of buyers than they sold to historically.

Radical change, which is uncommon, takes place when a fundamentally new approach for creating value arises and threatens to make obsolete all of the core assets and activities in the business. For example, the typewriter manufacturing industry was transformed radically when the personal computer was introduced.

The defining criteria for identifying the trajectory of change in a particular industry involve assessing different levels of threat from new technology, globalization, buyer tastes, and other factors. Where threats exist, they motivate change by exerting pressure on existing elements of the industry's revenue and costs. (Box 1-2 explains the relationship between Michael E. Porter's five-forces model of the elements of industry structure and industry evolution.) Innovation in an industry is vital to profitability under all trajectories of change, and innovation is vital to survival when threats are broad and intense. Furthermore, a firm's program of innovation—that is, its plans for investing in the business—becomes more productive if it takes advantage of the opportunities that arise as obsolescence occurs.

Threats can arise at two levels: to the industry's core activities and to its core assets. Core activities and core assets are central to the identification of an industry's trajectory, so it's worthwhile to clarify these concepts before going any further. The broad definition is that core activities and core assets drive value creation in the established industry before the threat arises. Assets are defined as items with durable value that are the property of the firms in the industry, and activities are defined as actions taken by firms to create profits. The word "core" identifies an asset

---

**box 1-2  Porter's Five-Forces Model and Drivers of Industry Evolution**

Industry evolution reflects changes in the way business is conducted. It may be driven from hundreds of sources and is usually triggered by multiple drivers simultaneously. To affect the way business is conducted, a shift in the environment must influence at least one of the five fundamental elements of industry structure, each of which has consequences for all firms in an industry: buyer power, supplier power, the threat of substitution, the intensity of rivalry, and the threat of entry. These five forces that shape industry-average profitability were identified by Michael E. Porter in his book *Competitive Strategy: Techniques for Analyzing Industries and Competitors*, published in 1980.

In brief, shifts in technology, demographics, regulations, trade barriers, and political conditions are some of the major drivers of change in the five forces. Porter's model is essential for understanding industry-average profitability and yet it leaves open a number of important questions about where changes come from, when the changes are likely to be systemic, and how firms can respond most effectively.

The framework presented here is complementary to the five-forces model and helps you to find answers for how your company can respond to the forces of industry change. It is built on the idea that the key to achieving sustained superior performance is *not* in trying to isolate a particular driver of change, but rather to understand the rules of industry change in the environment. Developing a successful strategy depends on understanding the implications of change for industry structure regardless of the driver.

---

or activity as central to the value created by the industry. Core activities and core assets are threatened with obsolescence when some sort of new approach carries the potential to make them irrelevant to value creation. (The next chapter includes a detailed discussion of how to identify activities and assets, how to determine whether assets and activities are "core," and what constitutes a true threat of obsolescence.)

Each of the four trajectories of industry evolution involves a different pattern in threats of obsolescence. When threats occur to both core assets and core activities, then the industry is confronted with Radical change. The absence of both types of threats means that the industry is changing Progressively. When only core assets or core activities are under threat, then change is Creative or Intermediating, respectively. Figure 1-2 shows the relationships.

Each of the four trajectories of industry evolution is distinctive in its implications for successful innovation. What's essential for successful innovation in one evolutionary environment may jeopardize profitability or even survival in another. As you'll see in subsequent chapters, some of the rules of industry change are definitive, while others are corollaries and guidelines. Under each trajectory, the rules of change act like barriers on a highway. These barriers establish the general route of travel but not which lane you drive in, how fast you go, or when you exit. Similarly, the rules of industry change carve out the direction of innovation but cannot tell you exactly how to invest, how quickly to innovate, or when to exit.[5] None of the trajectories of change is so restrictive as to define a single strategy for success, but each trajectory is definitive in determining the general direction of innovation.

### Progressive Change

Progressive evolution is the most common of the four types of industry change. On this trajectory, both core activities and core assets are stable, and firms within the industry tend to build on their established capabilities over time rather than abandon old ways of doing things in favor of something new. Under Progressive change, innovation tends to

---

**FIGURE 1-2**

## Trajectories of Industry Evolution

| Core Activities* | Core Assets** | Trajectory |
| --- | --- | --- |
| Threatened | Threatened | Radical |
| Not threatened | Threatened | Creative |
| Threatened | Not threatened | Intermediating |
| Not threatened | Not threatened | Progressive |

\* "Core activities" are recurring actions that create value both by making the industry's suppliers more willing to transact and by generating greater willingness to pay among the industry's buyers. This definition of value creation reflects ideas in Adam M. Brandenburger and Harborne Stuart, "Value-Based Business Strategy," *Journal of Economics and Management Strategy* 5:1 (spring 1996): 5–24.

\*\* "Core assets" are durable resources that make the firm more efficient or effective at performing core activities, and can include intangibles such as brand capital and knowledge capital. Core assets are threatened with obsolescence when a new approach accelerates their real rate of depreciation.

be relatively small in scale—companies excel by innovating incrementally in ways that don't rock their core positions. The discount retailing, long-haul trucking, and commercial airline industries are examples of industries evolving on Progressive trajectories.

On Progressive evolutionary paths, innovation typically revolves around constant feedback from buyers and suppliers. Growth usually involves geographic and product-line extensions by firms that seek to dominate the competition in their local areas. Companies in industries that are on a Progressive track do not have to put large amounts of capital at risk before learning whether an innovation has staying power; they have the opportunity to test the waters in a limited way and use what they learn from the test to hone their activities. Southwest Airlines has done this repeatedly. It tests new routes for buyer interest, operating feasibility, and weather delays. The new route has to fit the "Southwest model" of frequent turns at the gate to be acceptable. If the route meets its targets, it is continued; if not, Southwest pulls out and uses what it has learned to select the next route for testing.

Thus, in an industry on a Progressive evolutionary path, performance depends on two primary capabilities: the development of a highly efficient set of interlocking activities and the ability to respond quickly to feedback from buyers and suppliers.

### Creative Change

Creative industry evolution involves major innovation but not a threat to core activities, which means that the industry's relationships with buyers and suppliers remain relatively stable. The main difference between Progressive and Creative evolution is that under Creative change core assets are threatened with obsolescence.[6] What's so interesting about Creative change is that threats normally do not come directly from buyers or suppliers, but rather from competitors or new entrants. The Creative path is the least common form of industry evolution.

Examples of industries on Creative paths include movie production, pharmaceutical manufacturing, oil exploration, and fiction publishing. All are oriented toward a portfolio approach to the challenge of creating new assets over and over again. In these kinds of industries, profitability tends to depend on two types of innovation. First, organizations must innovate in modules to generate a series of commercially viable projects (i.e., feature films, blockbuster drugs, drilling sites, and book projects). Each commercialized project reflects the development of significant and unique new assets owned by the company. Second, companies tend to cultivate core activities that allow them to commercialize new projects successfully. These activities usually involve developing key relationships with consumers, merchandisers, distributors, vendors, or other players in the downstream or upstream chain.

The movie production industry evolves today on a Creative model. Successful film studios typically develop a portfolio of new films, each of which is a productive asset. Leading companies achieve superior performance partly because they maintain a network of complementary activities based on relationships with movie theater exhibitors and cable operators.

In pharmaceuticals, companies engage in large drug-development projects and then use their management skills to negotiate the FDA approval process and their marketing skills to commercialize newly developed drugs successfully. Oil and gas exploration involves managing a portfolio of exploration ventures. When a site is successfully developed, the industry's leading companies activate established relationships with refineries and distributors. Prepackaged software developers engage simultaneously in a range of new-product efforts with the hope that one or more will become best sellers. By applying well-honed skills at user testing, technical validation, and marketing, the industry leaders perpetuate their success.

As a result, in an industry on a Creative evolutionary path, performance depends on several primary capabilities: project management skills that allow a firm to develop a new asset efficiently and effectively, risk assessment capabilities for managing across a portfolio of projects, and the development of a network of complementary upstream and downstream relationships for commercializing a new product efficiently.

### Intermediating Change

Intermediating industry evolution, like Radical evolution, occurs when a new approach threatens an industry's core activities and thereby jeopardizes the firm's relationships with buyers and with long-time suppliers. However, unlike Radical evolution, the core assets in the industry are not threatened with obsolescence.

Intermediation typically involves massive changes in the structure of the information available to buyers and to suppliers. For example, the electricity transmission markets are undergoing Intermediation as deregulation provides consumers with distribution choices and online trading provides generators with multiple bids for their services.

As Intermediating change occurs, the markets for the industry's products—as well as for key raw materials, technology, and employees—may simultaneously become significantly more competitive. Intermediating transformation is surprisingly common, although not as common as Progressive change.

The difference between Radical and Intermediating change is that under the latter, the industry's core assets are *not* threatened with obsolescence, although their value depends on new buyer and supplier relationships. This can make Intermediating evolution even more difficult to manage than Radical change, because executives must find ways to preserve old capital and at the same time develop entirely new sets of relationships. By contrast, under Radical change, so few of the old activities and assets retain their value in the end that it may be easier to exit the business completely.

Under Intermediating change, performance depends on reconfiguring activities to create value in unprecedented ways. Consider the recording industry's artist-development capabilities (which include radio promotions, choreography, costuming, and image management, among other skills) and the auction industry's appraisal resources. Great old companies in these industries are dealing with the challenges posed by new online rivals by using their resources to support new activities that create value for a different set of buyers. Instead of incurring artist development as an expense, forward-thinking recording studios are beginning to sell artist-development services à la carte to aspiring musicians. The buyer and the activities have changed, but the core resource—artist-development capability—retains its relevance. Likewise, some traditional auctioneers, threatened by eBay, have taken their appraisal expertise online and offered (for a fee) to certify the value of online sellers' goods. By reconfiguring old activities in new ways, these companies are preserving their survival and staying afloat under Intermediation.

Today, automobile dealerships are undergoing a specific form of Intermediation called Disintermediation. Disintermediation occurs when the boundaries of an industry collapse inward because buyers and suppliers are each less responsive to the traditional bundling of core activities. In auto dealerships, Disintermediation is making obsolete some activities, such as aggressive selling and original financing, while it enhances the importance of other activities, such as vehicle preparation, representative financing, and servicing.

In an industry on an Intermediating evolutionary path, performance depends on the ability to unbundle old assets, to unwind established relationships without alienating buyers and suppliers unnecessarily, and to redeploy old assets in new ways, all while building new buyer and supplier relationships. Managing under this type of change is among the most difficult challenges in business because of the mettle required to leave old buyers dissatisfied, to leave old suppliers dormant, and to confront major organizational upheaval.

### Radical Change

Radical change occurs when a new approach threatens both the core activities and core assets within an industry, and is usually motivated by a massive technological or regulatory breakthrough. Buyer preferences shift dramatically, supplier capabilities become outdated, and old scale economies become fixed commitments that lock firms into outdated ways of doing business. As a result, the relationships between established companies, their buyers, and their suppliers are restructured. Today, the telephone-manufacturing industry—that is, the manufacture of conventional landline and cordless telephones—is undergoing Radical transformation as cellular telephony and wireless handsets become more popular. Because Radical change involves a sweeping and comprehensive threat, it is a relatively uncommon form of industry change (although not as rare as Creative change). When it does occur, the firms within an industry are hit hard with a stunning set of challenges.

Navigating Radical change successfully depends on developing a strategy that accounts for the transformation of the industry structure. One of the hard lessons of history is that the leaders in the emerging industry are rarely the leaders prior to the Radical change. It's very difficult for an industry leader to survive a Radical transformation, enter the emerging industry successfully, and then dominate the new industry as a pioneer.

Yet despite the challenges, there are strategic alternatives available to an established firm in an industry undergoing this kind of change. The number of alternatives is greatest if the firm recognizes the Radical change when it is just beginning. But regardless of when a firm recognizes what is happening, the critical challenge is to avoid deepening the firm's commitment to the old business. In an industry undergoing Radical change, performance ultimately depends on the ability to avoid redoubling investment in the business while continuing to extract value out of established assets and activities.

## Why Does the Pace of Change Seem Accelerated?

It is uncanny how many industry conferences begin with a speaker who talks about how the pace of change has accelerated over the past few years. In general, many executives feel that they are working harder and harder to maintain the performance of their businesses. How can this sense of accelerated change be reconciled with the claim that industry change takes hold over periods that span decades?

There are two answers to this question. The first acknowledges that the pace of change *has* accelerated over the last few years in some industries: Investment brokerage, long-haul trucking, broadcast media, and long-distance telecommunications come to mind as examples. Yet in all of these cases the recent acceleration in the rate of change simply reflects the reality that a broader transformation has been going on for decades and will continue for years. For example, the loss of confidence by many consumers in investment brokerage houses as the result of the conflict-of-interest scandals is only one facet of a decades-long transformation that reflects changing buyer preferences for advisory services, new sources of capital, the breakdown of information-based scale economies, and changes in incentives for scope economies through product bundling.

The second and more accurate answer acknowledges that the sheer scale of industry change may create an illusion of quick change. In other words, in some industries the pace of change seems accelerated because the scale of the transformation is so great. Think of discount retailing, where a dominant model that reflected Sam Walton's insights about distribution systems, store placement, store structure, and purchasing policies emerged several decades ago. Today, the industry shakeout associated with the rollout of the Wal-Mart model continues. For retailers that are not efficient, it may seem like the pace of change has accelerated, but in fact, only competitive pressure to conform has intensified. This pressure escalated over years as Walton and his successors invested incrementally to develop Wal-Mart's capabilities. For discount retailers without a long view on the profound significance of these changes for the entire industry structure, a confrontation with Wal-Mart during the last ten years may have led to surprising consequences, and as a result the pace of industry change may seem accelerated. However, careful analysis would have revealed the significance of the new discount retailing systems decades ago.

The idea of "dominant model" recurs frequently in this book. A dominant model exists when the leading firms in an industry organize their activities similarly because a single basic approach emerges as particularly efficient and effective and gains greater legitimacy than the alternatives.[7] Often network effects are at the heart of the adoption process. Examples are the hub-and-spoke model in overnight letter delivery and the branch network in retail banking. In automobile manufacturing, the dominant model is based on the combustion engine and on transmission and braking systems that are separated from the engine. Dominant models allow leading firms to develop the economies of scale and scope necessary to capture some of the value that they create, and changes in dominant models mark breakthrough transitions in industry structure.

While it's tempting to conclude that breakthroughs are common, research shows that the nature of change in an industry tends to retain its character through product and technology generations. The key to understanding this concept is to consider the way in which breakthroughs take hold rather than on the breakthroughs themselves. The nature of change (that is, the way that breakthroughs take hold) retains its character even when the pace of change heats up. When change does accelerate, the *rules* for successful innovation in a specific industry tend to stay the same. In the movie production industry, the pace of film development has increased substantially, but the way in which new films are conceived, developed, produced, and marketed has remained stable for decades, allowing for continuity in industry leadership.

Why does the character of change remain so constant? Because buyers, incumbents, and suppliers tend to be invested in established ways of doing things and require time to absorb, understand, and react to new opportunities. Since entrenched players may be threatened, old systems can be remarkably resilient. For example, the radial tire, introduced in 1949 by Michelin, represented a major technological advance over the bias-ply tires that preceded it, yet radials did not become dominant as the tire of choice until decades later because many automobile manufacturers were building heavy cars with cushy suspensions. Radial tires did not offer performance advantages in the prevailing car designs, and the car manufacturers were reluctant to absorb the risks and costs of changing the designs. The bumpier ride that radial tires offered was finally accepted only when consumer demand for greater fuel efficiency forced the redesign of American small cars and the processes for manufacturing them.

This same sort of difficulty in translating technological innovation into commercially successful products has occurred in a range of industries. Personal digital assistants (PDAs) were available long before businesspeople began buying Palm Pilots in droves in the late 1990s. Indeed, the Apple Newton (an early PDA) had been championed by former CEO John Sculley as early as 1993.[8] Companies experimented with long-distance selling for years before Sears Roebuck introduced its legendary catalog and transformed the general merchandising business in the late nineteenth century.

Even so-called radical innovations that represent major technical breakthroughs may not be commercialized successfully for years. In the case of PDAs, suppliers wanted to understand their obligations when they agreed to manufacture the components embedded in the new products. Buyers wanted to know that the PDAs they bought would be popular enough to assure a steady stream of applications software. The lesson: Once a breakthrough in buyer and supplier acceptance occurs, change may appear rapid despite years of failed effort by the industry to create the breakthrough.

So has the pace of change accelerated? Industries in which the pace of change has accelerated are in a *stage* of rapid change that is part of a larger evolutionary process. (The stages of evolution will be covered in detail in chapter 3.) The pace of change slows when buyers hold onto what's familiar, suppliers try to preserve their stakes, and competitors see little potential for profitability in the new environment. Even when the companies in an industry are committed to accelerating rates of adoption, the behavior of buyers and of suppliers will create drag on the pace of change in the industry. Consider the history of a major conceptual or technological breakthrough such as the emergence of the PDA. Buyers resisted the product until they felt assured that it would not soon become obsolete. Suppliers waited to make sure that they committed to a platform with staying power.

Given that the accelerated pace of change is often part of a larger process, companies should always strive for a thoughtful evaluation of the implications of change before reacting to it. Indeed, a company is more vulnerable to strategic errors when decisions are made quickly. By taking the time to understand the process of industry evolution, you can take a broad perspective and position yourself to recognize windows of opportunity when breakthroughs are most likely to take hold. The challenge is to develop a perspective on industry change early enough to maximize the available options.

It may be tempting to conclude that there is little that you can do about industry evolution because it unfolds over such a long period of time. Nothing could be farther from the truth. If you take one thing from this book, please let it be this: It is crucial to identify and understand the activities and assets that are working to your advantage as well as those that constrain your ability to adapt. The relationships that are most profitable may well be those that create the most constraints.

## Finding Opportunity in Industry Evolution

An understanding of industry change can serve as a platform for developing a strategy and a plan for innovation to navigate through transformation. The rules of industry change, which are defined in the next chapters in terms that reflect the five forces that shape industry structure,[9] are the linchpin in the process of gaining insight about opportunity and aligning your strategy. (See box 1-3 for a discussion of why strategy is important even in the face of major change to industry structure.)

Charles Schwab found unprecedented opportunity in the investment brokerage industry during the 1990s, and decided to commit his company to leadership in online discount trading in late 1997. At the time, many brokerages considered online trading to be a niche business that would appeal only to specialists and day traders in the long run. The conventional wisdom held that mainstream investors would discover the error of self-directed online trading as soon as the market went through a downturn.

A forward-thinking group of brokerage executives across the industry departed from the prevailing wisdom and was more optimistic about the impact of the Internet as a new channel. But the leadership team at Schwab went several steps further and reacted to the online opportunity as part of a larger transformation of the industry structure that involved the Disintermediation of brokerage. The transformation involved a

## box 1-3   Why Strategy Is Still Relevant, and How It Can Be Used to Exploit Industry Change

The concept of strategy has fallen out of favor among some executives because many have found that detailed plans become irrelevant as circumstances change. However, the real problem has been the misconception that a strategy is only a narrow plan for how to act. The true essence of strategy is a set of guidelines that describe how the firm will uniquely create and capture value.[a] Strategy guides decisions by executives, middle managers, field managers, and front-line employees in any organization. A clear strategy is particularly important at a time of rapid change, when decision makers throughout an organization are forced to make important inter-related decisions quickly and without extensive communication.

When a strategy is aligned with industry evolution, a firm's performance improves for three reasons:

1. Buyer acquisition and retention become significantly more effective and less expensive.

2. Supplier relationships become easier to manage.

3. Competitive threats diminish as the organization is perceived as distinctive.

The benefits of adaptation compound as the organization hits fewer dead ends in the development of new products and as investors become more confident that the organization is adapting at a sustainable rate that will work in the industry environment.

NTT DoCoMo, the subsidiary of Nippon Telegraph and Telephone (NTT) that invented and popularized i-mode telephony in Japan during 1999 and 2000, aligned its strategy with industry evolution by entering a new market at just the right time with a product that was perfectly suited to buyer needs. Teenagers were first to flock to the technology, which integrated Web access into a mobile phone. DoCoMo supplemented the package with applications available through vendors that could easily bill through the phone company for their services. i-mode quickly became just as popular in the business community. DoCoMo's subscriber base reached 32 million—about 25 percent of the Japanese population—just three years after the i-mode launch.[b] Investor enthusiasm led to the 2002 spin-off of the company by parent NTT, which retained majority ownership of the shares. This is an excellent example of how aligning strategy with industry change can position a company to seize opportunities quickly and profitably.

How did DoCoMo achieve this success? Its parent company, NTT, established DoCoMo expressly to pursue opportunities that were tied to changes in the industry structure. As the national telephone company of Japan, NTT had unparalleled access to information about buyer preferences and supplier capabilities. DoCoMo drew on its parent's knowledge capital and physical infrastructure to develop economies of scale quickly. The NTT brand name provided DoCoMo with an important economy of scope because it made the new organization instantly recognizable and credible among both buyers and suppliers.[c] Thus, DoCoMo achieved its success in the Japanese cellular telephony industry with careful alignment of strategy to exploit insights at NTT about buyer preferences, supplier capabilities, and the limitations of competitors.

a. In this book, I use the term "value creation" to describe how the firm deals with buyers and suppliers rather than with investors. The idea of uniqueness is critical to the definition of value creation. See Michael E. Porter, "What is Strategy?" *Harvard Business Review* (November–December 1996): 61–78.

b. NTT DoCoMo's 2002 *Annual Report.*

c. DoCoMo ran into difficulty as it grew increasingly independent from its parent, NTT. In particular, DoCoMo faced new challenges in aligning with industry evolution as it expanded into new geographic markets that evolved by different rules than the Japanese market.

sweeping breakdown in the economies of scope that had held brokerage and advisory services together.

As a result of insight about industry evolution, the Schwab brokerage made a major commitment to move all of the company's buyers to discount brokerage accounts. The drop in prices that accompanied the move was so dramatic that there was no chance of retrenching and moving back to the old model. It was a bet-the-company decision, yet its full-scale commitment allowed the company to achieve leadership as the industry began the major Intermediating transformation that continues today.

Understanding industry change allows you to make better assessments of the tradeoffs in a specific situation, such as those that confront leaders in the overnight letter delivery industry today. It's clear that secure encryption will *eventually* dampen demand for overnight letter delivery services by making it possible for documents to be delivered safely over the Internet faster and less expensively, but there's controversy about when secure encryption will become prevalent. For overnight letter companies, a tradeoff arises between reinvesting in the business and preparing for the inevitable decline of the industry. Federal Express, United Parcel Service, and the other overnight letter companies must avoid investing in dedicated assets such as distribution hubs that will lose value—even if it means losing competitive advantage as the industry declines. An analysis of industry change allows you to see the links between investment choices and the company's financial statements. It allows you to understand the tradeoffs in loosening your hold on a profitable business that may eventually deliver poorer returns in favor of a new model that may prove much more successful over the long term. The key is to understand the stages of the change clearly, to reinvest while the firm's position remains viable, and to stop reinvesting when the time horizon on change draws nearer.

This discussion of strategic decision making reflects the idea that history casts a long shadow. Many companies in the first decade of the twenty-first century are understandably reluctant to disturb activities that currently generate profits. Indeed, long-term relationships based on continuity in core activities account for the longevity of many established companies. But by understanding and capitalizing on the ways in which old activities generate value, and by jettisoning old activities when they no longer carry the potential to generate returns, your organization is much more likely to improve its performance over the long run. Rigorous analysis and an emphasis on the long term—which is often overlooked as companies rush to find solutions to unforeseen problems—provides the foundation for avoiding mistaken investment that cannot pay off.

Chapters 2 through 4 set the foundation for understanding the rules of change in a particular industry. By the end of chapter 4 you will be introduced to frameworks for understanding whether your industry follows a Progressive, Creative, Intermediating, or Radical trajectory. You will also be offered tools for evaluating the phase of a transformation, which is critical for understanding the best way to react. Chapters 5 through 7 discuss how to align strategy with industry evolution. A range of subjects is covered, including the repositioning of businesses within industries and diversification across industries. There's an emphasis in these chapters on providing you with the background necessary to formulate a strategy that exploits new opportunity while conforming to the rules of industry change.

# PART ONE

# Understanding Industry Evolution

# 2

## The Four Trajectories
## of Industry Evolution

CHAPTER 1 EMPHASIZED THAT your strategy *cannot* succeed if it violates the rules of change in your industry. The stakes are high even if you only want to understand how industry evolution affects the strategy you have in place. Yet careful analysis can deliver more than just an assurance that your strategy conforms to the rules of change. If your organization has the flexibility to redefine its strategy around the opportunities created by the trajectory of industry evolution, then the chances for improving your profitability are compounded. Great companies develop strategies that capitalize on untapped opportunity as change takes hold in the industry environment.

Rigorous diagnosis begins with a refined understanding of each of the four models of industry evolution: Progressive, Creative, Intermediating, and Radical. This chapter offers additional information on the background conditions for each model, describes their differences in detail, and outlines a few basic principles for determining which of the models applies to your situation.

### The Starting Point

Before you begin to diagnose which of the four models applies in your industry, keep the following principles in mind:

- *Every industry follows a trajectory.* The four categories outlined here are exhaustive. If you have difficulty in determining which of the four models applies to your industry, then you may be defining the industry too broadly. Chapter 4 contains diagnostic tools for evaluating industry boundaries.

- *Every industry follows just one of the trajectories.* The four categories are mutually exclusive. This point is subtle because there are overlaps in some of the characteristics of each of the four trajectories. For example, under both Progressive and Intermediating change, core assets are not threatened and serve as a source of stability. Under both Radical and Intermediating change, core activities are threatened with obsolescence. Thus, it is virtually inevitable that you will see characteristics of your industry represented in models that don't apply to it. The models are distinctive because they each rest on a unique *set* of defining characteristics. The acid test is in applying the criteria comprehensively to examine the status of both the core activities and the core assets in the industry.

- *Shifts between models are rare.* This is true because each model represents only the way in which change takes hold rather than the pace or specific character of the change. In the rare instances when a shift between models does occur, it is when a threat of obsolescence either crops up or goes away.

- *Structural change can be significant even when the industry does not face a threat of obsolescence.* Industry change occurs at different intensities, in different ways, and with different implications along the four trajectories. It is important to appreciate the potential magnitude of change even when the obsolescence of the industry's core activities and assets is not at stake. For example, the accumulated effect of many incremental changes in Progressive change can be transforming. Home Depot has continually upgraded its activities and created new assets to raise the standard for competing effectively in the home-improvement business. Competitors in the industry that do not confront the implications of Home Depot's strategy put their profitability and ultimately their survival at stake. Thus, be careful not to rule out the Progressive model prematurely just because obsolescence across the industry is absent.

### When Does an Activity or Asset Qualify as "Core"?

As you know from chapter 1, the criteria for evaluating which of the four models applies require identifying whether the industry's core activities and assets are under a threat of obsolescence. Progressive change occurs when neither the industry's core activities nor core assets are threatened while Radical change occurs when both are threatened. Along the remaining two trajectories either core activities or core assets, but not both, are threatened.

Before defining "core assets" and "core activities," it's worthwhile to clarify the difference between assets and activities. Assets are durable goods and services that are owned by the firms in the industry. Ownership exists only when a firm can claim the asset as tangible or intangible property. For example, a piece of equipment, a trademark, and a patent are all assets, but an employee's skills and a new R&D initiative are not assets. Following the conventions of the accounting system, it's useful to think of an object as durable if it would retain its character after lying dormant and unused. Property, plant, equipment, cash, inventory, and accounts receivables clearly qualify as assets. Brand capital and intellectual property qualify as assets if they would retain their potential to create value even after they were not in use for a year.

Activities are actions performed within the industry under corporate direction with the intention of creating revenue or of managing costs for firms—examples include purchasing, operations, human resource management, distribution, marketing, and selling. Activities tend to be integral to the relationships between the industry's firms and their buyers or suppliers. They lack durability and are drivers of income statement items on a company's financial reports.[1]

Once you've identified activities and assets, the next step is to evaluate which are "core." Here's the test: An asset or activity is "core" if the profitability of the industry as a whole would be materially diminished by the eradication of the asset or activity for some significant period of time.[2] (You can assume that the process of eradication in this thought experiment is instantaneous and pain-free.) In most cases, a year-long time horizon is sufficient for this evaluation. Thus, an activity or an asset qualifies as "core" if it could not be replaced within a year by some other asset or activity without damaging profitability.

This test may seem abstract but it's easy to use once you get the hang of it. The Coca-Cola brand is a core asset because industry revenues and consequently industry profits would be substantially lower a year from now than they are today if the brand were eradicated. It simply could not be replaced or recreated in a year. The lending activities in commercial banking are "core" because the industry's profitability would be lower a year from now if banks had to find some other way to meet the working capital and long-term borrowing requirements of corporate clients.

In applying this test, try to be as literal and specific as possible about what's getting eradicated. Imagine that all of the existing retail stores of grocery-store chains were obliterated instantly and painlessly. It would be virtually impossible to rebuild them all or to find other locations within a year, and therefore the existing stores qualify as "core." Keep in mind, though, that any individual store is not "core" for the grocery industry as long as it could be rebuilt or replaced within a year if it were eradicated and if the profits would return to their current levels within a year. This means that collectively the stores qualify as a core asset but individually no single store is a core asset. The implication is that a threat of obsolescence to a single store will not throw the grocery-store business into Radical or Intermediating change, but a threat to *all* stores at the same time will throw the business into Radical or Intermediating change.

As you analyze which activities and assets are core, start by looking at broad categories and drill down further when the broad activities and assets do not qualify as core. Then look at narrow categories and expand them when the narrow activities and assets are not core.[3] This dual approach assures that you identify all of the core activities and core assets in the industry.

Table 2-1 summarizes the major definitions that you need to identify core activities and core assets.

### The Threat of Obsolescence

The final step in assessing the implications for industry evolution is to evaluate whether core activities and core assets are threatened with obsolescence. To understand the situation in your industry, evaluate whether some change in circumstances lurks in the background that could diminish the value of the core activities or core assets. Is there something brewing that is likely to make today's core activities or core assets less productive in the future? Is the threat strong enough to create obsolescence?

The threat of obsolescence may emanate from a new technology, a change in government policy, the opening of new markets, or the breakout of war, for example. It also may originate in a shortage of a critical

TABLE 2-1

## Definitions for Identifying Core Assets and Activities

| | |
|---|---|
| **Asset** | An object qualifies as an asset only if it is: |
| | • *Durable.*    The object must retain its potential to create value even after lying dormant for a year. |
| | • *Property.*    The object must be owned by one or more firms within the industry. |
| **Activity** | An action qualifies as an activity only if it is: |
| | • *Controlled.*    The action must be directed by one or more firms within the industry. |
| | • *Profit-oriented.*    The action must be designed to increase revenues or lower costs or both for one or more of the firms within the industry. |
| **Core** | An asset or activity is "core" if it is essential to the value created by the industry in the following sense: Its eradication today (and continuing eradication for one year) would lead to diminished profitability as of a date one year from now, despite efforts to replace the eradicated asset or activity. |

raw material—for example, the overfishing of shellfish in some parts of the Atlantic has created a threat of obsolescence to the core activities of the local shellfishing trade in the affected areas. A threat often has multiple sources of origin. Shortages of shellfish were accompanied by a change in government policy that restricted access by fisherman to sensitive breeding areas. Thus, in the local shellfishing industry, both the raw material shortages and the policy changes created the threat.

Threats of obsolescence have varying impact, depending on whether they involve core activities or core assets (see box 2-1 for a discussion of how this kind of transformation differs from disruptive technology). Throughout this book, I'll refer to an industry under threat to core *activities* as undergoing Architectural transformation.[4] I've chosen this phrase because a threat to core activities involves at least the partial obsolescence of the revenue and cost structure of the business; an Architectural change thus occurs when the industry's buyer and supplier relationships are thrown into jeopardy and consequently the architecture of profitability is under fire.

I'll refer to an industry under threat to its core *assets* as undergoing Foundational transformation. Foundational change derives its name from the idea that core assets provide the industry with its durable structure. Without core assets, the firms in an industry own nothing of proprietary value. Foundational change occurs when the durable underlying structure that supports core activities comes under fire.

**box 2-1   Disruptive Technology, Architectural Change, and Foundational Change**

In 1997, Clayton M. Christensen's important book, *The Innovator's Dilemma: When New Technologies Cause Great Firms to Fail*, defined disruptive technologies as "technologies that result in *worse* product performance, at least in the near-term."[a] The idea here is that a disruptive technology does not immediately seem like a threat to the firms that offer established products because it offers less overall value to the mainstream market. Christensen goes on to explain that the threat posed to established firms by a disruptive technology may be great over the long term because the relative rate of improvement in the disruptive products may outpace that of the established products. It is difficult for established firms to justify investing in the new products principally because mainstream customers "generally don't want, and indeed initially can't use, products based on disruptive technologies."[b]

How does Christensen's idea of a "disruptive technology" relate to the ideas of Architectural and Foundational change illustrated in this book? There are three fundamental differences. First, the unit of analysis in this book is not a technology but rather an industry. Industries are more than markets; they are groups of firms that operate in the same product markets *and* the same markets for supplies such as raw materials (chapter 4 discusses this in detail). Where a disruptive technology is defined in terms of the market positioning of a product, an Architectural or Foundational change is defined in terms that reflect the value provided by an industry to suppliers as well as to customers.

Second, this book focuses on changes that can originate from any source— not only technological sources. Christensen is fundamentally interested in technological progress in a very broad sense. He discusses technological trajectories that may have implications for multiple markets and industries (although of course he defines disruptive technologies in terms of specific product markets). In this book, the focus is on the implications of change for established firms *regardless* of the source. Technology, deregulation, globalization, saturation of supply, and many other factors may influence and drive the changes discussed here. Sometimes change originates with a disruptive technology, but often it doesn't.

Third, the impetus for Architectural or Foundational change is conceived in terms of a threat that must have teeth but that doesn't always materialize into the failure of most established firms. In other words, the definitions of Architectural and Foundational change don't rely on the precise implications of the threat of obsolescence for the established firms. Christensen's "disruptive technology" is defined by reference to the *performance* of the established products, whereas Architectural and Foundational change are defined in terms of a threat to the *existence* of core activities and core assets. This book thus pays more attention to the options available to established firms as they weigh the performance implications of the threats.

Christensen's book and this one are similar in taking the perspective of firms in the established industry. Both adopt the assumption that executives want to do the right thing over the long run for their organizations. And both discuss the implications of change for organization structure, leadership, and investment.

a. Clayton M. Christensen, *The Innovator's Dilemma: When New Technologies Cause Great Firms to Fail*, (Boston: Harvard Business School Press, 1997).

b. Ibid., xvii.

Architectural and Foundational change need not occur at the same time, although sometimes they do occur simultaneously. Figure 2-1 summarizes the mapping between Architectural change, Foundational change, and the four trajectories. The Creative and Radical evolutionary paths involve Foundational change, and the Intermediating and Radical trajectories involve Architectural change. The relationships are the same as those depicted in chapter 1, but a new language has been introduced to summarize the threat of obsolescence.

How can you tell whether a threat is significant enough to motivate Architectural or Foundational change? To qualify, it has to be substantial enough to jeopardize the survival of more than one of the industry's leading firms, and it has to be general enough to affect all firms in the industry. In other words, the threat must truly arise at the *industry* level and must carry the potential to affect any firm that does not react strategically. Furthermore, the threat must be significant enough to lead to the actual obsolescence of a substantial portion of the industry's core activities or assets if it is realized. Live auctioneers have confronted a threat of obsolescence tied to eBay's extraordinary online success over the past five years. The impact of online auctions has been felt throughout the live auction industry.

**FIGURE 2-1**

## Nature of Change and the Trajectories of Industry Evolution

Architectural

|  | | Yes | No |
|---|---|---|---|
| **Foundational** | Yes | Radical | Creative |
| | No | Intermediating | Progressive |

Keep in mind that the threat does not have to materialize into the obsolescence of *all* of the industry's core activities and core assets to qualify as substantial. Indeed, in almost all industries under threat, widespread obsolescence does not occur. The typewriter, aircraft-propeller, and live theater industries all exist today. Some companies within these industries even flourish. Yet over the last half-century, in each of these industries the survival of more than one leading firm was at stake, and the threat was felt generally across the industry. The key to superior performance in these situations is in understanding the rules of industry change and adapting to opportunities as they emerge.

The following sections describe each of the four trajectories of industry change—Progressive, Creative, Intermediating, and Radical—in greater detail and provide case studies of firms that have wrestled with major challenges in the face of industry change. Box 2-2 provides estimates of the prevalence of each trajectory.

### The Rules of Change

There are ten rules of evolutionary change in industries. They fall into three categories: defining rules, corollaries, and guidelines. "Defining rules" are unshakeable, and hold in every situation in which change is under way. They are called defining rules because they are tightly related to the criteria for identifying the trajectory in the first place.

"Corollaries" are implications of the defining rules and almost always hold under a specific trajectory (indeed, exceptions are so rare that

## box 2-2   How Common is Each Trajectory?

Assessing the prevalence of each trajectory is difficult because it is hard to discern industry boundaries clearly in all situations and because reliable data is not available on the threat of obsolescence to assets and activities across businesses. Despite the difficulties, it is worthwhile to estimate how often each trajectory occurs in the economy to set the framework in context.

The following list reports the results of a rough estimate for the United States during the 1980s and 1990s.

Radical—18.9 percent

Creative—6.1 percent

Intermediating—32.1 percent

Progressive—42.9 percent

These estimates were obtained by aggregating profitability across each of the businesses of U.S. publicly traded corporations by the four-digit SIC (standard industry classification) code between 1981 and 1999. The dataset was based on the Compustat business segment reports and was screened in a number of ways to eliminate observations associated with poor industry definitions (i.e., industries labeled "not elsewhere classified"), entering and exiting businesses (i.e., because of anomalies in their reported income and assets), etc.

This process of aggregation yielded information on the average operating income and average assets for each of 726 four-digit industries in each of the eighteen years. The next step involved examining the amount of variation around the trend for each industry over time. Industries with substantial variation in their operating income were considered as subject to Architectural change. (Technically, an industry was considered to be undergoing Architectural change if the ratio of the standard deviation to the mean level of operating income was above average for the 726 industries.) Industries with substantial variation in their assets were considered as subject to Foundational change. (Technically, Foundational change was assumed if the ratio of the standard deviation to the mean level of assets was above the average.) After estimating whether an industry was undergoing Architectural and/or Foundational change, the trajectory was identified. The percentages reported here show the frequency of the estimates of each type among the 726 industries.

they can be difficult to find). Corollaries deal with three major issues: the clarity of industry boundaries, the terms of operational effectiveness, and the locus of innovation.

Defining rules and corollaries are summarized in table 2-2.

"Guidelines" are rules of thumb that describe how the elements of industry structure change given the broad conditions described by the defining rules and their corollaries. The elements of industry structure are expressed in terms of Porter's five-forces model for evaluating the profitability of an industry at a particular point in time (see box 1-2 in chapter 1). Changes to an industry's structure must work through these five forces to take hold.

## Progressive Change

Progressive change involves no threat of obsolescence to core activities or core assets. Coffee retailing, soft-drink bottling, long-haul trucking, and lumber milling all evolve on the Progressive model. Because buyers and suppliers are largely satisfied and because rivals tend to pursue distinctive positions, the industry's leaders can innovate by building on established activities. When an effort to innovate fails, the results aren't devastating. Companies quickly learn about the failure using feedback from buyers and from suppliers and can retrench without more than a temporary hit to performance.

### Progressive Case Study: Discount Retailing

Discount retailing in North America and most parts of the world is evolving Progressively. Figure 2-2 shows the principal activities in discount retailing.[5] The lines between the activities represent points of significant coordination and communication that occur within firms. For example, purchasing activities (at the upper left of the diagram) are tightly coordinated with merchandising programs because the promotion of a particular item can create a spike in demand that in turn leads to a greater number of orders. Purchasing is also tied to the screening and selecting of suppliers. If a candidate supplier cannot promise to deliver goods just-in-time to the discount retailer's distribution center, then the supplier may not be selected as a vendor. Purchasing is also tied to ongoing collaboration with suppliers. The most efficient discount retailers are known for integrating IT systems with those of reliable suppliers.

**TABLE 2-2**

## Defining Rules and Corollaries

| | Progressive | Creative | Intermediating | Radical |
|---|---|---|---|---|
| **Defining Rules** | | | | |
| 1. Robustness of core activities | | | | |
| • Major relationships | Stable | Stable | Unstable | Unstable |
| • Terms of competition | Stable | Stable | Unstable | Unstable |
| 2. Robustness of core assets | Strong | Weak | Strong | Weak |
| **Corollaries** | | | | |
| 3. Industry boundaries | Clear | Clear | Unclear | Unclear |
| 4. Operational effectiveness | | | | |
| • Dominant model | Interlocking activities | Project portfolio with support infrastructure | N/a | N/a |
| • Architectural transition | N/a | N/a | Deploying core assets outside long-standing relationships | Sustaining a profitable position and then exiting efficiently |
| 5. Locus of innovation | Links between activities | Modularized projects | Experimenting with asset deployment | Asset utilization; diversification as exit mechanism |

**FIGURE 2-2**

## Activities in Discount Retailing

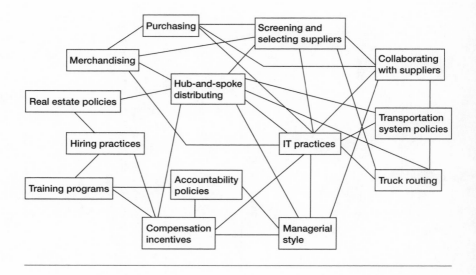

This analysis suggests that purchasing is a core activity in the discount retailing industry. Imagine that the industry's current purchasing activities were entirely eliminated and could not resume in their current form for a year. Industry profits would drop as companies strove to reinstate outdated methods for interacting with vendors—such as stockpiling inventory and working from paper order slips sent through the U.S. mail. Relationships with suppliers would be adversely affected. Some suppliers might be hurt so significantly that they would have to shut down operations or refuse to deal with the industry.

The profitability of the discount retailing industry would be hurt for other reasons as well. Because of the links depicted on figure 2-2, a wide range of related activities would become less effective. The retailers could no longer operate IT systems optimally. Coordination across suppliers would be damaged. Collaboration with suppliers to coordinate just-in-time systems would be ruled out.

A central feature of almost all Progressive industries is that almost all activities are core. The conclusions would be similar if the analysis were replicated on any other activity in figure 2-2. The centrality of the activity *system* is characteristic of industries on Progressive evolutionary paths (activities are related in simpler ways in industries on different evolutionary trajectories). Under Progressive change, the industry's stability arises from the links between activities rather than from any single proprietary activity, and as a result, a mapping of the links among activities tends to be complicated and messy.

Another characteristic of Progressive industries is that firms within the industry are open, not secretive, about what they do. Although it may seem counterintuitive, this openness poses relatively little risk to individual competitors because replicating the entire system of activities is difficult even though individual activities are easy to imitate. For instance, Wal-Mart is famous for inviting buyers, suppliers, dignitaries, pop stars, and even competitors to its Saturday-morning staff meetings. This isn't risky because Wal-Mart's efficiency rests on a virtuous circle between activities rather than anything secret. It's the tight coordination *among* activities and the constant adjustments in processes that account for Wal-Mart's profitability. Companies within Progressive industries are not secretive precisely because they want the revealed complexity of their system to deter outsiders. Because the system of activities in discount retailing is virtually impenetrable, its core activities are not threatened with obsolescence.

Similarly, the industry's core assets are not under a threat of obsolescence. In discount retailing, core assets include distribution centers, store locations, and brand capital. No new approach truly threatens to make these assets obsolete. Online retailing may be more convenient but the distribution of inventoried goods in low volumes from warehouses through a postal service is significantly more expensive than distributing them through discount retailers. Specialized superstores may offer better deals but cannot compete with discount retailers on product selection. The efficiencies in the discount retailing system continue to appeal both to buyers and to the vendors that sell into the discount retailing business.

The absence of both an Architectural and Foundational threat in the discount-retailing industry—and in all industries on Progressive evolutionary paths—makes for relative stability in the average profitability of the industry's leading firms. Firms go out of business because they fail to compete successfully, not because of a widespread threat of obsolescence to the industry as a whole.

The key to long-term survival and sustained superior performance in industries on Progressive evolutionary paths is a disciplined adherence to the dominant model for organizing core activities and core assets. The standards for operational effectiveness are too high to leave much room for error.

### The Rules of Progressive Change

Progressive change typically occurs through a long industry life cycle that spans many decades. The inception of the industry is often difficult to identify and visible only in retrospect: Sam Walton, who operated 30 discount stores in the rural Midwest by 1970, could not get vendors to deliver to his stores at reasonable prices; he thus built centralized warehousing and distribution centers that enabled him to buy in volume and lower the cost of goods sold. Progressive change usually ends when the industry is thrown into Architectural change by a threat to core activities.

#### Defining Rules

1. *Robustness of Core Activities.* Because core activities are not threatened with obsolescence, the industry's relationships with its buyers and with its suppliers remain relatively stable. Activities change incrementally to assure that the heart of the industry's approach to value creation is not disturbed. When changes are implemented, their value is quickly verified through feedback from buyers and from suppliers. The new value created by the change is distributed so that buyers, the industry, and suppliers benefit.

2. *Robustness of Core Assets.* The absence of a threat of obsolescence to core assets means that the firms within the industry can plan their investments carefully, without concern about engaging with competitors in a head-to-head race to make their commitments first. In other words, firms are not forced to innovate under a large-scale threat to the industry's foundation. As a result, the terms of competition— that is, whether firms compete on advertising, product features, merchandising, etc.—tend to change in ways that are predictable.

#### Corollaries

3. *Industry Boundaries.* The boundaries of industries that are changing Progressively are relatively easy to define because the dominant model for organizing activities sets a high standard

for efficiency in the business. (A notable exception to this rule occurs when the industry is just emerging.) A difficulty that occasionally arises has to do with the status of fringe firms. These firms are sometimes difficult to identify as insiders or outsiders because they are remote from the industry's leaders either geographically or in product features.

4. *Operational Effectiveness.* The dominant model in industries undergoing Progressive change emphasizes a system of interlocking activities. While each activity is relatively easy to imitate, the entire system of activities is difficult to imitate because of the ways in which the activities are coordinated. Often a powerful corporate culture emerges to coordinate choices made by dispersed employees.

5. *Locus of Innovation.* In industries undergoing Progressive change, innovation is usually most effective when it involves (i) adjusting the way that activities are coordinated, (ii) adding a new activity to the system, or (iii) improving information flows between activities. Large-scale projects that jar the entire activity system are usually less successful.

*Guidelines*

6. *Buyer Power.* Over time, buyers tend to become more aware of their preferences and often favor increasing convenience, which tends to increase their power. The power gain may be more than offset by increases in buyers' transaction costs, which become elevated as firms within the industry become distinctive and buyers become dependent.

7. *Supplier Power.* Suppliers invest in specialized capabilities as they tailor their activities to create value for the industry, which can raise their power (all else being equal). At the same time, suppliers' transaction costs tend to increase as they customize their activities for the industry and become more dependent on industry incumbents. Whether supplier power increases or decreases depends on the net effect of changes in supplier capabilities and transaction costs.

   A special note regarding employees (a type of supplier): Employees who are often unskilled at their points of entry into the industry accumulate skills that tie them to the industry. As a result, compensation for nonunionized employees tends to increase only incrementally over the course of a typical career. Employees may unionize to offset their lack of individual bargaining strength, in which case employee power may increase significantly.

8. *Threat of Substitution.* Substitutes for buyers tend toward incorporating more features or greater functionality, although at a higher price than the industry's products and services. Substitutes for suppliers tend toward offering greater opportunities for customization, although at the expense of volume. The net effect of the threat of substitution depends on the relative rates of improvement of the outside alternatives.

9. *Intensity of Rivalry.* The industry's incumbents attempt to manage rivalry by building increasing economies of scale and scope and by seeking to differentiate on geographic or product features. The best opportunities for building scale involve incremental changes in activity systems to incorporate insights achieved through experience and learning. The best opportunities for building scope involve incremental changes to coordinate activities more effectively. Incumbents work toward isolating themselves from the competition by building distinctive positions. As a result, market share tends to change hands only incrementally so that large annual shifts in market share between leading firms is relatively rare. Whether rivalry increases or decreases depends on whether firms are successful at building scale, building scope, and becoming differentiated fast enough to compel the exit of smaller and marginally efficient rivals.

10. *Threat of Entry.* New entrants may be attracted by the prospect of a stable return on investment in the industry, but the costs of entry increase in step with its rewards. Entry barriers accumulate as economies of scale and scope are built into the dominant model and as the complexity of the incumbents' activity systems raises the standard for efficient operations. Whether the threat of entry increases or decreases depends on whether outsiders correctly perceive the difficulty of catching up with the industry leaders in operational effectiveness.

### Performance Under Progressive Change

Progressive industries usually do not deliver either very high or very low profitability. When a dominant model takes hold, as in discount retailing, the return on invested capital to industry leaders may be somewhat higher than the national average, but these industries almost never rank above Creative industries. Over the long run, however, the leading firms in Progressive industries often generate high long-term returns on investment, once the fact that the initial investments aren't very risky is taken into account: Think of the returns at Wal-Mart and Southwest Airlines, for example. These companies were leaders in generating a high total return to shareholders over the 1980s and 1990s. This has to do with the adjustment for risk. Because investments are relatively inexpensive to reverse if they prove ineffective, investors can recoup their investments even when experiments fail. As a result, these firms can offer an impressive return to investors.

## Creative Change

Creative change occurs with a threat of obsolescence to core assets but not a threat to the industry's core activities. Examples of industries on Creative evolutionary paths include pharmaceutical manufacturing, oil and gas exploration, and motion-picture production. Companies in these industries engage in risky projects with the understanding that only some will pay off.

Leading companies in Creative industries exploit the fact that change is Foundational but not Architectural. This means that they use the strength of their relationships with key buyers and with the industry's suppliers to sustain themselves through the fits and starts of core-asset creation. Maintaining a system of core activities creates some stability, but there is an overtone of constant crisis in industries on a Creative evolutionary path because there is no stable foundation to the business. Companies must create core assets well before they can realize a return on their investments. Creativity is required in the broadest possible sense: Companies achieve superior performance by bringing products to market that were conceived years in advance.

Achieving leadership—that is, market dominance over time—in industries on Creative paths requires sustaining a system of core activities that equip the company to launch projects sequentially when they are ready for market.

Firms that successfully navigate through industries on Creative trajectories can achieve very high profitability. High profits in turn tend to attract entry by firms that undertake big, unconventional projects in the hope of becoming Cinderella stories. These ongoing threats of entry coupled with the overtone of constant crisis may tempt you to conclude that your industry is undergoing Radical change rather than Creative change. Yet the ongoing stability of buyer and supplier relationships reflects that change is not Architectural, and great companies in industries undergoing Creative change use this stability to their advantage.

The key to long-term *survival* in an industry on a Creative trajectory is in developing a system of supporting activities so that commercialization of projects through the organization is as efficient as possible. The key to *profitability* is in creating new products and services that capitalize on core assets that were conceived years in advance. *Sustaining* high profitability depends on creating successful new products and services repeatedly—becoming a home-run hitter—by creating a portfolio of projects and by cultivating the skills necessary for the disciplined management of each creative project.

### *Creative Case Study: Motion-Picture Production*

The motion-picture production industry is on a Creative evolutionary path. Hollywood film studios engage in several projects simultaneously while maintaining a system of relationships with actors, directors, scriptwriters, distributors, and exhibitors. With luck, a studio produces a few major hits in a year.

In the 1950s, 1960s, and 1970s, the dominant formula for motion-picture production became entrenched and the industry moved into maturity. The formula for making motion pictures is so familiar that we take it for granted:

- Most Hollywood films feature one to three famous stars.

- Films typically run about two hours.

- Each film falls into a genre (e.g., comedy, romantic comedy, drama, thriller, action).

- Movies are often released in the summer and around the December holidays.

- Major production studios are located in one of several large centers, most notably Hollywood California.

- Production budgets (which cover scriptwriter royalties, actor salaries, staging, and costuming, for example) are normally established at least a year in advance of the release of a film.

- Exhibitors bid for the rights to show films before they are completed.

Occasionally innovation occurs in this formula. *Star Wars* redefined the science fiction genre by combining a compelling and dramatic storyline with unprecedented special effects. *Fantasia* extended the adult animation category with an unusual storyline that incorporated classical music. Yet most innovation in the industry occurs within the established framework to create new assets—durable, owned property—that can be exploited within the industry's system of core activities.

Films are the core assets of the motion-picture studios and are constantly threatened with obsolescence. As a consequence, the studios regularly invest in a portfolio of risky projects with the hope that at least one will succeed. By most reports, the production budgets for features films have increased over the past twenty years. This means that the firms lay out more and more capital in advance of achieving box-office revenue. At the same time, the outlays required to compete effectively as a leader in the industry have escalated even more dramatically than for the average firm in the business. This means that the risks involved in pursuing a leadership position are even greater than the risks required to stay in the game. For filmmakers with an ambition for leadership, the risks are worthwhile only because the profits on blockbusters can be substantial.

This pattern is typical of Creative change. In motion-picture production, profits have expanded, which creates an incentive to spend more on making a film with blockbuster potential. In pharmaceuticals, a patented blockbuster drug requires the investment of more than a decade and hundreds of millions of dollars in development expense.

A critical feature of almost all industries on Creative evolutionary paths is the lag between the initial investment and the materialization of a revenue stream. It takes time to build the core asset before it can be commercialized. The lag creates inherent risk in the process of creating new assets. In motion pictures, the production cost is incurred before the studio gets definitive information about the value of the film in the marketplace. In the pharmaceutical industry, firms commit to drug development without any assurance of FDA approval.

Risk is high because the revenue stream cannot be predicted accurately when projects are initiated. Feedback from buyers and from the industry's suppliers is delayed until projects are finalized, packaged, and formally introduced to the market. If you were a film executive with a romantic drama in development that starred Gregory Peck and Audrey Hepburn, it's true that you could have conducted market research while the film was under development to project interest in seeing the movie on the July Fourth weekend in 1953, but odds are that the prediction would have been inaccurate. Interest in the movie would have depended on the weather, the other available movies, the reviews, and a range of other factors that would have been impossible to predict with any certainty months in advance.

This problem of unreliable buyer feedback is endemic in Creative industries because the character of assets cannot be perfectly predicted and because there is a long lag before they are commercialized into products or services. The lag forces firms in Creative industries to anticipate future demand—they have to stay ahead of the curve so products align with buyer preferences when the products are finally released. Given the unreliability of this forecasting effort, the leading firms in an industry sometimes experiment with risky projects that ultimately fail. And occasionally, an unknown filmmaker can achieve a surprising breakthrough that drives an unexpected surge in profitability. The only constant is that the performance of an industry on a Creative evolutionary path is volatile.

In Creative industries, invention also occurs around core activities. These activities tend to be stable and form the basis of economies of scale and scope, which in turn soften price competition. In motion-picture production, invention occurs as companies discover new ways of distributing their products. By the 1990s, Disney, Sony Pictures, Warner Brothers, Paramount, and many other film producers owned cable stations, broadcast networks, as well as traditional movie theaters. Domestic box-office receipts in traditional theaters accounted for less than 20 percent of the revenue from a typical film, with revenues from foreign, cable, and video-cassette sales accounting for most of the rest. This diversity in revenue sources reflects efforts to lower risk by creating scope in channels to market.

Yet despite volatility in profits, the industry's leading firms do not often lose their dominance. Companies sustain their market positions in two major ways. First, they develop specialized expertise in project management to create new core assets. By sponsoring a portfolio of projects, a motion-picture studio increases the likelihood of achieving a hit during a specific year. Second, leading companies develop core activities that are critical to project launch and that are difficult to imitate. Examples include distributing and vendor relationships. Even if an outsider develops a single project successfully, typically it cannot penetrate the leadership ranks because it does not have access to these supporting systems of core activities.

The dominant model in motion-picture production involves engaging in a portfolio of film projects and in nurturing key relationships with actors, directors, scriptwriters, distributors, promoters, exhibitors, and reviewers. Key relationships assure the longevity of the leading firms. By taking on a series of projects concurrently, the leaders develop economies of scope in project management that allow them to lower costs and improve the odds of success on individual films. Most large movie studios can recover from a series of box-office flops because they have relationships that keep the odds high for success on the next project.

### The Rules of Creative Change

Creative change generally begins as entrepreneurs seek out ways to successfully manage the risks of commercializing projects. In motion-picture production, oil and gas exploration, and pharmaceuticals, this means rationalizing a system for project management as well as for distribution. Creative change usually ends when the industry is thrown into an Architectural transformation by a threat to core activities.

The ten rules for competing effectively in an industry undergoing Creative change are also categorized as defining rules, corollaries, and guidelines:

#### Defining Rules

1. *Robustness of Core Activities.* Core activities are crucial to the stability of industries on a Creative path because core assets are threatened. Indeed, it is the stability of the industry's core activities that holds the industry's leaders in place. As a result, firms tend to expand and develop core activities over time.

2. *Robustness of Core Assets.* Core assets are threatened with obsolescence, which creates an imperative need for their renewal among firms that seek superior performance. Because the industry's leading firms maintain a complementary system of core activities, they have the greatest incentive to create new core assets that can form the basis of newly commercialized products and services (each of which may have its own short shelf life). Because of the risk in the development of each new core asset, the industry's leaders develop systems where projects are modularized.

*Corollaries*

3. *Industry Boundaries.* Boundaries are relatively easy to identify in industries that follow Creative paths, although questions occasionally arise regarding the status of a fringe of small firms that lack a network of key relationships (i.e., core activities). These small enterprises may look like one-hit wonders rather than firms with real staying power.

4. *Operational Effectiveness.* The dominant model in industries undergoing Creative change usually involves managing the development of new core assets on a portfolio model to assure that failing projects can be cancelled easily without jeopardizing other projects and without creating a risk that the activity system will lie dormant for too long. The standard for operational efficiency in supporting core activities and in creative project management tends to increase and to be high in industry maturity. The culture of industries on Creative evolutionary paths tends to reward superstars (e.g., movie actors, research chemists, and insightful geologists) with high status.

5. *Locus of Innovation.* Innovation is usually most productive when it occurs in modularized projects that are each designed to yield new products and services. Large-scale projects with long development times are crucial for value creation. At the same time, innovation may occur incrementally in the network of supporting core activities.

*Guidelines*

6. *Buyer Power.* Buyers attach high value to products and services that are new and that tap into unprecedented new material or are surprising in some way. Because products are often experiential (i.e., their full value depends on the experience of consuming them), buyer preferences can evolve unpredictably. Transaction costs tend to decrease as the industry strives to make it easy for buyers to try new products, thereby lowering buyers' switching costs. Increases and decreases in overall buyer power depend on the evolution of underlying preferences.

7. *Supplier Power.* Several types of suppliers work within the industry. Those engaged in creating core assets tend to have the greatest power and status, and try to retain low switching costs to force firms within the industry to bid for their services. For example, some talented superstar employees who are integral to project management are compensated at unusually high rates. Suppliers that support core activities have less power and status: They build specialized capabilities and raise their transaction costs in the process. For example, a large cadre of employees engaged in supporting activities develop industry-specific skills over their careers and cannot command high salaries unless they unionize. The overall level of supplier power depends largely on whether suppliers can develop enough specialized expertise to stimulate competition among firms within the industry for their services.

8. *Threat of Substitution.* Substitutes for buyers tend to offer a different experience or a different mode of accessing a similar experience to those offered by the industry. The most potent substitutes for suppliers are those that threaten to attract creative talent, perhaps by providing an alternative way to commercialize creative output. Increases and decreases in the threat of substitution depend on relative rates of improvement in both the creative experience and in ease of access to the experience.

9. *Intensity of Rivalry.* Firms within the industry attempt to manage rivalry by building increasing economies of scale and scope. The best opportunities for building scope involve a

portfolio of projects, each designed to generate a new core asset. The best opportunities for building scale tend to arise through coordination of supporting core activities. The annual market shares of the industry's leaders tend to be volatile in industries undergoing Creative change because of differences in success at commercialization. Similarly, the rate of industry growth can be volatile because of unpredictable shifts in buyer preferences, supplier capabilities, and project management. Firms are secretive about their plans for innovation because imitation is only partly deterred by the system of supporting core activities. If word were to get out about a new idea for building a core asset before it was constructed, the company would be vulnerable to imitation. On balance, the level of rivalry depends on the successes of the industry's firms at building distinctive identities based on differences in creative capabilities.

10. *Threat of Entry.* New entrants are often attracted by the prospect of the high return on assets that accompanies a hit product. Occasional entry occurs as an outsider successfully develops a new product or service, and yet longevity and superior performance depend on cultivating a network of supporting core activities. Entry barriers accumulate on project-development skills, the network of supporting activities, and the scale required to amortize risk across a portfolio of projects. Incumbents can retaliate against new entrants by capitalizing on their superior access to buyers and to suppliers. The level of the threat of entry depends on outsiders' perceptions of the tradeoffs between the rewards to a proprietary hit product and the costs of obtaining access to a supporting network of core activities.

### Performance Under Creative Change

Industries on Creative trajectories often generate better profitability on average than industries on the other evolutionary paths. However, the greater profits are tied to risks. While industry leaders and some breakthrough entrants achieve outstanding performance, the majority of firms may struggle financially. The temptation to attempt entry is great because the rewards of success are enormous, even though most new entrants fail. As a result, there is significant dispersion in the profitability of high and low performers. While some firms in industries on Creative paths achieve unparalleled profitability, others post significant losses.

## Intermediating Change

Intermediating change, a form of Architectural transformation, involves a threat of obsolescence to the industry's core activities and often occurs when changes in information flows make new ways of transacting more efficient. Intermediation usually leads to a major reshuffling of relationships among the industry, its buyers, and its suppliers, with many corporate casualties along the way. Like Radical change, the threat to core activities under Intermediation rarely leads to the total eradication of the established industry, although several leading firms may undergo bankruptcy or merger. Examples of Intermediating industries are automobile dealerships, coffee importers, and energy distributors.

Unlike Radical change, core assets retain their relevance under Intermediation. The threat to core activities but not to core assets creates a difficult management challenge: Performance ultimately depends on developing new relationships and reconfiguring activities while preserving brand capital, knowledge capital, and physical resources. The ultimate goal is to preserve profitability in the established business while stripping it of its most valuable core assets.

### Intermediation Case Study: Auto Dealerships

Intermediating transformation can take hold in any established industry, on any prior evolutionary path, and at any stage. When it occurs, Intermediation imposes a whole new set of rules onto the industry. The auto dealership industry was evolving Progressively through the mid-1990s when a threat of obsolescence to core activities emerged. Advances in automobile manufacturing improved car longevity to the point where the frequency of purchase began to drop dramatically. (All else being equal, a 50 percent increase in the durability of a car means that it lasts 33 percent longer and that auto dealerships thus see buyers a third less frequently.) With less frequent buying, price competition rose to ferocious levels, margins slipped, and dealerships began to go out of business. The threat of obsolescence to core activities meant that the rules of Progressive change were immediately invalidated. A new set of rules that reflected the industry's Intermediation was in place.

The auto dealership industry began its Intermediating transformation years before the popularity of online auto services like Autobytel.com, but the growth of online services accelerated and contributed to the transformation. At first, the online services provided only information about car costs and features. After a few years, the services expanded their functions to handle the transfer of offers between consumers and car dealerships. Some even began to offer financing and insurance. Buyers were attracted by the opportunity to negotiate at arm's length, especially given the unsavory reputation of car dealers and the convenience of online services. These new functions made for complex relationships between the online services and the traditional auto dealers. Because the dealers paid fees to the online service companies in exchange for referrals, the dealers were both buyers and competitors of the online providers (see figure 2-3).

As the online service providers grew and Intermediation progressed, it became clear that many of the traditional activities in the business were becoming less prevalent. Edgy personalized selling and local marketing were becoming less important. As consumer dependence on Internet services increased, dealerships found it inefficient to

**FIGURE 2-3**

## The Intermediation of Auto Dealerships

**Traditional Core Activities**

**Activities of Online Auto Services**

continue to employ large numbers of salespeople. The threat to selling and marketing activities was materializing into the actual obsolescence of traditional activities.

Yet Intermediation did not threaten to make the auto dealers' core assets obsolete. Inventory, local reputation, showroom presence, and service bays retained their relevance to buyers. As traditional marketing and selling activities lost their relevance, auto dealers used many of their other assets, such as locally held inventory, a physical store, and local brand capital, to complement the online selling process.

With time, the value created by car dealers operating on the traditional dominant model began to drop even more dramatically. Some dealers persisted with the old ways of doing business, thus creating unprecedented excess capacity in the business and further exacerbating the need for change. Core assets retained their relevance when configured in a new way to work in tandem with online services, but the transition proved to be too painful for many established dealers. The traditional auto dealers had the *potential* to create value in tandem with the online services but could only realize this potential by dramatically changing their core activities. In effect, the online services had cut a slice out of the traditional auto dealers' value chain and found a way to build businesses around a subset of their activities (see the shaded area of figure 2-3).

As Intermediation progresses in the industry, the survival of many auto dealers depends on taking advantage of core assets that retain their value. The whole structure of relationships between the auto dealers, manufacturers, and buyers is affected. Some dealerships have failed after years of unsuccessful attempts at restructuring and as a result more than 8 percent of U.S. auto dealers went out of business during the 1990s.[6] Succeeding in this kind of environment requires the grit to take core assets out of a business in which they currently generate profit and to move them into an emerging business in which profits have yet to materialize.

### The Rules of Intermediation

Under Intermediation, the threat of obsolescence commonly originates with some sort of change in information flow that causes buyers and suppliers to become disenchanted with old ways of doing business. The newly available information is usually of major significance and can make new markets possible. As a result, companies no longer have to coordinate activities internally and can buy products and services on free markets. Occasionally, companies have to take on new activities to get access to a new market. For example, many automobile manufacturers integrated into auto financing in the 1950s to get access to the consumer market. Intermediation ends only with the threat of obsolescence to the industry's core activities. This usually occurs because of vast consolidation that leaves in place only enough capacity to serve a group of residual buyers.

### Defining Rules

1. *Robustness of Core Activities.* Because core activities are threatened with obsolescence under Intermediation, the industry's relationships with its buyers and with its suppliers are unstable. Firms must find ways to sustain profitable relationships despite increasing concerns among buyers and suppliers about the viability of transactions over the long term.

2. *Robustness of Core Assets.* Core assets are not threatened with obsolescence and retain their ability to create value in industries undergoing Intermediation. To actualize the value creation over the long term, the core assets must be reconfigured to support new kinds of transactions that involve different activities. However, over the short term, the core assets yield their greatest value in traditional uses. As a result, firms within the industry struggle with the tradeoffs of preserving critically valuable resources in old, profitable relationships versus redeploying resources in new ways.

### Corollaries

3. *Industry Boundaries.* Under Intermediation, industry boundaries are difficult to identify. At first, the new approach may seem like a new segment or niche within the established industry. Because the new approach involves a threat to core activities, it constitutes a separate industry. The trick to identifying the boundaries of the Intermediating industry is to keep in mind that they are the same as they were prior to the Architectural threat. Because the new approach involves a different set of core activities (even though it may rest on the same core assets), it is a different industry that evolves by a different set of rules.

4. *Operational Effectiveness.* Under Intermediation, no dominant model serves as a centerpiece of industry evolution. Performance reflects the abilities of the firms within the industry to manage the transition in core activities effectively and to extract value from the core assets that retain their value. Profitability over the short run depends on preserving core assets as long as possible in established relationships, even as the relationships come under threat. Survival and profitability over the long run depend on finding ways to use the core assets in new kinds of relationships. The key to operational effectiveness is in balancing these competing demands despite the enormous strain on the organization.

5. *Locus of Innovation.* Innovation is usually most productive when it takes one of two forms: first, when it provides firms within the industry with ways of capturing value from core assets in new relationships, and second, when it softens the tension between preserving old relationships and pursuing new relationships. The most successful forms of innovation often involve finding new ways to transact with old buyers and suppliers so that established relationships aren't entirely abandoned.

*Guidelines*

6. *Buyer Power.* Major changes in transaction costs allow buyers to transact with the industry more efficiently, but the precise nature of the effect on buyer power depends on contextual factors. The threat to core activities in the industry may spill over and also threaten the industry's buyers, causing buyers to scramble to sustain themselves and diminishing buyer power in the process. On the other hand, the threat to core activities in the industry may not spill over, and buyers may find themselves struggling to find ways to get out of old relationships with the industry. On balance, the net impact on buyer power depends on how buyer preferences change in relation to outside options as well as on the degree to which buyers are locked into dealing with the industry by their prior commitments.

7. *Supplier Power.* Under Intermediation, suppliers operate under uncertainty about their long-term prospects for dealing with

the industry. As a result, there is a significant disincentive to reinvest in capabilities that will further lock suppliers into their positions. This disincentive is complicated by countervailing pressures if the suppliers' industry is also threatened with obsolescence. Suppliers may scramble to improve their efficiencies in an effort to retain their viability in the short run. The implications for overall supplier power depend on the success of suppliers in finding new ways to transact that maximize the value available through the new approach.

8. *Threat of Substitution.* The most significant threat of substitution under Intermediation is the new approach, which promises to make obsolete a significant portion of the industry's core activities. The threat may involve attracting buyers and suppliers into new ways of transacting, or the threat may bypass buyers and suppliers entirely and threaten to make them obsolete along with the industry. Either way, the threat of substitution tends to intensify over the course of time under Intermediation.

9. *Intensity of Rivalry.* A number of factors contribute to the escalation of rivalry in industries undergoing Intermediation. First, economies of scale in core activities break down. Secondly, significant excess capacity can arise as the industry's incumbents struggle with barriers to exit in their fixed core assets. At the same time, the industry's incumbents may be able to pursue strategies that allow them to manage rivalry effectively. Some of the principal mechanisms for managing rivalry include: (i) economies of scope across product lines that partly offset the threat of obsolescence; (ii) partnerships with buyers, suppliers, rivals, and outsiders in the emerging industry; (iii) distinctiveness arising from differences in systems for migrating core assets from the old to the new approach. The net result may be either an improvement or deterioration in the terms of competition, although deterioration is more common under Intermediation.

10. *Threat of Entry.* Barriers tend to arise around core assets rather than core activities and may increase the direct costs of entry. As Intermediation progresses, the threat of retaliation by in-

cumbent firms typically becomes central to entry deterrence. The threat of entry may either decline or increase within each stage of Intermediation, but over the long course of the transformation, the threat almost always declines.

### Performance Under Intermediation

The performance of an industry undergoing Intermediation is typically volatile and deteriorates over time. While leading firms may initially dominate the business and retain their profitability, the threat from reconfigured competitors eventually becomes significant. There is a strong incentive to preserve core assets by redeploying them into a new business (which is often the business that creates the threat to the industry in the first place). For example, many traditional auto dealers are focusing on providing specialized services in the online-supported auto selling business. The restructuring itself creates unprecedented costs that can damage profitability significantly. As a result, the profitability of most industries undergoing Intermediation is unusually low.

## Radical Change

We are conditioned to think of many changes as radical, but the evidence suggests that truly Radical transformation of industry structure is not common. Radical transformation, which involves both Architectural and Foundational change, is defined by a threat of obsolescence to both an industry's core assets and core activities. The commercial railroad industry was changed Radically by interstate trucking's smaller loads, greater flexibility in the timing of shipments, greater flexibility in pickup locations, and broader range of destinations. One of the key events that created the threat of obsolescence was the construction of the interstate highway system in the 1950s and early 1960s. Today, the railroad industry continues to evolve by the rules of Radical change.

The financial planning industry is also undergoing a Radical transformation tied to the availability of abundant information for managing money. Rather than pay for services from a financial planner, investors can do their own research online, and develop a plan using prepackaged software. Many of the principal suppliers to the financial planning industry—the investment specialists who serve as advisors—are also on the job market largely because they lack the sophisticated technical skills to satisfy a new breed of investors. The financial planning industry is likely to evolve by the rules of Radical change for decades to come.

Under Radical change, buyers and suppliers to the industry become less inclined to continue dealing in traditional ways. At the same time, established companies face an incentive to shed resources and capabilities that once lay at the foundation of value creation. The result of Radical transformation is typically a thoroughly reconfigured industry that operates at a reduced scale. As the process of Radical change advances, a war of attrition can arise as leading firms compete for the last remaining viable positions in the industry. The difficulty is that wars of attrition are almost never worth it because firms spend more during the war than they earn subsequently in the diminished industry.

### Radical Case Study: Typewriter Manufacturing

The typewriter industry is nearing the end of a Radical change largely attributable to the introduction of the personal computer. Indeed, the transformation has been so profound that you may be surprised even to think of typewriters as precursors to personal computers. The main link between the personal computing and typewriting industries is in how the products are used—we now do our word processing by PC rather than by typewriter—but just about everything else is different. First, PCs are usually distributed from manufacturers to consumers either directly or through value-added resellers. Typewriters are usually distributed through specialized distributors that call on corporate accounts and that sometimes operate Main Street offices. Second, PCs and typewriters are manufactured using different kinds of components. PCs use modularized electronic components and are easy to assemble, while typewriters are manufactured on integrated designs. Third, buyer purchase criteria differ substantially. Corporate purchasing agents are often concerned about preserving the value of inventoried spare parts in their decisions about typewriter purchases, while decisions to purchase PCs are based on price, service, and available features. Finally, PCs are subject to much greater economies of scope than typewriters in that they offer many functions besides word processing. Of course, this is only a partial list of the ways in which the PC and typewriter-manufacturing businesses differ. The bottom line is that each industry is evolving by a very different set of rules. PC manufacturers focus little on competition from typewriter manufacturers, but typewriter manufacturers must be constantly vigilant about developments in PCs.

Keep in mind that the typewriter manufacturing industry is distinct from PC manufacturing and follows a different evolutionary trajectory. It is typewriter manufacturing that is going through the Radical transformation (not the PC business, which is on a Progressive trajectory). Typewriter manufacturing was thrown into Radical transformation as soon as it became clear that PCs carried the potential to make typewriter manufacturers' core activities and core assets obsolete. When a shift like this happens and an industry is snapped into Radical transformation, the trajectory of change in the old industry is superseded by a new set of rules. Everything is called into question. Prior concerns about how to compete in the typewriter industry (such as how consumers would react to smaller models with more sophisticated components and higher price tags) give way entirely to the new question of whether the installed base of typewriters will soon become wholly irrelevant.

In general, Radical transformation can take hold in any established industry. Yet despite the force of Radical change it does not take place instantly. You can still find a typewriter in many office buildings, although of course few companies spend as much money on typewriters as they did twenty years ago. Why is the change so slow? Because the prior infrastructure built around typewriters locked buyers, distributors, suppliers, and competitors into their relationships. The suppliers of ink cartridges, spare parts, maintenance, and training for typewriters all provided important services that typewriter buyers gave up reluctantly. In fact, PC users were initially concerned about the stability, security, and reliability of their machines. To break through the value created by the typewriter industry, the PC industry had to offer enough benefits to overcome the risks and costs of switching.

### The Rules of Radical Change

Radical transformation begins as soon as the threat to core activities and core assets becomes clear. Recall that the key question for identifying whether an activity or asset is "core" is to evaluate whether the industry's profitability would be damaged if the activity or asset were eliminated for a period of a year. If the activity or asset is irreplaceable (in the sense that profitability would suffer), then it is "core." Radical transformation occurs when both core activities and core assets in the industry are confronted with an actual threat of obsolescence. The transformation ends only when the threats are eliminated. If the threat never abates, then the industry never emerges from Radical change.

### Defining Rules

1. *Robustness of Core Activities.* Because core activities are threatened with obsolescence, relationships between the industry, its buyers, and its suppliers are unstable. Shifts in the distribution of value lead buyers and suppliers to reevaluate their incentives to continue to invest in dealing with the industry.

2. *Robustness of Core Assets.* Core assets are threatened with obsolescence, which creates instability in the terms of competition. Firms within the industry are constantly confronted with questions about whether to recreate core assets to remain competitive or whether to scale back their commitment to the business. The tradeoffs between these choices change over time.

### Corollaries

3. *Industry Boundaries.* Under Radical change, the industry's leaders are clearly distinguishable, but questions may arise about the status of firms that represent the threat of the new approach. Keep in mind that industry boundaries are more or less the same as they were prior to the Architectural threat. The new approach evolves by a different set of rules. Firms that participate in both the old and new businesses become diversified and must compete effectively in each business separately to remain a viable competitor in both businesses over the long run.

4. *Operational Effectiveness.* Survival depends on finding new uses for durable assets and activity systems that lose their capacity for creating value incrementally. In many industries, the threat of obsolescence initially stimulates a renaissance in the established industry, and may lead to a long period in which the industry remains competitive with the emerging approach. Profitability in the established industry depends on sustaining the industry's system of core activities and core assets as long as possible. Firms in industries undergoing Radical transformation often deal with the challenge by diversifying, but only oc-

casionally are they able to lead in the industry that represents the Architectural threat. More often firms succeed by applying their activities and assets in industries that are not directly related to the emerging business that represents the Architectural threat.

5. *Locus of Innovation.* Innovation occurs at two levels in industries undergoing Radical transformation. The first involves finding ways to operate efficiently in the industry under threat by scaling back commitments, by avoiding over-investing in the business, and by capitalizing on previously untapped opportunities to create value for buyers. The second level of innovation involves finding ways to diversify into businesses that may not initially seem related to preserve the value of core activities and assets.

## Guidelines

6. *Buyer Power.* Under Radical transformation, major changes in transaction costs occur as buyers confront new alternatives. Because changing to the new approach may involve incurring substantial set-up costs or risk, buyers may delay, thereby providing the established industry with an opportunity to rejuvenate its value creation. Transaction costs of the new approach tend to decline, and buyer retention through this mechanism may be more difficult to accomplish. Similarly, buyer preferences tend to develop in relation to outside options. As a result, while buyer power may ebb and wane through the course of Radical transformation, the long-term trajectory is toward higher buyer power until only a circumscribed segment of very loyal buyers is left.

7. *Supplier Power.* Suppliers may initially work in partnership with the industry to improve efficiencies and keep the industry viable. In this effort, their power may shift as new kinds of dependencies between suppliers and the industry emerge. As the number of firms and suppliers in the industry begins to drop, suppliers may gain power but become increasingly vulnerable to industry contraction. As a result, they may face an incentive to stop investing in their capabilities. The industry's incumbents may integrate vertically to assure access to key

raw materials and services. Thus, over the long course of the transformation, supplier power may increase and decrease, but the trajectory is toward higher supplier power.

8. *Threat of Substitution.* The threatening new approach represents a significant substitute for dealing with the established industry. The threat may originate in attracting away buyers and suppliers, or it may entirely displace buyers and suppliers.

9. *Intensity of Rivalry.* Economies of scale and scope in the established industry are critical for retaining efficiency, and tend not to break down during the course of Radical change because there is little opportunity for their partial redeployment in the newly emerging business. Instead, firms within the industry tend to reinvest in developing efficiencies by escalating economies of scale and scope. Firms may develop partnerships with old rivals and then even consolidate through mergers and acquisitions in an effort to manage excess capacity. While these efforts may be partly successful, excess capacity nonetheless tends to develop, especially as the transformation advances. The recommitment of firms to the industry may be enhanced through vertical integration to assure access to key supplies and downstream distribution channels. Rivalry may be partially mitigated as firms seek out new segments and new opportunities for differentiation. As a result, firms within the industry may be able to manage the terms of competition. Whether the intensity of rivalry increases or diminishes depends on their success in this effort.

10. *Threat of Entry.* New entrants into the business tend to be deterred first by the formidable systems of core activities and core assets in the business, and then by perceptions of retaliation by incumbents. Because the prospects of a reasonable return on investment are poor, the threat of entry generally remains low.

### Performance Under Radical Change

The profitability of industries undergoing Radical change—measured by return on invested capital—is often high until the transformation becomes advanced. At first, the leading firms within the industry usually fend off the threat of obsolescence temporarily. As the threat becomes significant, consolidation begins to occur but surviving firms can often keep their profitability high by avoiding too much investment in the business. In the advanced phases of the transformation, profits may drop dramatically as the industry's mainstream buyers defect and as the war of attrition between surviving firms advances. Of course, Radical change carries a significant threat to firm survival, especially for industry leaders.

## Playing By the Rules

Although rare, it is possible for an industry to shift between evolutionary trajectories. The criteria for a shift lie in whether a new threat of obsolescence emerges or fades away. When a new threat emerges, then an industry is snapped onto a new path. The path depends on the nature of the threat (i.e., in whether Architectural and/or Foundational change is under way). When an old threat fades, the structure of the industry evolves by a different set of rules that depend on whether a residual Architectural or Foundational transformation continues.

Industries almost always start out on either a Progressive or Creative trajectory because the firms within the industry have a strong incentive to create a clear, dominant model for organizing activities in a way that allows them to capture value. Industries begin on a Creative rather than Progressive path when core assets must be created before their commercialized value can be assessed.

In both Progressive and Creative industries, pressure may build up for change in the dominant model. As a result, the industry's approach to value creation may become threatened with obsolescence and an Architectural change may occur as the industry is catapulted onto either a Radical or Intermediating path. Both Radical and Intermediating transformation occur over long periods and threaten the competitive standing and profitability of established leaders.

After the restructuring of activities over time—on the order of decades—the threat of obsolescence may fade, marking a transition back to a Progressive or Creative path.[7] A company that has survived from the beginning confronts renewed opportunity to secure competitive position, although often on a smaller scale and often based on a very different approach. Sears survived Radical change in catalog retailing during the mid-twentieth century by becoming dominant in general merchandise retailing. Until recently, Sears continued to publish a catalog, although catalog sales had become much less significant to the company's overall revenue stream. Today, the best option for Sears may be to diversify into businesses in which its brand name and merchandising capabilities carry more long-term value than they do in general merchandising.

Shifts between trajectories do not happen frequently. It can take decades for the trajectory of industry evolution on a single model to run its course. In fact, it is virtually unheard of for an industry to go through a transition between evolutionary trajectories more frequently than once in ten years.

The rules in play under an evolutionary trajectory establish boundaries on effective strategies. Each trajectory carries strong implications about the kinds of innovation that lead to sustained superior performance. Developing a strategy that exploits the opportunity in industry evolution depends on understanding the phase of change under each trajectory. A company that recognizes a transformation early generally has access to a broader range of attractive options than a company that recognizes the evolutionary path late in the process of change. By innovating to take advantage of the specific character of the trajectory the firm can substantially improve its chances of achieving a superior return on investment over the long run. The next chapter describes each of the phases of change, and chapter 4 offers diagnostics both for evaluating which trajectory applies and for understanding the phase of change in the industry that you are examining.

# 3

# How Change Unfolds
# on Each Trajectory

C HAPTER 2 DEFINED the four major trajectories of change, and showed that every industry follows just one trajectory. The next step in applying these concepts toward better performance is to understand how each trajectory unfolds through a series of stages. Crafting a strategy that exploits the transformation of the industry structure depends on an approach that takes advantage of the timing of the transition and the kinds of pressures that will be brought to bear on competitors. The inflection points between stages can provide opportunities for surprising rivals and improving competitive position. This chapter builds on your understanding of the four evolutionary phases to discuss how and when these opportunities emerge.

Some broad themes characterize strategies that make the most of each phase. Early in the process of change, the most attractive alternatives often involve the building of options that can be exercised later. As change progresses through its central stages, the stakes become clearer and firms may have to compete vigorously to survive. Often this involves drawing upon options created earlier. As industry evolution progresses into its advanced stages, companies may confront tradeoffs between concentrating resources in their industry and aggressively diversifying into new businesses in which the potential for value creation is greater. The common challenge is winding down commitment to the current industry without damaging short-run profitability.

Figure 3-1 summarizes the stages of change for each of the four trajectories of industry evolution. The character of the stages depends on whether change is Architectural but does not directly depend on whether change is Foundational. Under Progressive and Creative evolution, the "life cycle" model applies. Some readers may be familiar

FIGURE 3-1

## Stages of Change

| Trajectories of Industry Evolution | Description | Model of Transition | Phases of Transition |
|---|---|---|---|
| Progressive | Not Architectural, Not Foundational | Industry life cycle | Fragmentation Shake-out Maturity |
| Creative | Not Architectural, Foundational | | Decline |
| Intermediation | Architectural, Not Foundational | Phases | Emergence Convergence Co-existence |
| Radical | Architectural Foundational | | Dominance |

with this model, which is often held up as a standard for understanding industry evolution. Because the life cycle model is so intuitive, many executives are accustomed to using it to guide their decisions about transformation. The trouble is that the life cycle model does not *always* apply and can lead to dangerously incorrect conclusions when change is Radical or Intermediating. Figure 3-1 shows that under Radical and Intermediating (i.e., Architectural) transformation, a different model of staged change is relevant. This more nuanced model is discussed in the next section.

## Models of Change

The life cycle model of Progressive and Creative change involves stages of fragmentation, shakeout, maturity, and decline. The following are brief descriptions of each of the stages:[1]

1. *Fragmentation.* Industries begin in a period of fragmentation as companies experiment with different approaches to a market. Many firms offer a variety of products, and each operates at low volumes. Companies tend to be entrepreneurial, privately owned, and focused on serving narrow geographic areas with a limited number of products. Benchmarking is uncommon because competitors use different processes.

2. *Shakeout.* In time, industries go through shakeout. Shakeout occurs because a *dominant model* emerges for generating value on a large scale. The dominant model generally is substantially more efficient than other approaches and gains legitimacy as influential early adopters promote it through their networks. Volumes grow quickly as the industry adopts the dominant model and generates unprecedented value for buyers and for the industry's suppliers.

3. *Maturity.* Industries eventually enter a mature phase in which growth in volume slows. The industry structure becomes remarkably stable with little change in the rank of leading firms.

4. *Decline.* When volumes begin to drop, an industry moves into decline. Competition can take on new intensity. As competition heats up, companies often search for incremental efficiencies in an effort to recover profitability. Leading firms may compete in wars of attrition, resulting in poor performance for all competitors.

Figure 3-2 summarizes the industry life cycle.

Even though the life cycle model does not apply, Radical and Intermediating transformations do move through phases: emergence,

**FIGURE 3-2**

## The Life Cycle for Progressive and Creative Change

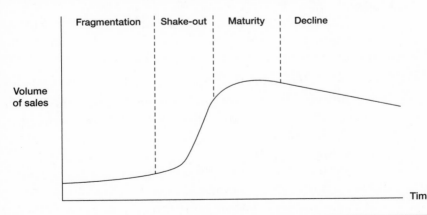

convergence, co-existence, and dominance. The following are brief descriptions of each of these four phases:

1. *Emergence.* The initial period of emergence is characterized by experimentation with new approaches to value creation that buck conventional wisdom in an established industry. The defining characteristic of the emergence stage is that the inventive effort is specifically focused on making the traditional dominant model in an established industry obsolete. At this stage, however, the efforts occur on a relatively small scale. For firms in the established industry, the threat of obsolescence to the industry's activities warrants attention but may not be significant enough to compel immediate restructuring.

2. *Convergence.* A single new approach for creating value is identifiable as central to the threat of obsolescence, but the traditional industry continues to dominate the emerging industry in volume of sales. The defining characteristic of this stage is that growth in volume under the new approach is high enough to allow for convergence in the sizes of the new and traditional industries. As the new industry gains in volume, leaders in the traditional industry may react by reconfiguring some of their activities.

3. *Co-existence.* During a period of co-existence, buyers and suppliers become increasingly sophisticated at evaluating the new approach. Volume growth in the emerging industry may slow, but it continues to outpace any residual growth in the established industry. The old industry may go through a temporary renaissance as a result of the increasing sophistication of buyers and of suppliers as well as defensive efforts by industry incumbents to manage an increasing intensity of rivalry and threat of substitution.

4. *Dominance.* During the final phase, dominance, the rules for competing effectively in the traditional industry are superseded by the rules of change under the new approach. Buyer preferences, supplier capabilities, and the terms of competition are all defined in reference to the emerging industry. As a result of the popularity of the new approach, volumes in the traditional industry stop growing and may even begin to decline. The threat of obsolescence materializes as firms exit the industry through consolidation, merger, and bankruptcy.

When industry change is Architectural, the process of transformation can seem like a life cycle even when it is not. For example, an industry undergoing Radical transformation moves through a phase in which companies consolidate, buyer needs change, and vertical integration and disintegration occur. Because these changes can also occur in industries undergoing Progressive or Creative change (i.e, during shakeout), it is easy to fall prey to the tempting—but mistaken—conclusion that the Architectural threat is absent in an industry that is going through a Radical transformation.

Consider the explosion of innovation in landline handsets that accompanied the threat from wireless telephony. Handsets of unprecedented portability and clarity were introduced to the market in an effort to defend share against wireless. Landline handsets appeared to go through a renaissance with improved cordless telephones and lower prices on conventional phones. To the untrained eye, the landline handset industry may have seemed as though it were going through a shakeout in which the best response was to defend market share against the upstart segment. In fact, the industry was evolving by a separate set of rules that had nothing to do with the life cycle, and the escalation of commitment to the landline handset business was probably among the worst strategic moves under the circumstances.

The introduction of the wireless telephone had thrown the landline handset industry into a period of Architectural change in which the core activities of the landline handset industry were threatened with obsolescence. The entire structure of the cellular-handset manufacturing business differed so substantially from landline handset manufacturing that it threatened to make obsolete virtually all of the core activities of the traditional industry. By committing to the expansion of capacity in landline handset manufacturing, the established companies were throwing good money after bad. The escalation in capacity would spark price competition later as landline handset volumes inevitably began their decline.

Please keep in mind that it is the *established* or *traditional* industry, and not the new industry, that goes through Architectural change. In landline handset manufacturing as well as others undergoing Architectural change, the phases of the transformation are defined by comparison with the new approach. In addition, the emerging industry evolves by a different set of rules than the industry that is under threat. There is an asymmetry: In the emerging industry, change is almost always

Progressive or Creative when the advanced phases of transformation are not defined by reference to the traditional industry. The following sections describe in detail the stages of the life cycle under Progressive and Creative change and the phases of Radical and Intermediating change.

## The Life Cycle of Progressive Change

You'll recall that Progressive Change is under way in the long-haul trucking, commercial airlines, and home goods retailing industries, as well as in other businesses in which neither core activities nor core assets are under a threat of obsolescence. Think of national coffee retailing, where Starbucks has exemplified a dominant model over the past twenty years. Under Progressive change, innovation tends to involve incremental change and life cycle phases tend to be long.

### Fragmentation: Experimentation on a Small Scale

An initial period of fragmentation may require years to unfold. The principal activity during this period is widespread experimentation by entrepreneurs seeking to find an operating formula that yields significantly more value than competing approaches. Early experimentation with personal computers occurred in corporate labs, hobby shops, garages and attics as entrepreneurs sought to build prototypes that could become standard for the business.

At this stage, experimentation is often so subtle and indistinct that the new companies appear to operate in a niche within an established industry. For example, discount retailers Wal-Mart, Kmart, and Target initially operated on a small scale and with narrower product lines than department stores. As a result, the emerging discount retailing industry seemed to be a specialized segment of the general-merchandise industry, which was led by companies such as Sears and Montgomery Ward. By carving out a narrow market position, the discount retailers did not pose an immediate threat to the general-merchandise leaders.

Yet there were a number of critical choices that made the entrepreneurial discount retailers successful at instigating a new industry. First, they initially targeted buyers that were underserved by general merchandisers. Wal-Mart focused on small towns, while Target and Kmart focused on suburban markets. As the companies built efficiencies, the viability of the new approach became apparent, and the new discount retailing industry took form. Simultaneously, the general merchandising industry was thrown off its Progressive path and into Radical transformation.[2]

Second, the discount retailers dealt mainly with different suppliers than those selling to general merchandisers. Wal-Mart, Kmart, and Target carried more branded goods and perishables, which required unprecedented activities for managing vendor relationships. The discount retailers provided the branded goods manufacturers with high-volume outlets that in turn allowed the vendors to lower their own costs and become more competitive with the unbranded suppliers to the general merchandise industry.

As Wal-Mart, Kmart, and Target expanded in product and geographic breadth, they built economies of scale to lower costs below those of the traditional general-merchandise leaders. In other words, the more products they carried and the more stores they opened, the lower their costs per unit sold. Declines in cost translated to declines in prices, which put enormous pressure on Sears and Montgomery Ward.

While the geographic footprint of each firm overlapped with those of the others, a degree of geographic specialization began to develop. A virtuous circle had emerged, with benefits for geographically dispersed buyers, branded-goods manufacturers, and the discount-retailing leaders. The fragmentation phase of discount retailing ended with clarity about the dominant model for organizing activities in the business.

### Shakeout: The Dominant Model for Organizing the Industry Emerges and Inefficient Firms Exit Slowly

One of the classic features of the life cycle model is an inflection point that occurs after one or more entrepreneurial firms discover a "dominant model," which is an approach of compelling efficiency that promises to become the centerpiece of organization in the industry. The adoption of dominant models also depends on achieving legitimacy—often through early championing by influential users and suppliers.

Shakeout following the establishment of a dominant model may require decades to occur. For example, in overnight package delivery through the 1970s, carriers used different systems to distribute packages directly between cities. Some operated on a small number of point-to-point routes using company-owned planes while others predominantly contracted with commercial airlines for package-carrying capacity. Systems for package drop-off and pick-up were quite varied.

Then, during the 1970s, the efficiency and legitimacy of the hub-and-spoke system became clear. This system involved sending packages from all over the country to a central location for sorting and redistribution. It was not at all obvious from the outset that the best way to move a package from New York to Washington, D.C., was via Memphis, but in practice the system allowed carriers to expand volume and to reduce the number of daily point-to-point flights. Despite the efficiency of the hub-and-spoke system, a handful of point-to-point delivery companies survived into the 1980s.

The shakeout took so long because the power of the dominant model emerged slowly and incrementally. Achieving the potential of the hub-and-spoke model required building out the activity system to its full scale over several years. In many situations (including overnight letter delivery), constructing the new system involves investment that is substantially greater than required to maintain the outdated system, and thus an impediment to adoption can arise.

The net result is that established firms that don't operate on the dominant model may be only slightly disadvantaged and therefore can post profitability that's just slightly below the industry average for a long period of time. Executives in these firms may be willing to tolerate the inferior performance, hoping to catch up eventually with the industry leaders.

History shows that these hopes are usually misplaced. The firms committed to the dominant model benefit from experience, which reinforces efficiencies and expands legitimacy. Meanwhile, firms that get stuck in catch-up mode almost always fail in the end. Furthermore, their failure is drawn out; the firms endure prolonged periods of diminishing profitability before it becomes clear that exit is the best option.

### Maturity: Secure, Stable Returns over a Long Period

Industries undergoing Progressive evolution usually go through long maturity phases in which they benefit from incremental improvements that don't disrupt the core of the business. Companies can test changes to the activity system without irrevocably changing their profiles because their *overall* competitive positioning is so secure. The result is powerful reinforcement of existing advantages through incremental improvements.

Many of the most successful firms in industries undergoing Progressive change have been celebrated for their constant improvement. Southwest Airlines' employee-suggestion system continues to generate many ideas for incremental efficiencies even after more than thirty years of operation as a low-cost airline. Wal-Mart, Starbucks, and Federal Express constantly test new ways of adding efficiencies to their models, even after spending over a decade in clear leadership positions.

In most industries that evolve along the Progressive trajectory, the profitability of leaders is only moderately high during years of maturity, with the real payoff coming through stability in their competitive advantages. "Competitive advantage" occurs when companies have achieved both operational effectiveness on the dominant model and gone further to offer distinctive value in some way. For example, Starbucks is not only a great coffee importer and roaster—it also delivers a unique coffee experience. Federal Express delivers overnight letters on schedule more than 99 percent of the time and also provides tracking services and more retail locations than its rivals. Both Starbucks and Federal Express achieve premium prices as a result, whereas Wal-Mart not only achieves the extraordinary efficiencies demanded of discount retailers, it goes further and leverages its distribution, IT, and procurement experience to operate at lower costs than its closest rivals. The benefit to the consumer is lower prices and the benefit to the company is higher revenues.

Investment analysts tend to view the stocks of Wal-Mart, Starbucks, and Federal Express as lower-risk securities than those of companies in Creative industries because their positions are relatively stable. Occasionally, however, industry leaders cannot achieve even moderate profitability because they are so focused on adhering to the dominant model that their strategies lose distinctiveness. A high-profile example of this phenomenon has occurred in the U.S. airline industry, where firms are plagued with an inability to achieve reasonable returns on their investments despite impressive operational efficiencies. The problem is that incremental improvements that might have served as a basis for competitive advantage for one airline are engulfed by the dominant model and become standard operating procedure for all of the other airlines. The leading firms in the industry—with the exception of Southwest Airlines—are not distinctive enough to prevent buyers from switching based on price. Because the infrastructure in the business is fixed, the greater efficiencies end up generating excess capacity that can lead to persistent price wars; these in turn damage industry profitability. Southwest Airlines is the exception because it has carved out a distinctive competitive position—based on smaller airports, the exclusive use of 737s, and frequent travel across route pairs—that protects it from some of the problems facing the larger trunk carriers.

Except in unusual situations like U.S. airlines, industries undergoing Progressive change tend to be stable in maturity because buyers are satisfied by the improvements in value delivered by the industry. Because industry change is incremental, suppliers are rarely jarred by radical changes and are satisfied as well by the stability in their trading relationships. The result is a set of stable relationships that persist.

### Decline: Shortages of Supplies or Shifts in Buyer Preferences Cause Volumes to Drop Slowly

The decline of an industry on a Progressive path often begins with a small shift in buyer preferences or with a shift in the supply of raw materials. Consider the impact of petroleum fuel shortages (a decline in raw-material supply) on the independent trucking industry in North America. Before the cost of fuel rose, independent truckers offered their corporate clients access to fast, personalized service, even when it meant traveling with partial loads and an empty truck on backhaul. Rising fuel costs changed the economic tradeoff between flexibility and efficiency in favor of efficiency. Because independent truckers did not operate in networked logistics systems, they became inefficient and the industry moved into decline.

The slow process of decline in Progressive industries can create sustained performance problems for industry leaders, but because profits tend to drop gradually, industry leaders may resist exiting. Often, the first reaction for an established company as the industry moves into decline is to search for additional incremental efficiencies. This is not usually a long-term solution, however, and in time reinvestment leads to diminishing marginal returns. At that point, retrenchment becomes the best approach.

The point of demarcation from maturity to decline is a drop in industry volumes. In an industry on a Progressive path, the drop in volume occurs for one (or more) of three reasons.

- *Company dominance.* First, a single company (or a small group of companies) comes to dominate the industry. The lack of competition causes rising prices, a drop in quality, and a slowdown in incremental innovation. As a consequence, the industry's volumes stop growing and decline begins.

- *Saturated demand or supply.* For instance, retail laundromats have been in decline because more and more homeowners, educational institutions, hotels, and housing agencies own their own laundry machines. Similarly, there is a shortage of plumbing services in some parts of the world because young people don't pursue the training required to become plumbers in the same proportion as they formerly had.

- *Threat of substitution.* A threat of substitution from outside the industry can lead to the perception that the industry no longer delivers value compared to some other alternative. For example, the decline of the rail transport of non-agricultural goods occurred in many countries as commercial air freight became less expensive.

Regardless of the reason for the change, a strategy for dealing effectively with industry decline requires the discipline to avoid escalating the firm's fixed costs as volumes diminish.

## The Life Cycle of Creative Change

Industries on a Creative evolutionary path tend to be characterized by the introduction of major new products that have been developed at substantial risk to the sponsoring firms. To manage the risk of failure, the industry's leading firms typically take on a portfolio of projects, each of which involves investment that occurs years in advance of commercialization. You'll recall that examples of industries on Creative evolutionary paths include pharmaceutical manufacturing, oil and gas exploration, and motion-picture production. Because they do not undergo architectural change, the life-cycle model applies to industries on Creative paths. However, the life-cycle phases in Creative industries take on a different shape from those in Progressive industries. The fragmentation and maturity phases tend to be long, but shakeout and decline may occur relatively quickly.

### Fragmentation: Multiple Stages of Extensive, Varied Experimentation

The early phase of Creative change generally involves three stages of experimentation: first on the entire mode of product design and delivery, second on the nature of core assets, and third on supporting core activities. The industry's dominant model emerges only with the completion of all three sub-stages. Because the phases are cumulative, entrepreneurial activity may ebb and wane several times through the fragmentation stage.

#### The First Sub-Stage of Fragmentation

In the first sub-stage of fragmentation, entrepreneur inventors who attract any attention at all often are viewed as crackpots or eccentrics. For instance, around the beginning of the twentieth century, entrepreneurs came up with so many different automobile designs that old movies depicting them seem comic. Many early pharmacists who ground herbs and boiled roots drew jeers and condemnation. The effectiveness of their remedies was limited by the lack of standardization in formulating treatments and lack of communication among pharmacists about successful formulations.

Similar problems arose for the earliest programmers in PC applications-software development. Entrepreneurs that experimented with programs such as VisiCalc and MacDraw were considered hobbyists in some quarters. The commercial viability of products was limited by diversity in hardware and operating-system standards. And, in motion-picture production, companies experimented with the length, subject, recording, and projection mechanisms during the early stages.

The end of the first stage of experimentation occurs as entrepreneurs begin to develop a system in which the company manages the development of new products separately from the systems used for commercializing products. Through the separation, the entrepreneur can become more efficient in project development. Risky activities that carry the largest chance of failure are contained and modularized to prevent damage to core activities when failure occurs. For example, most leading pharmaceutical manufacturers are organized functionally, with R&D projects separated from marketing and sales activities. As a result, the marketing and sales functions continue to operate even when particular R&D projects are canceled.

### The Second Sub-Stage of Fragmentation

During the second sub-stage of fragmentation, entrepreneurs become more focused and more effective in developing projects that can be used as core assets. For example, in motion-picture production during the early 1930s, companies began to devote their resources to the feature film rather than to shorts and documentaries. In applications software during the 1980s, companies began to build for the Windows and Macintosh operating systems. During the 1950s, entrepreneurs in the pharmaceutical industry began to rely on scientific experimentation in the creation of new formulations, with clinical trials as supporting activities.

Focused experimentation makes a company better at project management, and therefore expertise begins to accumulate. In the 1980s, applications software developers learned how to diagnose and test new code, and how to become more efficient by incorporating proven code for specific functions like printing instead of writing new code into each new program. Newcomers enter the industry, begin benchmarking, and learn from the failures of predecessors.

### The Third Sub-Stage of Fragmentation

In the third sub-stage of fragmentation, companies learn to protect their successes at project development by developing a support system of core activities. They test different mechanisms for dealing with key suppliers, developing distribution systems, and marketing to end-users. In PC applications software, entrepreneurs tried distributing new products in shrink-wrapped boxes and through original-equipment manufacturers (OEMs). Microsoft, for instance, began to sell application software such as its Office suite through PC manufacturers like Dell and Compaq, which installed the programs on PCs before they were shipped to buyers. In the film-production industry, motion-picture studios began to develop relationships with theatrical exhibitors to ensure access to theaters for movies once they were completed. Pharmaceutical companies experimented with distributing drugs directly to patients, through doctors, and through a hybrid prescription-pharmacist system.

The experimentation phase of industry development ends when the dimensions of risk become clearly identified, a dominant model begins to emerge, and companies striving for industry leadership begin to converge on that model. Because the experimentation process is cumulative, early entrants with experience at either project design or supporting activities may have an edge over later entrants. Then, as the field of viable entrepreneurs narrows, the fragmentation phase ends and shakeout begins.

### Shakeout: Rapid Escalation of Volume on the Dominant Model

Not all companies that survive the fragmentation phase also survive the shakeout phase. Many car manufacturers of the early twentieth century, including Olds, Durant, and Nash, were bought out during the industry's shakeout phase, mainly because they were not committed to building the distribution and marketing capabilities necessary to compete effectively. During shakeout, the dominant model takes shape and continues to develop as companies scramble to acquire the core assets necessary to secure first-mover advantage. Because the fragmentation stage is long and involves several sub-stages, the shakeout often occurs quickly.

During shakeout, survival often depends on developing cost-effective core activities. Many biotechnology firms with great new products barely break even because they must license their molecules to large pharmaceutical firms. The small biotech companies simply do not have necessary core activities for shepherding drugs through the FDA approval process (e.g., the infrastructure necessary to conduct human trials) and then for marketing drugs to doctors (e.g., large, specialized sales forces). In other words, to survive shakeout and thrive as an industry leader, a company must have both skilled project management capabilities as well as core activities. The frustration of having superior project management without supporting core activities is particularly vivid in the pharmaceutical industry, in which biotech firms have been successful at the painstaking process of new-drug discovery only to find that commercialization is impossible without a large pharmaceutical partner.

The shakeout phase of industry development is short because the dominant model is clear at the beginning of the period. Companies that cannot develop the assets and skills necessary for superior performance must confront the consequences as investors, board members, and corporate executives react to the operational ineffectiveness. As a result, many companies retrench to supplier positions, streamline their activities, or exit altogether.

### Maturity: High Variability Across Competitors in Profitability

During industry maturity, the profits of large firms can be among the highest in the economy. Firms with extensive project portfolios secure leading market positions, while smaller firms with a single successful project must strike deals with rivals or spend extensively on supporting activities. As a rule, profitability is generally associated with size, with exceptions for firms in niche or specialized markets.

While the profitability of industry leaders is high on average, it is also volatile. Pharmaceuticals, motion-picture production, applications software, oil and gas exploration, and investment banking are all characterized by variation in the performance of mature firms. In motion-picture production, the leading studios—Disney, Paramount, Warner Brothers—routinely shift in share rank, but rarely does a new company enter into the top tier.

Because the stakes are high, brinksmanship in competition is common. Firms compete for key suppliers, channels, and buyers. Secrecy abounds about specific project ideas and about early indications of project success. Rumors fly regarding new policies and plans for changing the supporting infrastructure. Companies compete vigorously for talent, raw materials, specialized channel access, and end-user attention. Profitability is maximized as companies adjust the timing of project launches in response to competitive conditions.

### Decline: Diminishing Ability to Generate Valuable Assets

Industry decline may be driven by saturation of demand or by exhaustion of key supplies, and is marked by a drop in industry volume. The trigger for *volatile* decline is a waning ability to take on successful new projects, which leads to an unpredictable revenue stream. For example, some observers have argued that the pharmaceutical industry is nearing decline as classic methods of drug discovery fail to yield major new treatments.

In Creative industries, profits may drop dramatically, as they did when baseball went on strike in 1994, and then recover, as they did with the home-run derby in baseball during the late 1990s. As the process progresses, industry leaders become saddled with excess capacity, and organizations struggle to shed resources that are no longer economically viable.

In industry decline, companies experience increasing difficulty in finding new projects that appeal to buyers. As the automobile industry enters decline, the leading companies may find that they have difficulty attracting accomplished designers, engineers, and marketing talent. To defend themselves, some automobile companies are introducing exciting niche products that appeal both to buyers and engineers. As the opportunity to develop such new projects dwindles, the industry is often sustained by a few key blockbuster products that continue to sell.

Profitability during the decline phase may not drop immediately as firms aggressively manage their costs and defend against the change in structure, but a drop in profitability becomes inevitable as volumes fade. In this situation, firms consider a range of alternatives. Some delay their exit to the point of no return as they compete for a diminishing group of buyers and suppliers. Others try to specialize in project management or supporting activities but find it difficult to attract former rivals as buyers.

With time there's less ambiguity about the industry's future. Companies ultimately must choose to redeploy their activities in both project management and in core activities into related industries or, in extreme situations, retire unproductive assets through merger, alliance, or bankruptcy. This is what happened to many companies that originally specialized in operating amusement parks. Most have diversified geographically and into related business in which their creative capabilities can be most productive.

## The Phases of Intermediating Change

Industries on Intermediating evolutionary paths are confronted with changes in the boundaries of their businesses. Former buyers and suppliers may become competitors. As companies struggle to redefine their relationships with buyers and with suppliers, they find themselves with too much capacity in some functional areas and too little in others. Intermediation requires extensive rebalancing and represents one of the most challenging competitive situations in business.

As indicated earlier, Intermediating and Radical change are Architectural, and as a result, the life-cycle model is not relevant. Instead, these types of changes occur in four phases: emergence, convergence, co-existence, and dominance. However, the process of Intermediating transformation often occurs more quickly than Radical transformation: on the order of a decade rather than several decades. Phases are irregular in length and are difficult to predict, and periods of rapid change may be followed by stagnancy, only to resume.

This section lays out the phases of Intermediating transformation. It's important to keep in mind that the transformation occurs only in the *established* industry. The industry that represents the new approach typically evolves on a Progressive or Creative path by a different set of rules. For instance, the live-auction industry is currently going through Intermediation, with core activities such as appraisal, storage, and marketing coming under fire from online auctions. But the online auction industry is evolving on a Progressive path, with a dominant model defined by eBay's approach.

### Emergence: New Ways of Transacting Threaten the Value Created Through Core Activities

In 2003, the investment brokerage industry was in the first phase of an Intermediating transformation that had been sparked by a number of related factors. Several large investment brokerage houses had diversified into investment banking. In this dual role, the organizations were committed to representing the interests of both the investors purchasing securities and the corporations selling them, and problems arose when these interests conflicted. Charges filed by New York State's Attorney General, Eliot Spitzer, claimed that the investment banks generally favored corporate interests over investor interests. In advising investors about securities, the brokerages allegedly made biased recommendations that unjustly favored their own interests. The public outcry was intensified because the scandals coincided with widespread investor disappointment at the end of the dot-com bubble.

As investors struggled to develop and deal with a new understanding of the dual roles of their investment advisors, signs of a new approach in investment brokerage materialized. Nonintegrated investment brokerage houses like Charles Schwab and Edward Jones gained credibility, while mutual fund companies began to experiment with a broader range of offerings to satisfy investor needs. Some investors began to close accounts with the traditional investment banks and open them with Schwab and Jones. Others closed their accounts and began dealing with mutual-fund companies that were not integrated into investment banking. These changes were motivated by a widespread desire to invest in instruments that would generate returns for investors rather than profits for the brokerage house.

At the same time, the corporations that offered securities began to experiment with new ways of raising money from investors. Some former investment banking corporate clients even tried offering securities directly to the public, avoiding the traditional brokerages altogether. New kinds of securities designed both to protect investors and to raise capital for specific projects began to appear. Independent research and rating organizations gained attention.

It is unclear today exactly what kinds of transactions will predominate in the investment brokerage industry of the future. What is clear is that the brokerage industry has moved from a Progressive structure into a period of Intermediation. Investors are no longer satisfied with prior terms of access to trading services, and corporations have been forced by regulatory scrutiny and legislative consequences to offer their securities on terms that fairly represent their financial prospects.

This fuzziness about the new approach is characteristic of the emergent phase of Intermediation. Indeed, in investment brokerage a number of different models for new transactions are being tested. Some brokers are experimenting with providing advisory advice independently of trading services, while others are bundling unbiased research-based advice with trading. In short, there are several candidates for organizing transactions and years may pass before a new dominant model emerges. What is clear is that the traditional brokerages are under unprecedented pressure to configure their activities differently.

### Convergence: A New Approach Begins to Permeate Established Relationships and Intensifies the Threat

In the early years of the twenty-first century, the music publishing business is in the convergence phase of an Intermediating transformation. Perhaps you have never downloaded music over the Web, or have done so only a couple of times, but it is likely that you know someone—perhaps a teenager—who downloads songs habitually.

The implications of online distribution for the music publishing business are profound. Today it is unclear whether legal protection will be potent enough to stop free downloads. Even if legal protections take hold and are enforceable, the music industry is undergoing transformation. Why? Because the introduction of online music distribution is occurring simultaneously with another major transition in music publishing: The era of the long-lived pop star seems to be giving way. Staple artists such as the Beatles, the Rolling Stones, Bruce Springsteen, Fleetwood Mac, and Madonna are becoming rare. Now the trend in the music business is toward shorter careers for top artists.

The traditional structure of music publishing, which evolved on a Creative path, has been propelled into Intermediation, and the transformation has progressed into the convergence stage. Core activities of the traditional industry structure—such as the ways in which artists are recruited to sign with a label—are coming under fire. Under a traditional arrangement, artists sign a six- or seven-album contract that effectively binds the artist to the recording studio for five to ten years.[3] The artist retains royalty rights of 10 to 14 percent on receipts earned by the publisher on albums. In exchange, the music company develops the artist (by influencing the music, enhancing the artist's image, teaching singers how to dance, etc.), promotes the music (on radio stations and through other advertising), arranges and pays for tours, and records and distributes albums. When the term of the original contract expires, an artist can attempt to attract competing bids from various music publishers. Some artists (including David Bowie, Nirvana, Madonna, and Prince) have elected to form their own labels and take on the responsibilities of music publishing directly rather than cede 100 percent of their gross receipts in exchange for a 10 to 14 percent royalty.

The Intermediation of music publishing reflects several fundamental challenges to the structure of the business. First, buyers who download songs generally don't want all the new songs on an album or CD. I might download Ricky Martin's "Livin' La Vida Loca" but not his other material. The preference of buyers for particular songs makes Internet downloading attractive because it is easy on the Internet to download a single song without buying others on the album. Single-song downloading compounds the trend toward shorter musician careers by further emphasizing specific hits rather than a collection of songs on an album.

The Internet changes the recording industry profoundly because it changes the economics of signing an artist to a contract that specifies a number of albums. As more and more single songs are downloaded, the idea of the "album" has less meaning and therefore multiyear contracts become less attractive to the studio. The inevitable result is that contracts with artists must be written on different grounds with the impact of the Internet reflected in the terms.

Second, the downloading of songs from the Internet threatens to make obsolete other core activities in traditional music publishing. When artists have short careers, it becomes less feasible economically to devote resources to dance lessons, costuming, musical training, and even promotional activities. Developing garage bands into commercially successful artists becomes harder to justify as the returns on each artist drop. Sending an artist on an expensive promotional concert tour becomes impossible when the album only breaks even. With fewer follow-on record sales, concert ticket prices rise to reflect actual event costs, which in turn diminishes attendance and makes it even more difficult for an artist to tour. In short, the development, promotion, and touring activities of the traditional music publishers are threatened with obsolescence.

Third, the diminished revenues from selling fewer songs and charging lower prices per song create an incentive for consolidation across the industry. After a period of curtailed expansion, the industry is confronted with losses and cost-cutting pressure. Less efficient companies have been forced to consider merger, bankruptcy, and diversification.

This pattern of effects in music publishing is characteristic of the challenges that face traditional companies during the convergence phase of Intermediation. The new approach has emerged and the implications have become clear. Buyers are responding to streamlined products and services that offer high convenience at low prices. Companies scramble to respond as the nature of the product changes.

### Co-Existence: The Value Tied to Core Activities Creates Incentives for Collaboration

By the time Intermediation reaches the co-existence phase, the threat from the new approach is clear. As companies in the emerging industry struggle to redeploy valuable assets, a strong incentive emerges to collaborate with pioneers of the new approach. At the same time, traditional companies may collaborate with key buyers and suppliers to stave off the threat.

The auto dealership industry of North America is in the co-existence phase of Intermediating transformation at the beginning of the 2000s. You'll recall that the business was thrown into Intermediation by the emergence of online trading services as well as by the increasing durability of automobiles, which in turn created excess capacity in the industry. Some traditional dealers are coping with the challenge by signing collaborative agreements with Internet service providers like Autobytel or AutoNation (an integrated dealer and Internet service provider). While a cadre of dealerships is developing collaborative relationships with online auto service providers, the vast majority of dealerships cannot find partners on the new model. The reason has to do with the declining demand for dealer services, which had preceded Intermediation. Several leaders in the online auto services industry have restricted by contract the number of dealers with which they work. The thousands of independent dealers that are either unaffiliated or weakly affiliated with online providers continue to operate principally along the traditional approach.

The auto dealers that have found ways to collaborate with online providers generally have much better prospects both for survival and profitability than those that remain with the traditional model. At this writing, there are signs that many independent traditional dealerships may not be able to find ways to preserve their core assets. Many are going into bankruptcy while those that that have survived are consolidating with former archrivals in a particular geographic area.

The process of Intermediation in auto dealerships is not complete, however. A definitive dominant model in the online industry has not yet emerged as many online service providers continue to experiment with new ways of transacting. Delays in commitment by companies on the new model create high short-term costs, which in turn creates an umbrella that softens competitive pressure on traditional dealers. Those that have survived may face even more intense pressure in the future.

### Dominance: New Ways of Transacting Dominate Established Approaches

The next time you look for a job, you may do something that you never did before: conduct your search online. It is now easy to learn about companies, find out about the competition for jobs, and get information about compensation packages through online investigation. In short, the Intermediation of bricks-and-mortar job-placement agencies has moved into a phase in which online activities are dominant. While offline job placement may continue to occur in specialized settings, it is clear that the industry has gone through a fundamental transformation.

There are several reasons for the change. First, in many professions, searching online job sites rather than specialized trade publications is more convenient because the listings are up to date and the indexing of jobs by type and by geography makes a focused search easier. For many job seekers and recruiters, the loss of personal service and personalized counseling available through job-placement agencies has been superseded by the convenience of online searching.

Second, as the job market became tight in the late 1990s, many job seekers and recruiters preferred to cast a wide net rather than to restrict themselves to the matches favored by job-placement agencies. Effectively, the attributes most favored by the recruiters were those at which the traditional agencies operated at a disadvantage.

Third, conflicts of interest skewed the recommendations of some agencies. Because job-placement agencies were typically paid a portion of the recruit's salary as a fee after successful placement, the agencies had incentives to recommend the most qualified and expensive person available for a particular job. Candidates tended to end up in jobs that were not challenging, and recruiters tended to hire candidates that were expensive and sometimes overqualified for specific roles.

The Intermediation of job placement occurred in a number of phases. Some of the earliest experiments involved moving job placement agencies online, evaluating usage patterns, and adapting the sites to integrate desirable features. With time, companies began to specialize in specific facets of job placement, with personal interviews becoming less important. A new crop of services emerged both for candidates and recruiters. As the co-existence phase took hold, Monster.com and Hotjobs.com gained share and experimented with an even larger number of services, including personalized counseling. Norms of disclosure in the industry began to change as the sites offered more information to candidates about job characteristics. Today, online job-placement services dominate the traditional job-placement industry.

To summarize, Intermediation can provide opportunities for established firms to migrate their capabilities into a new environment. The challenge is finding a way to develop new relationships without destroying valuable resources in the process.

## The Phases of Radical Change

Radical change occurs when an industry's core activities and core assets are both threatened with obsolescence, which in turn creates a dramatic challenge for companies in positions of leadership. Yet the threat is not quickly realized. The phases of a Radical transformation are irregular in length, and their timing is difficult to predict.

Industries undergoing Radical change move through multiple phases, but as with Intermediating change, the phases do not follow a life cycle. To understand the nature of the phases, it is critical to take the point of view of an established industry and investigate how a new approach influences the standing industry structure. Keep in mind that the industry that represents the new approach is likely to be evolving on a different trajectory and by a difference set of rules than the industry undergoing Radical change. The PC industry is evolving on a Progressive path while the typewriter manufacturing industry goes through Radical transformation. The process of Radical transformation may take decades. Once it begins, Radical transformation supersedes any other type of change occurring in an industry.

### Emergence: The Threat Emerges in a Small, Strategically Important Segment

Most of us in North America, Europe, and the developed countries of Asia would agree: In twenty years, we will transmit important documents through secure, verifiable, electronic channels rather than using overnight package delivery. In the long run, secure e-mailed documents will be more convenient, quicker, and less expensive to deliver than a letter printed and delivered on paper.

The inevitability of this outcome creates a threat of obsolescence to both the core activities and the core assets of companies in overnight letter delivery, including Federal Express, United Parcel Service, and Airborne. Once secure, verifiable, electronic delivery is available, the existing core activities of the overnight delivery companies (such as pick-up, recording, sorting, flying, additional sorting, and drop-off) will no longer create value. And the core assets of the overnight delivery companies (such as truck fleets, airplane fleets, and hub-and-spoke sorting centers) will not be necessary to support value creation under the new approach. As is typical in this situation, the skills required to achieve leadership in encryption software are quite different than those held by the overnight letter companies. The overnight letter delivery industry, which had been evolving on a Progressive path, has been thrown into Radical transformation.

The rules of the prior Progressive path are suspended even though the technology necessary to deliver documents securely and verifiably is in its infancy today. Many practical questions have not yet been answered. Is a signed document from your computer binding? What if you claim that you didn't send it? Will you be responsible for reporting misuse of your computer much like you are responsible for reporting misuse of your credit card? Will the recipient bear responsibility for verifying the origins of electronic documents?

There are signs that answers may be coming soon. In Massachusetts, a judge recently ruled that an electronic discussion of the terms of sale on a property was binding even though a formal purchase and sale agreement had not been signed.[4] With each legal decision that clarifies contractual obligations, the threat to the assets and activities of the overnight package delivery industry becomes more intense. The point of no return has passed. Companies have begun to buy encryption software with the intention of using it to transmit documents securely. As more companies come to rely on secure encryption technology, the threat will mount.

In overnight letter delivery and in many other industries beginning the process of Radical transformation, the threat often develops in a significant but limited segment of the market. Thus with document transfer, the companies most likely to rely first on encryption systems are those that routinely send a lot of secure documents, but where the stakes on fraudulence around a single document are not too high. Examples include travel agencies that send airline tickets and insurance companies that verify claims. Even organizations that adopt secure online delivery are likely to continue to use overnight letter delivery for their documents where traditional systems for verification—the sender's signature—are especially valuable. Financial institutions continue to use overnight package delivery to validate large trades, for instance.

With secure encryption technology developing only in a segment, it's easy to assume that the new approach will never appeal to mainstream buyers. Market research may even validate the idea that encryption technology is relevant in only a narrow segment, claiming that mainstream buyers may initially have difficulty in understanding how they will react in the future when legal remedies and business conventions for dealing with electronically delivered documents are established. The impression that secure electronic delivery will be limited is reinforced if you examine the behavior of buyers that are experimenting with secure encryption: These buyers also use overnight letter companies. The temptation is to consider the threat as minor[5] but the real problem is that market research does not work very well in these situations. It is important not to succumb to temptation. The Radical transformation of overnight letter delivery is only in its earliest phase, and this is the short window of time in which the overnight letter companies have the greatest range of motion in creating strategic options for the future.

### Convergence: The Threat Intensifies as Activities Under the New Approach Become Organized More Efficiently

In the convergence phase of Radical transformation, the new approach begins to attract significant profit that would otherwise be earned by traditional companies; in other words, profits begin to be lost to the newcomers. The commercial landline telephone industry in the United States is currently facing the convergence of the wireless industry because a significant number of buyers who would otherwise order landline service are opting instead for wireless products.

In this phase of Radical transformation, traditional companies often try to partner with new entrants into the emerging industry for access to technology and key supplier relationships. The companies that adopt the new approach may be responsive because they can achieve access to buyers through traditional providers. But in general, the incentives of companies in the emerging industry to engage in partnerships are somewhat lower than the incentives for traditional companies. The reason has to do with the stakes: In the emerging industry, the incentive is enhanced profitability; in the established industry that is undergoing Radical change, the stakes can be survival.

The accumulation of knowledge about the new approach becomes a focal point of activity. Wireless firms in the United States conduct extensive research on digital transmission, consumer behavior, channel

effectiveness, and supplier efficiency. This knowledge constitutes a formidable asset at the foundation of the new industry structure, and compounds the threat to core assets in the traditional industry undergoing
Radical transformation. The potential for progress is great, and the research pays off handsomely. The costs of delivering service are dropping dramatically as wireless companies build new activities on the assets that they have accumulated. The threat of obsolescence has become
intense in the traditional landline industry.

The convergence phase ends and the co-existence phase begins
when the emerging industry builds enough volume to make clear the
threat to the traditional industry's relationships.

### Co-Existence: Tension Builds as Competition Mounts Between Old and New Approaches

In the co-existence phase of Radical transformation, competition
between traditional companies and new entrants in the emerging industry becomes intense. No longer do companies make the mistake of considering the new approach an irrelevant fad, and the vulnerability of the
established industry becomes clear.

At this phase of Radical transformation, established companies can
no longer avoid the reality that their industry structure is changing dramatically, and that the traditional dominant model is deteriorating in its
ability to deliver value. It becomes more difficult to fend off the threat by
leaning on relationships with key buyers or suppliers; long-term buyer
relationships are challenged, companies begin to reorganize, and mergers may occur; partnerships between traditional and new firms often fall
apart as the new approach gains power and attention; and survival depends upon an uncompromising strategy for dealing with the challenges.

At the same time, the co-existence of the new and the established
industries reveals limitations of the new approach. In many situations,
the dominant model of the new industry has been clarified by this point,
and because the emergence of a dominant model involves committing
to tradeoffs, the disadvantages of the new approach also become clear.
During the mid-1980s, while personal computers were widely heralded
as a major breakthrough, many users were frustrated with the amount
of time required to load and configure software and peripheral hardware. This frustration opened up an opportunity for typewriter manu-

facturers to meet the needs of conservative buyers with extra service and assurances of stability.

One of the most poignant features of Radical transformation at this phase may be a temporary resurgence of innovation on the older, traditional model. For instance, in a major effort to fend off PCs, typewriter manufacturers in the early 1980s introduced a spate of new features, including self-correction tapes, long-life batteries, and miniaturized chassis. Family farms in the American midwest became more efficient through the introduction of new agrichemical and harvesting technologies when threatened by large-scale agriculture based on the cost-effective application of modern agricultural chemicals. The innovations inspired by threats to survival may be significant enough to perpetuate the traditional model for years.

The co-existence phase of Radical transformation ends and the dominance phase begins when the rules of competition in the established industry are set in the new industry.

### Dominance: The Industry Must Create Value on Terms Defined By the New Approach

In the final phases of Radical transformation, the new approach dominates the old approach. The PC industry now dominates the typewriter industry as the mass market of buyers has become comfortable with the new technology. In the dominance phase, most buyers stop running the old systems in parallel with the new. In many office-supply cabinets today, you cannot easily find a typewriter ribbon or an eraser cartridge, and typewriters are discarded rather than repaired when they break. Suppliers to traditional companies begin to exit the business, and shortages of raw materials, parts, and skilled labor on the traditional model may occur. For devoted typewriter users, it is becoming more difficult to find a shop that can repair their machines.

The dominance of the new approach does not always involve total obsolescence of the traditional way of doing things. Today, railroads continue to serve passengers traveling significant distances as well as daily commuters. While other forms of transportation now dominate the passenger railway industry, the railroad companies continue to create value for a significant minority of buyers and suppliers. The same pattern is likely to hold in the future, when secure, verifiable electronic delivery based on encryption technology dominates overnight letter delivery. The overnight letter delivery business is likely to survive but operate on a smaller scale and with a different cost and revenue structure.

The critical difference between the co-existence and dominance phases of Radical transformation is that the traditional industry now must create value on terms that are driven by the new approach. Railroads are compared to passenger cars and airplanes, and the standards for on-time performance, convenience, and comfort are defined by the newer technologies. If you look at the professional live theater industry, you'll see that it is now in the dominance phase of a Radical transformation. Even accomplished theater companies struggle financially while consumers spend increasing amounts on film and broadcast entertainment. Ironically, the threat posed by the new model has inspired significant innovation. Many traditional theater companies have introduced a broad range of new practices, including spectacular staging, historically informed reinterpretations of classic scripts, and featured superstars (often from film). Even as theatrical companies have taken heroic steps to demonstrate their value, the revenues of film studios continue to grow at untouchable rates. With each new innovation, the threat posed by the prerecorded entertainment industry on the traditional live theater industry becomes painfully evident.

As traditional companies struggle to survive, the new industry follows a different, more powerful set of rules defined by a new trajectory of change. The railroads must define their value relative to the airlines, although airlines generally do not put railroads at the forefront of their competitive decisions. With the emergence of greater efficiencies around the dominant model in air transportation, the final phase of Radical transformation in passenger rail travel is occurring. The survivors are those railroads that compete effectively by the new rules, often on a smaller scale than during their heyday.

In sum, Radical transformation eventually yields a dramatic and irrevocable change in the underlying structure of an industry. Yet the process of transformation may take decades to unfold, and yields significant opportunities for profitability along the way.

## The Implications

Opportunities to improve performance depend in a precise way on the stage of industry change. This chapter makes the point that the process depends on whether the trajectory is Progressive, Creative, Intermediating, or Radical. Understanding the stages of change allows you to make contingency plans for adapting to future changes in the environment. You can improve your reaction time, avoid overinvestment, and envision unconventional options by anticipating how the structure of an industry will evolve. By investing early to take advantage of the changes, you can lower the costs of innovation by tailoring your approach to the environment.

The stages of Architectural transition (which apply to Radical and Intermediating change) have a different character from the the conventional life cycle (which applies to Progressive and Creative change). You may make a host of dangerous mistakes if you formulate strategy as if the company is following a classic life cycle when in reality the industry is undergoing Architectural change. Consider the following types of issues that confront firms in industries undergoing Architectural change:

1. The company may over-commit to and over-invest in the old technology. You can spend too much to renew landline handsets when in fact the opportunities in the industry are limited and diminishing.

2. The company may miss opportunities to earn profits in the industry undergoing Architectural change. Landline handset manufacturing and many other industries undergoing Architectural transformation offer significant opportunities for profitability. Exploiting them requires operating by the rules of the Architectural transformation, some of which involve creating partnerships between the established (landline handset manufacturing) and the emerging industry (wireless handset manufacturing).

3. Companies may miss opportunities to enter the emerging industry by migrating activities out of the established industry. IBM, a leader in mainframe computing, adapted its corporate sales force to gain position in personal computing.

For both Architectural and non-Architectural change, the stages of the evolutionary path are defined by hard criteria that involve assessments of industry volumes. When an industry follows a conventional life cycle (i.e., because it is Progressive or Creative), the stage depends on inflection points in volume growth. When change is Architectural (i.e., Radical or Intermediating), the phase depends on inflection points in the relative growth rates of volumes in the established industry and in the new industry. These inflection points are described in detail in chapter 4. Chapter 4 also presents a number of related tools for identifying the trajectory and phase of change that's relevant in the industry that you are examining.

The second part of this book, beginning with chapter 5, offers a number of insights on how firms have used their understanding about the nature of industry change to seize opportunities and improve performance.

# 4

## Assessing the Nature and Stage of Evolution in an Individual Industry

THIS CHAPTER OFFERS a series of tools for diagnosing the trajectory and stage of change in your industry. In diagnosing industry evolution, it's easy to become distracted or confused by the immediacy of buyer demands or by a competitor's actions, or to get derailed by colleagues who have never thought much about industry evolution. Despite these challenges, clarity about the trajectory and stage of change is critical for developing a strategy that delivers consistently high performance. Acquiring clarity depends on a deep understanding of the four trajectories and the discipline to assess the stages of change accurately.

The process of diagnosis can be split into four steps: defining the industry, identifying whether change is Architectural, identifying whether change is Foundational, and identifying the stage of change. These steps are not as daunting as they may seem initially. Under most circumstances, you can work through the four steps with the senior leadership team over a relatively short period—without a consulting team or a major commitment of time—by focusing carefully on the specific issues outlined here.

### Step One: Defining Your Industry

The first step toward achieving a comprehensive understanding of industry evolution is to define the industry clearly using a process that is accepted and understood by all members of the executive team. While defining industry boundaries may seem straightforward, it is uncanny how often executives—even within the same firm—disagree over how they should be drawn.

There is a long history of controversy in the United States and abroad about how industries should be defined—that is, how industry boundaries should be drawn—in light of the of antitrust laws, which are designed to prevent and punish unfair competition. The companies accused of antitrust violations almost always argue that industry boundaries should be drawn widely to encompass the largest possible number of competitors. Those accusing the companies of unfair behavior nearly always claim that industry boundaries should be drawn narrowly. The U.S. Department of Justice has published guidelines intended to help the courts find a middle ground, but judgment is required in every case.

Part of the problem is that there are no widely accepted criteria for defining industry boundaries. Yet despite the difficulties, careful industry definition is important for several reasons. The first is that there can be a steep price for making a mistake. If an industry is defined too broadly, the temptation is to diagnose industry change as Architectural, which could lead you to dismantle activities that should be supported and sustained. Too narrow a definition, on the other hand, can lead to complacency by diverting your attention from critical changes in industry structure.

The second reason is the potential influence of internal politics. Division heads with varying responsibilities and backgrounds often see the world through different lenses. The senior leader of one product division, given the leeway, might understandably draw the industry's boundary lines differently than the leader of another division. Gone unchecked, the differences could cause the analysis to become hopelessly stalled or even compromise its accuracy. A formal process prevents these problems from occurring. It can also keep managers from becoming mired in discussions before they are ready. By focusing only on industry definition as a first step, the executive team can then move efficiently into discussions about the character of the industry evolution and its implications for strategy. The goal at this early stage is to keep the process moving by holding off discussion of implications until industry definitions are established. Bear in mind that endless negotiations over boundaries can lead a company to miss critical windows of opportunity for securing competitive position. One of the primary goals of this chapter is to offer techniques for avoiding this problem.

Finally, a consistent and disciplined process makes it much easier for diversified companies to ensure that the same criteria are being used for industry definition across various lines of business. The goal is to avoid a broad definition of an industry in one division and a series of narrow definitions in another division. It's also important to make sure that industry definitions deal with commonalities in the buyers and suppliers across different divisions. Disney's theme parks appeal to many of the same buyers as its film-production business, but clearly the theme-park industry is distinctive from the film-production industry.

Making the judgment that two industries are different gets harder when the activities in the divisions are similar. For instance, a provider of homeowner property insurance may also offer auto policies. Is the firm competing in one or two industries? By clarifying in advance that the industries are different, the two divisional executives can then proceed into a detailed analysis without having to compromise by creating a single characterization that conflicts with their distinctive experiences.

A warning before moving on: Every industry definition has its detractors. Even with a formal process, not everyone will agree with the final decision, and there may have to be some compromises along the way. Progress depends on accepting the industry definition and proceeding with the analysis on the understanding that subsequent techniques are flexible enough to accommodate the full range of relevant issues.

To define boundaries, it is necessary to examine whether competitors share common buyers and suppliers, common intent, and common technical platforms. The following sections explain the criteria in detail.

### Common Buyers and Suppliers

#### Common Buyers and Common Suppliers

If a group of firms shares both the same buyers and suppliers, then they qualify as members of the same industry, regardless of the other two criteria. Common competitor intent and common technical platforms are useful as supplementary criteria when judgment is required to determine whether buyer commonality and supplier commonality are strong enough to justify treating the firms as direct competitors within the same industry.

It's easy to find examples of companies that share the same buyers and suppliers. For instance, General Electric and Philips Electronics both sell light bulbs and target the same consumer. Movies from Warner Brothers and Paramount may star the same actors and target the same customers. Cookies from Kraft may look just as good to you in the grocery store as cookies from Nabisco and may incorporate many of the same ingredients provided to the companies by common suppliers. There is little question that each of these pairs of firms are competitors, and that the industries in which they compete should be defined broadly enough to encompass both firms in each case.

The more difficult case arises when you suspect that a group of firms should be classified within the same industry but they appeal to different buyers or different suppliers. Two cases arise. The first involves situations in which companies target either the same buyers or work with the same suppliers, but not both. The second covers situations in which companies deal with neither the same buyers nor suppliers. The following sections discuss the issues arising in these two situations.

### Common Buyers or Suppliers

When two companies deal with only some common buyers *or* common suppliers, the question is whether the commonalities are strong enough to qualify the competitors as members of the same industry. There are a number of cases that fall along this spectrum. First, consider Coca-Cola and Delta Air Lines, both of which have large offices in Atlanta, Georgia. The companies work with several common suppliers: local trucking companies, service facilities, and even some employees who have worked first for one and then the other company. Yet most analysts would agree that the degree of commonality between Coca-Cola and Delta is insufficient to qualify the two companies as direct competitors in the same industry.

Now consider a somewhat different situation in New York City, where investment and commercial banks compete for buyers and key employees. In markets for corporate finance, investment banks advise companies that are considering issuing securities to the public. Commercial banks often advise different decision makers within the same companies on managing their cash flow. Thus, there is a sense of buyer commonality, but the decision criteria and processes are somewhat different. On the supply side, some of the employees who are qualified for investment banking also may be qualified for commercial banking and vice versa. Should investment and corporate banking be considered distinct industries or is the commonality in their buyers and suppliers sufficient to qualify them as direct competitors within the same industry?

This question is more complicated than the question about Coca-Cola and Delta Air Lines because the investment and corporate banks share some buyers as well as some suppliers. In practice, buyers use varying criteria to make decisions about raising capital through investment and commercial banks. Some corporate clients readily issue securities to raise capital while others work with investment banks only periodically. In general, for the largest segments of corporate clients, the decision to pay an investment bank for advisory services is influenced only marginally by the fees paid to commercial banks for their advisory services. Because the decision to buy each type of service is not motivated by consideration of the fees charged by the other, the degree of buyer commonality can be considered relatively low.

What is the fundamental logic here? It rests on the decision criteria of the common buyers at the point when they decide to purchase services from each company. Economists often use a rule of thumb that involves calculating the "price elasticity of demand" and the "price elasticity of supply." The intuition behind these rules is simple. If a significant drop—approximately 5 percent—in the price charged by commercial banks would cause a corporate buyer to switch from working with an investment bank to a commercial bank, and if a 5 percent drop in investment banking prices would cause a corporate buyer to switch from a commercial bank, then the criteria used by the buyers across the two businesses is close enough to support the hypothesis that they are in the same industry.

Next, consider the question of industry definition on the criterion of supplier commonality. The 5 percent rule also can be applied to supplier relationships: If an increase of 5 percent in the compensation paid by commercial banks would cause a key employee to switch from working at an investment bank to a commercial bank (and vice versa), then there's evidence that the two businesses are part of the same industry. The investment banks and commercial banks are separate industries for the same reasons as Coca-Cola and Delta: Employees do not switch between jobs in investment banking and commercial banking often enough to create a high degree of commonality in supply relationships. If the 5 percent criterion is met for both buyers and suppliers, then the judgment is conclusive: The two businesses are indeed part of the same industry. Thus, under these assumptions, the investment banking industry and commercial banking industry should be defined separately.

In practice, judgment is required to conduct this thought experiment and to forecast how buyers and suppliers would react to a 5 percent change in prices. The insight from the economists' methodology is the idea that the judgment should be made from the *buyers'* and the *suppliers'* points of view. When companies share common buyers but not common suppliers, the standard for commonality should be high. Burger King and McDonald's are generally considered members of the same industry despite the fact that they have different suppliers because buyers regularly compare products from the two companies.

The logic here is also helpful for understanding whether a company is moving into a new industry when it tries to meet different needs for a group of its buyers. Think of Lou Gerstner's actions at IBM during the turnaround he led in the mid-1990s. When Gerstner took the helm in 1993, IBM held leading positions in both the mainframe and PC hardware businesses, each of which lacked the potential to support the company's goals for profitability and growth (but for different reasons). Gerstner spent considerable time talking with IBM's corporate clients about their needs.[1] The result was a decision to offer networked e-business solutions. Did this move represent diversification into a new industry? Using the criteria laid out in this section, the answer is yes because networked e-business solutions involved a different set of suppliers, and because the buyer purchase criteria differed so substantially from those used to evaluate mainframe and PC hardware products. There was enough of a difference in buyer purchase criteria to disqualify the two businesses as parts of the same industry.

One more note: The fewer buyers and suppliers that are common across two or more sets of firms, then the greater the test for cross-price elasticity should be. In other words, for the companies to qualify as members of the same industry, those few buyers and suppliers that do overlap have to view the companies as close alternatives, and the 5 percent threshold should be ratcheted down. Another rule of thumb to consider is that 25 percent or more of buyers or of suppliers must have virtually *no preference* between the alternatives presented by the two groups of companies for the companies to qualify as members of the same industry. For example, Boston's teaching hospitals employ physicians who also run highly specialized private practices. The private practices compete directly with the teaching hospitals in advising patients, who are generally indifferent about whether they see a particular physician in private practice or at the hospital. It follows, then, that the industry definition should be broad enough to include both the teaching hospitals and the private practices.

### No Common Buyers or Suppliers

When companies do not share common buyers or suppliers then the criteria for defining the industry to include them as competitors should be most stringent. Yet there are important situations in which companies do compete directly and should be considered as part of the same industry despite the fact that they share no buyers or suppliers. These situations tend to arise when competitors each write contracts with different buyers and suppliers, or when purchases occur sporadically.

Consider offset and gravure printing as an example. (These technologies involve using ink-laden plates and engraving to transfer images.) Companies in this business print everything from magazines to phone books to catalogs to brochures. Because the transportation costs are so high for delivering large volumes of printed and bound materials, these companies tend to be geographically distinctive and work with localized suppliers as often as is economical. Leading firms write long-term contracts with large companies such as cataloguers and magazine publishers. When contracts come up for renegotiation, two printers may each bid for the business. Imagine the case where a contract is renewed with the same printer as previously. Here, two offset printing companies may share no buyers and no suppliers and yet compete vigorously to steal business from one another.

Competition of this sort can occur in a variety of situations. Retailers with different geographic bases may compete intensely at local points of contact. A manufacturer with a specialized product may appeal to buyers and suppliers in a niche that is also targeted by a more diversified competitor. A service firm may aspire to win business from a rival with long-term relationships that are difficult to penetrate. In each of these situations, the firms in the business may deal with different buyers and different suppliers, but the industry should be defined broadly enough to encompass the firms because the presence of competitors is so important to the dealings of each.

Defining industry boundaries in these situations requires careful judgment. A first step is to apply the 5 percent rule described earlier (i.e., if both buyers and suppliers would switch for pricing terms that were better by 5 percent, then the competitors qualify as members of the same industry). Sometimes, though, it is difficult to know how buyers and suppliers would respond to a 5 percent change in pricing because so little switching has occurred historically. In this case, supplementary criteria that deal with competitor intent and technical platforms may be useful. The next two sections lay out these alternatives.

### Shared Competitive Intent

Identifying industry boundaries by reference to common buyers and suppliers may be impractical or incomplete because of the difficulties of assessing how buyers and suppliers would behave if the terms of the deal were to change by 5 percent. Geographic differences, alliances, long-term contracts, or recent entry may make it difficult to assess whether two firms compete closely enough to justify including them both in the definition of an industry. For example, the route structures of Virgin Atlantic Airways and Continental Airlines are quite different, and yet both firms target transatlantic business buyers. Should each firm be considered part of the transatlantic airline industry? It's hard to know whether Virgin Atlantic and Continental are responding to each other's pricing behavior (because price changes in this business are so complex), and as a result, the case on buyer commonality is unclear. The case on supplier commonality is more straightforward, as 25 percent of the employees of each company are qualified for jobs at the other company. Yet confirming information on industry boundaries would be helpful for validating a conclusion that Virgin Atlantic and Continental should indeed be considered competitors in the transatlantic airline business.

In situations like this, competitor intent provides significant information on how an industry should be defined. When Disney entered the cruise line business, it signaled an intention to compete with other cruise lines for family vacations. Common competitive intentions may be enough to justify including a firm within the industry even if the competitors do not serve exactly the same buyers and suppliers. Most cruise lines do not cater to families, yet Disney may still cut into the market share of competitors' business. Common intention is relevant to industry definition when it deals with a firm's goals for attracting buyers and suppliers.

Competitive intentions are relevant only when the intention is backed by the ability to conduct the desired business. To be considered a viable competitor, a company must have ramped up activities to the point where it could reasonably deliver on its intentions. This does not mean that a company must have the capacity to fulfill all incremental business immediately but it does mean that the company must have enough capability to ramp up activities quickly if necessary to fulfill a contract. This criterion rules out outsiders with only a *desire* to become viable. Because Virgin Atlantic and Continental clearly have the capability to attract each others' transatlantic business if necessary, they meet the criterion of common intent.

### Shared Technical Platforms

Direct competitors within the same industry operate on a common technical platform. This means that many of the employees qualified to work at one company are qualified for employment at another. It also means that buyers attracted to the products of one firm would opt for the products of a competitor if the preferred provider were to go out of business. By relying on the same basic technologies, companies across the industry create value in parallel ways.

This criterion is the most difficult to implement in practice. It should be used only *after* the range of candidates for industry definition is narrowed down using criteria based on common buyers and common suppliers, and common competitor intent.

The first purpose of this criterion is to rule out industries defined so broadly as to cover multiple technical generations. (Keep in mind that the buyers may be the same in these situations, but not the suppliers.) Consider the printing business. The traditional technology for large-scale projects such as magazines, catalogs, and telephone directories is offset printing, where equipment is physically complex and massive and operating skills are acquired only with years of experience. New digital technology for printing was initially not as cost effective for large printing projects. However, the costs of digital printing have since dropped dramatically while the costs of offset technology are not changing as fast.

According to the criterion of shared technical platform, the offset printing and digital printing industries are distinct. Digital printing is evolving on a Progressive path, and has driven the offset printing industry into Radical change. If the industry boundaries were diagnosed incorrectly, the analyst might be tempted into the conclusion that offset and digital printing were evolving in the same way. Because change in the digital business is so dramatic, it would be tempting to conclude that a Radical transformation is under way in both the digital and offset businesses. This conclusion would obscure important opportunities for improving performance in digital printing by investing by rules that conform to Progressive change. In general, this criterion—the technical platform—rules out these kinds of mistakes.

The second purpose of this approach is to avoid defining an industry too narrowly. Microbrewed beer is manufactured and delivered using the same fundamental processes as popular and premium beer (such as Anheuser-Busch's Busch and Budweiser). The criterion of a common technical platform supports the idea that microbreweries and general breweries compete within the same industry. Thus, in general, a common technical platform tends to broaden industry definition to include close competitors with the capability to attract each other's buyers and suppliers, regardless of competitor intentions.

## Step Two: Determining Whether Change Is Architectural

After you have established the boundaries of the industry in step one, you can begin the processes of determining whether change is Architectural and Foundational. Clear industry boundaries are necessary if you are to identify exactly those activities and assets that are central to the business and that may be subjected to threats of obsolescence.

The second step in the diagnosis of industry evolution is to determine whether change is Architectural. Recall that Architectural change is defined by a threat to the core activities in an industry and that the term "core" indicates that an activity is essential to an industry's value creation and therefore to its current profitability. Because each core activity has a direct impact on the relationships between the industry, its buyers, and its suppliers, each core activity can be tied directly to both the revenue and cost streams of the industry.

How can you tell whether an activity is essential to value creation? When faced with this question, try to imagine what would happen to industry profitability if the activity were to be disallowed entirely and immediately.[2] If the profitability would drop substantially, then the activity is a core activity. For example, if soft-drink bottlers were prevented from making direct store-door delivery to supermarkets, both the industry's costs and revenues would be affected. Revenues would decline faster than costs, causing a drop in profitability. As a result, store-door delivery qualifies as a core activity.

Research is an example of an activity that does *not* qualify as a core activity because it influences today's costs but not today's revenue. This doesn't mean that research is unimportant. Indeed, a firm's ability to innovate rests on activities performed today that create value in the future. It's just that Architectural change in the industry structure is defined only by reference to activities that influence both revenues and costs *today*.

Architectural change tends to occur on a broad scale and generally involves a threat to an industry's dominant model for organizing its core activities as well as the activities themselves. Keep in mind that a threat alone defines Architectural change. In most situations, the threat is not fully realized—that is, not *all* activities become obsolete. For the threat to be credible, though, the new approach must affect the ability of the industry to create value by influencing both buyer willingness to pay and supplier willingness to sell.[3] In almost all cases, Architectural change eventually leads to a widespread transformation of an industry's activities and the eventual exit of several major firms—perhaps even more. Architectural change ends when the industry no longer operates under a threat to its core activities.

Chapter 2 defined "core activities" as recurring actions that make the industry's suppliers willing to sell and the industry's buyers willing to buy. Thus, core activities involve the industry's buyers and suppliers. An activity qualifies as "core" only if profits would be substantially affected if the activity were ruled out, as is the case with soft-drink bottlers that rely on store-door delivery to support revenue. The mental exercise of determining which activities are "core" to an industry is itself illuminating.[4] The following list describes a few activities that are core in the discount retailing industry, where Wal-Mart, Kmart, and Target compete:

- Trucking merchandise from central distribution centers to stores

- Negotiating with merchandise vendors centrally

- Operating warehouse stores in malls with large parking lots

The following is a list of activities that are not core:

- Operating a particular model of truck

- Negotiating in Bentonville, Arkansas, with a specific vendor

- Operating a store at a particular address in a small city

The activities in the first list are core because discount retailers would have to find fundamentally new ways of running their businesses without them, and, as a result, the value that they create and their profitability would diminish substantially. The activities in the second list are constituents of the activities in the first, but they are not core because the industry could create value without them. A corollary is that the activities in the second set are not characteristic of the dominant model for discount retailing. The dominant model in an industry is made up only of core activities for achieving operational effectiveness.

Don't be fooled into a diagnosis of Architectural change if you see a threat of obsolescence only to activities that affect buyers *or* suppliers. Again, core activities influence both buyers and suppliers simultaneously. When an industry's activities for dealing with buyers become obsolete, Architectural change is not necessarily the root cause.[5]

How many core activities must be threatened for an Architectural change to occur? It depends. The key is that the new approach must create enough of a threat—either across core activities or within specific core activities—to affect overall buyer willingness to pay and overall supplier willingness to sell. (Recall that "value creation" by the industry is defined as the difference between the willingness of *all* buyers to buy and the willingness of *all* suppliers to sell.[6])

Put another way, Architectural change occurs when the dominant model in an established industry creates less value than it used to because a new approach emerges that affects the behavior of one or more significant groups of buyers and of suppliers. Remember that value creation is defined in terms of buyer willingness to pay, which puts a cap on prices, and of supplier willingness to sell, which puts a floor on costs. Value creation may erode before profitability erodes because of the gaps between prices and buyer willingness to pay, and costs and supplier willingness to sell. In practice, what this means is that the threat initially makes the industry's buyers and suppliers increasingly uncomfortable with the changing terms of the deals that they get by continuing with the established industry. Even if their next-best alternatives are not immediately more attractive, the trends are working against continuing old relationships.

For example, Architectural change occurred when savings and loan institutions (S&Ls) were threatened by investment management companies and commercial lenders in the 1980s. At first, S&L depositors, borrowers, and employees simply had their eyes on the burgeoning investment-management companies, their mutual funds, and the prolif-eration of specialized lenders. In 1980, there were about 4,000 federally insured S&Ls in the United States that together held assets of approxi-mately $600 billion and that paid moderate interest rates to depositors in an environment of unusually high interest rates.[7] The S&Ls had been stressed by the business cycles of the 1970s, but deposits had been growing at stable average rates. Everything seemed to change as mutual funds offered by investment management companies became widely available and as the impact of the second oil shock in the late 1970s cre-ated unprecedented pressure on interest rates.

With time, the depositors and employees of the S&Ls began to re-alize that mutual funds offered better deals for investors willing to ab-sorb additional risk. In the mid-1980s, the largest mutual fund, Fi-delity's Magellan Fund, returned more than 20 percent on average. The S&Ls saw an explosion in deposits as competition among them for funds led to major increases in interest rates. Between the end of 1982 and the end of 1985, deposits in S&Ls rose 56 percent, but insolvencies also rose to unprecedented levels. At the same time, talented employees fled the S&Ls to pursue jobs in investment management, commercial banking, and even investment banking, and borrowers sought special-ized lenders that offered better mortgage rates. By 1989, there were fewer than 2,900 federally insured S&Ls remaining in the United States, more than 500 of which were insolvent; the surviving S&Ls posted losses in that year of more than $17 billion. The S&L industry had been catapulted into Architectural transformation.

Today, Architectural change is occurring in the landline telephone services industry. Landline telephone service—historically dominant in telephony—is threatened by wireless technology. In Japan, the number of fixed telephone lines dropped for the first time in 1997, indicating that the threat of obsolescence is taking hold.[8] Use of wireless phones in some European countries has surpassed use of landlines. In rural Tanza-nia, landline service may never be installed on a large scale. Given the cost of maintaining landlines over long distances, wireless technology is cheaper and more convenient.[9]

As a rule, Architectural change usually takes hold in a specialized group of buyers and suppliers and then migrates to other groups within the industry. The newly forming industry may coexist for years with the established industry, steadily attracting volume and threaten-ing the survival of the incumbents. If the established industry survives the transition and becomes stable, then it is fundamentally changed with a new dominant model at its center. The horse-and-carriage trade, once a major form of transportation in New York City, went through an Architectural transformation many decades ago, and yet carriage rides are still available in New York. It's just that the entire dominant model has changed. The number of carriages, the way the rides are marketed, and buyer purchase criteria are all very different than they were in the industry's heyday.

When Architectural change begins, it's often difficult for executives to see because the company's core activities may become threatened with obsolescence without complaint from the buyers and suppliers.[10] The reason is that the change almost always begins with buyers and suppliers that are out of the mainstream.[11] For instance, in the 1980s, many corporate clients of large telecommunications companies rejected wireless service as inferior to landline service because of unreliable dial tone, narrow geographic range, and dropped calls. Leaders in the land-line business—like leaders in many established industries—could only learn a limited amount about the true potential of the new technology by asking customers to forecast their needs. Figure 4-1 summarizes the challenge. Leaders in mature or declining industries are often con-

FIGURE 4-1

## The Effect of Architectural Change

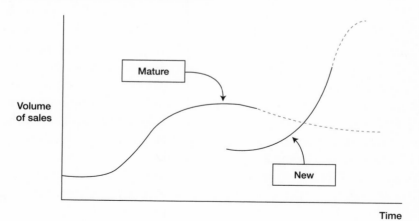

fronted with seemingly unimportant threats from outsiders who seek to create a new approach that is initially inferior to the established model. As Clayton Christensen notes in *The Innovator's Dilemma*, the most important buyers in the industry generally find the new approach inferior because technical performance on established criteria is worse than on the existing dominant model.[12]

The threat to established leaders leads to consolidation as a new dominant model emerges and the new industry becomes much more appealing to the mainstream. As buyers and suppliers defect from the traditional industry, the established leaders on the old dominant model have little chance to preserve their positions in the new industry. Because they are so invested in the old model, they are reluctant to abandon it and often hold on as long as possible to their existing buyers and suppliers—for better or worse. For example, by the late 1990s, wireless technology had improved to the point where signals were clear and calls were reliable. In fact, some corporate clients even issued wireless handsets instead of landline telephones to new employees. While the core group of loyal landline clients had not abandoned their partnerships with the regional telephone companies, wireless technology had a significant impact on the survival, short-term profitability, and long-term profitability of the landline incumbents.

The acid test for understanding whether Architectural change is occurring is to examine whether buyer willingness to pay and supplier willingness to sell are dropping. There is a significant advantage to this approach over those advocated by prior authors, who have often recommended looking historically at changes over time. The problem with an historical analysis is that the causes and effects of Architectural change are very difficult to isolate and identify. A new technology may motivate Architectural change, but ultimately the effect on the industry structure depends on a variety of related factors that are often difficult to understand without the benefit of hindsight. For example, the Apple Newton, an early personal digital assistant, had the potential to drive Architectural change in the address-book manufacturing industry, but it did not. Why? Because the product was ahead of its time, which is one of the risks of moving first to commercialize a technology. Personal digital assistants gained momentum only with the introduction ten years later of products like the Palm Pilot and Blackberry. The success of these later products depended as much on buyer readiness to accept the new technology as on the quality of the products themselves. By focusing on changes in buyer willingness to pay and supplier willingness to sell, you can identify an Architectural change without relying on a qualitative historical analysis.

## Step Three: Determining Whether Change is Foundational

The third step in the diagnosis of industry evolution is to identify whether change is Foundational, which occurs when core assets are at risk of obsolescence. A core asset is defined as essential to the value created by the firm,[13] and is sometimes called a "core capability" or "critical resource." Core assets support activities that are integral both to revenues and to costs in exactly the sense described earlier.

Think of brand capital in the soft-drink concentrate business. If it were entirely and immediately eliminated, then nobody would know anything about Coke or Pepsi—which demonstrates that brand capital is integral to our willingness to pay for either product. Without brand capital, the soft-drink concentrate industry's profitability would drop right away and would likely never recover. Contrast this with the ice-cream shop industry on Cape Cod, where locally owned businesses tend to command market share. There's a shop called "Sundae School" that has a regular following. If the "Sundae School" brand were entirely and immediately eradicated, the profitability of the shop would drop temporarily, but the owners of the establishment would probably be able to recover within a year, especially since the shop would operate from the same location as it always had. Brand capital is a core asset in the soft-drink concentrate industry but not the Cape Cod ice-cream shop industry.[14]

Foundational change differs from Architectural change in that it focuses on core *assets* instead of core *activities*. The difference between a core activity and a core asset is that assets are durable and retain value even when they are not in use.[15] Core assets lie at the foundation of economies of scale and scope. They are owned and controlled by the firm, and therefore have durability that can outlive their deployment in a particular economic setting.

Foundational change occurs when the core assets of an industry are threatened with obsolescence by a new approach. Keep in mind that the threat alone defines Foundational change. Just as with Architectural change, the threat usually is not fully realized and not all core assets that are threatened will eventually become obsolete, but the threat must be credible to qualify as the source of Foundational change. In the end, credible threats most often cause the obsolescence of a significant proportion of the industry's core assets (although usually not all of them). For example, consider the threat to independent automobile service stations, which had been in decline when the Foundational threat from the quick-lube industry took hold. The quick-lube industry threatened to make obsolete the local reputation and physical capital of independent service stations. In the end, not all independent stations have actually gone out of business, but so many have that no surviving independent station can take its ongoing viability for granted.

Foundational change may or may not accompany Architectural change. Understanding the difference between Foundational and Architectural change rests on appreciating the difference between core activities and core assets. You'll recall from chapter 2 that core activities are recurring actions. By contrast, "core assets" are durable resources that can stand idle for some time (normally more than a year) without losing their potential to create value. As chapter 1 indicated, core assets are threatened with obsolescence when a new approach accelerates their rate of depreciation. As an example, think of the portfolio of patented drugs owned by the major pharmaceutical companies. These assets are constantly threatened with obsolescence as firms engage in R&D to develop new blockbusters. Once regulatory authorities approve a new drug, the value created by old drugs with similar therapeutic purpose can drop dramatically.

There are many industries that are asset-intensive but where assets are not regularly threatened. The commercial trucking business is not undergoing Foundational change because no new approach currently threatens to accelerate the rate of depreciation on the trucks or on any other asset in the business. Similarly, the commercial airlines industry is not undergoing Foundational change because no new approach is making the planes (or other assets) obsolete. Asset intensity is not a signal of Foundational change.

An asset qualifies as "core" by the same criterion that applies to activities: Profitability (measured by return on invested capital) would be substantially affected if the asset were eliminated. The following list describes a few assets that are core in the soft-drink concentrate production industry:

- The legislated right to long-term, exclusive contracts with bottlers conferred by the Soft Drink Interbrand Competition Act of 1980

- Trademarked logos

- Brand capital

The following list of assets owned by soft-drink concentrate producers are *not* core:

- Trucks

- Existing stocks of vanilla, caramel, and other ingredients

- Headquarters buildings

The activities in the first list are core because the soft-drink concentrate producers would have to find fundamentally new ways of running their businesses without them, and, as a result, value creation and profitability would diminish substantially. The activities in the second list are not core because the industry could easily replace the existing stock if it were eliminated. Coca-Cola, Pepsi, and the other concentrate producers would quickly recover their value creation by purchasing more trucks, replenishing the stock of ingredients, and moving to another headquarters building if the existing assets were no longer available. But companies in the industry would find it very difficult to recover if their exclusive rights, logos, and brand capital were eliminated.

One of the key characteristics of core assets is that they influence interaction between the industry and both its buyers and its suppliers at the same time. For instance, the right to long-term, exclusive contracts with bottlers, which was created in the United States by the Soft Drink Interbrand Competition Act of 1980, provides soft-drink concentrate producers with the ability to award exclusive contracts by geographic area. Of course, this has a direct influence on buyer willingness to pay, since the value of a bottling franchise is substantially enhanced by the guarantee of no direct competition from a representative of the same manufacturer. The contracts also influence supplier willingness to sell.

The major soft-drink manufacturers negotiate with the providers of key raw materials on behalf of their bottlers, which would not be feasible if the bottlers themselves were competing locally.

To what extent must core assets be threatened for Foundational change to be under way? The threat must cause a decline in total buyer willingness to pay and total supplier willingness to sell, each of which should be calculated by aggregating across all of the buyers and suppliers in the industry. Let me clarify: Each buyer has a willingness to pay, and each supplier has a willingness to sell. By adding the willingness to pay across all buyers that deal with any firm within the industry, you can calculate total buyer willingness to pay, and by adding the willingness to sell across all suppliers, you can calculate total supplier willingness to sell. The industry's core assets are threatened if each of these totals drops because of a threat to core assets. Keep in mind that the totals don't drop if one firm in the industry steals business from another. The threat must affect the industry as a whole.

The threat of asset obsolescence may originate from within the industry or from outside the industry. Consider the movie production industry, which is undergoing Foundational change because core assets— that is, the portfolio of films—are constantly being threatened by new films that distract buyers from last month's big hit. This threat occurs repeatedly across the industry— and as a consequence filmmakers are in the business of creating new assets to get an edge on the competition. Similarly, the pharmaceutical industry's portfolio of drugs depreciates faster than it would if there were no pressure from new blockbusters. In both film-production and pharmaceuticals, the threat usually originates from within the industry, but is potent nonetheless. In other situations, the threat of obsolescence originates outside the boundaries of the established industry: Typewriter manufacturing and overnight letter delivery are all undergoing threats that originate externally.

Unlike Architectural change, which usually takes hold in a specialized group of buyers and suppliers, Foundational change generally arises in the mainstream of the industry. But like Architectural change, Foundational change occurs over a long period. Indeed, in an industry that is not changing Architecturally, the impetus for Foundational change may be built into the dominant model.

The acid test of Foundational change is that the value created by the industry is declining because of a threat to the industry's core assets.

A comprehensive study to assess whether Foundational change is under way involves:

- Identifying the hierarchy of assets in the industry

- Evaluating which assets are core by assessing whether the industry's ability to create value would be affected if the assets were eliminated

- Understanding which core assets are indeed threatened by a new approach

- Evaluating whether the value created by the industry is diminishing because of the threat

### Determining the Trajectory of Change Based on the Assessments

Now that you've defined the boundaries of your industry and determined whether your industry is undergoing Architectural and Foundational change (through an assessment of threats to core activities and assets), you're ready to put it all together and answer fundamental questions affecting your firm's future by determining which trajectory you are on. Your industry is undergoing

- *Radical change* if both Architectural and Foundational transformation are under way

- *Intermediating change* if Architectural but not Foundational transformation is under way

- *Creative change* if Foundational but not Architectural transformation is under way

- *Progressive change* if neither Architectural nor Foundational is under way

Once you have determined which of the four types of industry change applies, the next challenge is to delve into the more detailed aspects of the particular stage of industry evolution that is under way. Identifying the stage will allow you to place your firm within a context of change, and provide you with the background necessary to evaluate your current strategy and future needs.

## Step Four: Assessing the Stage of Industry Evolution

You'll recall that the industry life cycle is only relevant for industries on Progressive or Creative paths. For industries on Radical or Intermediating trajectories, the life cycle model doesn't apply because the transformation does not track the development of a dominant model that shapes the industry structure. Radical and Intermediating transformations also occur in phases, but these phases have a very different character than a life cycle. The principal questions addressed here are:

- What is the stage of the *life cycle* occurring in an industry undergoing Progressive or Creative change? Is it fragmentation, shakeout, maturity, or decline?

- What is the phase of the *transformation* occurring in an industry undergoing Radical or Intermediating change? Is it emergence, convergence, co-existence, or dominance?

Chapter 3 describes the stages in detail, but not exactly how to determine which stage is under way in a particular industry. For both Architectural and non-Architectural change, the stages of the evolutionary path are defined in broad strokes by hard criteria that involve assessments of industry volumes. When an industry follows a conventional life cycle (i.e., because it is Progressive or Creative), the stage depends on inflection points in the *growth of industry volume*. When change is Architectural (i.e., Radical or Intermediating), the phase depends on inflection points in the *relative growth rates of volumes in the established industry and in the new industry*. The precise criteria are described in the sections that follow.

### Determining the Stage of the Industry Life Cycle

The best way to assess the stage of the industry life cycle is to step back and look at what is happening to industry volume. Here are the definitive criteria to use for identifying the evolutionary stage in your industry.

#### The Point Between Fragmentation and Shakeout

The initial fragmentation phase tends to be accompanied by low volumes. When shakeout occurs, volumes increase dramatically. Many researchers identify the inflection point between fragmentation and shakeout as the year in which the *rate* of growth in industry aggregate volumes increases quarter over quarter. This is a dramatic time: An increasing growth *rate* occurs only when the absolute level of sales accumulates faster and faster each quarter.

### The Point Between Shakeout and Maturity

The point of demarcation between shakeout and maturity occurs when the rate of growth in aggregate volume stops increasing. To avoid coming to mistaken conclusions based on temporary fluctuations in volume, many experienced analysts look for the year in which the rate of growth drops in four successive quarters. Keep in mind that growth continues in maturity; it's just that the rate of growth is lower than it was historically.

### The Point Between Maturity and Decline

When volumes drop in an absolute sense, then the industry has reached the point of decline.

### Additional Criteria

Even after you carefully identify the inflection points between the stages of the life cycle based on changes in volume, you may be concerned about whether you are basing your assessment on an anomaly in volumes. For example, a downturn in the business cycle can cause volume to decline temporarily and then rebound. If this happens, you may want to look for evidence to back up your hypothesis about the stage of the life cycle. The most reliable confirming evidence comes from tracking the dominant model in the industry. By assessing patterns in the technical performance of the dominant model, it is possible to resolve ambiguity in the pattern of aggregate industry volume. The technical performance of an industry is an idiosyncratic measure that increases over the life cycle, such as fuel efficiency in the automobile industry.

The advantage of this confirming measure is that the rate of improvement in technical performance tends to be more stable than industry volume. The disadvantage is that there is no formula for finding the measure of technical performance in a particular industry. In each industry, the dominant model is unique. Finding an appropriate measure of technical performance involves identifying a central indicator of the industry's efficiency and effectiveness at creating value. Hence, measuring improvement on the dominant model requires judgment and may not be definitive, and yet tracking progress on the dominant model can provide important confirming evidence in the following ways:

- Rapid acceleration in technical performance marks the point of transition between fragmentation and shakeout. In automobile manufacturing, the transition between fragmentation and shakeout is associated with the introduction of the Model T, which was produced using assembly techniques that radically improved manufacturing efficiency.

- The point of demarcation between shakeout and maturity is associated with a deceleration in rates of improvement in technical performance. The automobile manufacturing industry hit this point in the 1960s as the rate of increase in manufacturing productivity began to slow.

- When technical progress on the dominant model hits a physical limit, the industry generally reaches a point of decline. By many accounts, the automobile industry hit the point of decline in the 1990s, as manufacturing productivity rates leveled off. The argument for decline in automobile manufacturing rests on the observation that cars incorporating combustion engines cannot be made much more cheaply without sacrificing fuel efficiency or safety (features on which buyers are generally unwilling to compromise).

Despite its attractiveness, the absence of a definitive method for identifying technical efficiency makes this approach unreliable. In automobile manufacturing, the central measure of technical efficiency on the dominant model is tied to the costs of producing safe, fuel-efficient cars. In overnight package delivery, the measure is tied to the costs of reliable, on-time distribution. Because there is no single definitive measure of performance, it's hard to know whether you have conceptualized the dominant model accurately. As a result, it's not a good idea to rely on the dominant model as the primary indicator of the stage of the life cycle. In most cases, investigation into the dominant model only can provide powerful confirming evidence to *complement* an assessment based on industry volume.

### *Determining the Phase of Radical or Intermediating Change*

Tracking aggregate industry volumes alone won't work for assessing the stage of Architectural transformation in industries going through Radical or Intermediating change. The challenge is in assessing how quickly the new approach is overtaking the established one.

To make the assessment, take the point of view of the older, established industry that is undergoing the Architectural transformation. It is easy to become distracted when a new approach sparks an Architectural transition in more than one established industry at the same time. The emergence of the PC threw both typewriter manufacture and minicomputing into Architectural transitions, although the transitions began at different times. Because the transitions in the typewriter manufacturing and minicomputing industries began at different times and occurred at different rates, the processes must be tracked separately.

The most reliable method for measuring the stage of an Architectural transition is to examine the *relative* volumes of the established industry and the new approach that embodies the threat. The criteria are described in the following sections.

#### *The Point Where Emergence Begins*

As a new approach emerges, its volumes tend to be small but the growth rate is greater than in the established industry. For example, the number of auctions held by eBay and other online auctioneers was initially smaller than the number held in flea markets and state fairs, but the rate of growth in online auctions was much higher than in live auctions. The first stage of Architectural transformation—the emergence phase—is marked by growth in the new approach and also by an overwhelmingly greater level of volume in the established industry. In other words, the high rate of growth in the new industry may be striking, but the discrepancy in the volumes of the old and new industries is so enormous that convergence doesn't occur. Because the established industry is growing simultaneously with the new approach, the actual obsolescence of activities is far off into the future—but the wheels are in motion.

#### *The Point Between Emergence and Convergence*

The convergence phase begins when the growth in the new approach is high enough to allow the new industry to gain ground on the established industry. This may sound as though it would be a foregone conclusion given that growth is required for the prior Emergence stage but it is not. To see why not, consider what has happened to the soft-drink concentrate industry. The absolute volume of soft drinks consumed annually in the United States in 1993 was estimated at 48.9 gallons per capita, and the annual rate of growth was 2 percent.[16] The absolute volume of bottled water in the same year was 10.5 gallons per capita and was growing at 6 percent annually. Growth in consumption of bottled water was higher than growth in soft drinks, but the rate of growth was not sufficient to cause convergence in the volumes of soft drinks and bottled water.[17] The convergence phase of the transition only occurs when the relative growth rate of the new approach is high enough to allow for decreases in the absolute difference in the volumes across the old and new approaches.

### The Point Between Convergence and Co-existence

An Architectural transition moves from the convergence phase into the co-existence phase when the growth rate in the new industry begins to slow (but remains higher than the growth rate in the established industry). Landline and wireless technology coexist today. Music recording currently co-exists with the online distribution of music. In each case, the new approach continues to grow but not as fast as it had before. The old and new approaches have settled into a period in which each accounts for a significant share. For the threat of obsolescence to continue (i.e., for the transition to continue as Architectural), the new approach must grow at a fast enough rate to gain volume on the established industry. Yet the growth rate is almost always slower than in the convergence phase. During co-existence, firms in the established industry may be lulled into a false sense of security about the supposedly fading threat of obsolescence.

### The Point Between Co-existence and Dominance

Eventually, the new approach comes to dominate the established industry and the industry moves from the co-existence to the dominance phase. The transition to this period of industry evolution is marked by greater volume in new industry than in the established industry. Some examples of this process: the volume of personal computers sold annually, which is now substantially higher than the volume of typewriters. The volume of consumer goods hauled by commercial long-haul trucking is now substantially greater than the volume hauled by rail. A majority of North Americans now use the Internet to research new car purchases rather than only going to car dealerships to learn about different models.

The old approach may retain its viability for some time despite being dominated by the new industry. For instance, conventional auto dealers, typewriter manufacturers, and commercial railways survive and may even prosper after they become dominated by new approaches. The key feature of this kind of transformation is that the new approach creates enough of a threat to the survival of established firms to define the terms of competition.

### A Final Transition

Industries undergoing Architectural transformation may face a final transition. In time, the Architectural transformation may end and the industry may move back onto a Progressive or Creative evolutionary path. This occurs—and the industry moves to a stable, non-Architectural evolutionary trajectory—once the industry's activities for dealing with both buyers and suppliers are no longer threatened. The horse-and-carriage industry in New York City, once thrown into an Architectural transformation by the subway and the automobile, is now on a Progressive path. After a short period of fragmentation, a dominant model emerged that involved carrying tourists and romantics through Central Park. The industry has hit a new maturity, where growth is slow and business is stable.

### Additional Criteria

The transition through stages of Architectural transformation is best measured by examining relative volumes on the old and new approaches, but this measurement can be hard to make. For example, shifts in the business cycle may make it difficult to assess patterns in relative volume. If there is ambiguity, then there is a reliable mechanism confirming the stages of Architectural change, which is to examine how the established and new industries satisfy buyers.

During the emergence phase of the Architectural transition, buyers that switch from the established to the new industry must compromise on some product attributes. Electric cars today perform better than conventional automobiles on fuel efficiency, but they are smaller and their maximum speeds are lower. Music downloaded over the Internet may be more convenient to obtain than a CD in a store, but it cannot be played as easily on most stereos. Downloading music initially appealed to young people with a great appetite for music but without much money. eBay's earliest buyers did not attach much value to the physical experience of sorting through goods before auction at a flea market or state fair. An industry in the emergence stage of an Architectural transformation offers products that continue to be judged as superior by mainstream buyers in the largest segments of the market, but that are judged as inferior by buyers in specialty segments where specific attributes of the new product are highly valued.

The convergence stage is associated with a shift in relative performance across attributes as breakthroughs occur in the new industry. As an Architectural transformation proceeds, firms in the new industry face steeper learning curves than firms in the established industry. As learning accumulates, the performance of new products may improve dramatically. In 1999, it took about twenty minutes to download a song off the Internet (assuming an up-to-date modem and processor), while in 2002 it took less than a minute. Improvements in the convenience of Internet downloads made the new approach more popular. At the same time, online auctioneers developed mechanisms for signaling reliability, such as eBay's rating system.

The co-existence phase begins when mainstream buyers rate the overall value of new products as about the same as old products. New products perform excellently on one or more attributes that had not been considered critical in the established industry. Old products are highly valued on conventional attributes. But the net result—as mainstream buyers weigh the advantages and disadvantages of each class of products—is that the overall value provided is comparable. Wireless telephones are now nearly as reliable and clear as landline telephones, especially in urban areas, and they continue to be a lot more convenient than landline phones.

The dominance phase begins when new products are judged as better than established products on all major aspects of performance that are valued among mainstream buyers. The subway and automobile displaced the horse and carriage for commuters in New York City. The new approach even outperformed the horse and carriage for most tourists. The fact that a segment of tourists remained interested in the carriage accounted for the survival of the established industry on a small scale.

In summary, the phases of Radical and Intermediating transformation may take as long to unfold as the stages of an industry's life cycle.

Because it is so pervasive in its implications, it is virtually impossible for Architectural change to occur rapidly and yet the implications of Architectural change for the industry's incumbent firms are profound. The short-term performance of a firm in an industry undergoing Architectural change depends on the phase of the transformation and the firm's strategy for dealing with the Architectural challenge. Long-term performance—both in terms of survival and profitability—depends on developing a strategy for unwinding the organization's commitment to the business.

## Implications

The purpose of this chapter is to provide you with criteria for defining the boundaries of the industries in which you compete, identifying the evolutionary trajectory, and determining the stage of change in your industries. Because the implications of industry evolution can be monumental, executives often desire to move slowly, to study the situation extensively, and to compromise in conclusions about the implications, but the delays associated with further study may be unnecessary and the compromises that generate buy-in may lead to profound mistakes. The fact that you have time to react to industry change does not mean that you should avoid dealing with it by becoming stuck in endless analysis.

You can avoid unnecessary delay and damaging compromises by following the steps laid out in this chapter. The criteria laid out here lead you to a definitive conclusion about the trajectory of change in the business you are examining. Armed with this assessment, you can move toward a strategy for addressing the challenges and opportunities in your environment—even if the strategy involves taking smaller steps today to create options for the future. Part II of this book provides an overview of the challenges and discusses many of the approaches that have been pursued successfully by firms in a wide range of industries under all four trajectories and at all stages of change.

**PART TWO**

---

# Aligning Strategy
# with Industry Evolution

# 5

## Conforming to the Rules of Change Within an Industry

THIS CHAPTER BEGINS a new section that explores how to develop a strategy that capitalizes on your understanding of the trajectory and stage of change in your industry. Chapter 5 examines the prerequisites that arise from industry evolution for effective strategy within a particular business. To pick up an analogy from chapter 1, the prerequisites describe what a firm must do to keep within the barriers at the sides of the highway. If you can't meet the prerequisites required for success in your industry given its trajectory, then your chances of survival and for a minimal level of acceptable profitability are negligible.

Chapter 6 reviews many of the tactics that are available to firms for taking advantage of the opportunities created by change within a particular industry. While it is impossible to be comprehensive, the goal of Chapter 6 is to show how firms have used an understanding of industry evolution to achieve better performance than the competition.

Chapter 7 goes further, addressing the implications of industry change for a firm's level of diversification across different business units. The questions here have to do with the advantages and disadvantages of using a portfolio strategy to cultivate relationships across business units that are in different industries. While all the issues you face cannot be anticipated here, chapters 5 through 7 equip you to make better strategic choices and invest in innovation programs more productively. This section of the book identifies a number of core themes and issues that regularly arise in industry evolution and illustrates how strategy can become more effective by accounting for them explicitly. It starts by offering a number of principles for conforming to the rules in industries undergoing Architectural and Foundational change (see box 5-1).

---

**box 5-1   The Difference Between Prerequisites and Strategic Choices**

"Prerequisites" are "givens"—that is, actions that a firm absolutely *must* take to survive and achieve a minimal level of performance. For instance, it is a prerequisite to adhere to the dominant model in the mature phase of an industry undergoing Progressive change if you intend to survive for the long term. Similarly, it is a prerequisite in an industry in the advanced phases of Radical transformation to migrate activities and assets out of the business. Prerequisites are axiomatic for firms that plan to achieve a reasonable return on investment within the industry.

Strategic choices, which are discussed in chapter 6 and the second part of chapter 7, have a different character than prerequisites because they involve selecting between two or more attractive alternatives. Strategic issues arise when a firm must make tradeoffs between choices that are mutually incompatible but that each have advantages. For example, a new entrant with a hit product in an industry undergoing Creative change has to decide whether or not to try for more hits and thereby commit to participate in the industry for the long haul. The advantage of trying for additional hits is that the firm may be able to earn a significant return by capitalizing on its unique capabilities in the business. The advantage of choosing not to develop additional assets is that the firm doesn't have to take on the risk of failure. Both choices are justifiable under different circumstances. The essence of strategy is in making a contextually robust choice, and effective strategy depends on a detailed understanding of the opportunities in the industry as well as the firm's capabilities for exploiting them.

The analogy to traveling on a highway is again useful. Strategic choices within a business unit—that is, those that describe how a company will compete effectively within a particular industry—are akin to choices about how fast to travel and which lane to take. Strategic choices regarding corporate strategy—that is, those that describe how a company will compete across industries—are like choices about how to deploy a fleet of trucks across the highway system. Business-unit and corporate strategy each involve prerequisites and strategic choices.

---

## Prerequisites Under Architectural Change

You'll recall that Architectural change occurs when the core activities in a business come under a threat of obsolescence, and that it is associated with Intermediating and Radical transformation. As a consequence of an Architectural threat, the industry's relationships with buyers and suppliers become strained and organizations face considerable pressure to create value in different ways.

The central challenge under Architectural change is in finding a way to preserve core activities and relationships as long as they are profitable and then to efficiently decouple the core activities when they begin to damage profitability. Forecasting the inflection point and preparing an organization to make such a major change in orientation require massive effort, extensive planning, and unparalleled leadership. The prerequisites are the inviolable principles of competing effectively in this situation, which fall into five categories, summarized in table 5-1.

*1. Take the perspective of the industry's buyers, and constantly evaluate and re-evaluate their best alternatives to dealing with the industry. Adjust your offering of products and services over time to reflect your buyers' true underlying interests instead of just their short-term willingness to pay.*

Under Architectural change, your buyers are faced with new alternatives that they may never have considered. The implications of the new alternatives for buyers may be as straightforward as having to drive to a quick-lube shop instead of a service station to get an oil change. While driving to a quick-lube is easy for the buyer, its implications are certainly not straightforward for the service-station industry, which went through an Architectural challenge that began as quick-lube stations were introduced.

When Architectural change occurs, buyers may be confronted with alternatives that require profound changes in their entire systems of activities, as when jet engines were first introduced to commercial airlines. The airlines were initially concerned with how jet propulsion would affect braking systems, fuselage size, runway lengths, and crew training, to name a few. As a consequence, the jet-engine pioneers worked closely with the airlines in the decades after World War II to deal with the implications of the technology for the airlines' activities as a whole. Delays in adoption by the airlines were not a signal of the failure of jet engines but rather a period in which further technical development solved the buyer's problems. For propeller-engine manufacturers, the magnitude of the threat was temporarily obscured by the development process. This example illustrates how important it is to assess the viability of a new alternative from the buyer's point of view.

**TABLE 5-1**

## Principles for Competing Under Architectural Change

| Principle | Implications |
|---|---|
| 1. Take the perspective of the industry's buyers | • Develop and redevelop market research designed to extract reliable information about changes in preferences—challenge conventional wisdom.<br>• Acknowledge the presence of new and attractive alternatives for the buyer.<br>• Track the ways in which your buyers are investing in alternative products to understand shifts in incentives.<br>• Repeat the analysis in each stage of the downstream chain. |
| 2. Take the perspective of the industry's suppliers | • Work collaboratively to ease suppliers' transitions out of the industry.<br>• Become less dependent on proprietary inputs.<br>• Simplify the demands you place on suppliers.<br>• Subcontract to guarantee commitment and lower costs. |
| 3. Track changes in segments of the business | • Measure carefully how segment boundaries change over time.<br>• Expect unconventional segment definitions.<br>• Centralize decisions about the allocation of resources across segments.<br>• Concede unattractive segments to the competition and channel resources into attractive segments. |
| 4. Interpret organizational conflict in terms that reflect market pressures | • Acknowledge the legitimacy of the views held within different divisions serving different market segments.<br>• Provide effective leaders with the authority to resolve disputes through resource-allocation decisions. |
| 5. Evaluate competitors as potential allies | • Constantly evaluate the strategic options available to competitors.<br>• Map competitors' performance by segment to understand incentives.<br>• Identify common threats and opportunities for alliances with former competitors to defend the industry structure.<br>• Develop the capability to engage in and operate alliances efficiently. |

As an Architectural change takes hold, buyers may continue to purchase from you but for different reasons than prior to the threat—your survival and profitability depend on understanding these changes in detail. Sometimes buyers continue to purchase from the industry because they are locked in by prior commitments. It is usually not in your long-term interest to take advantage of willingness-to-pay that arises from prior commitments that buyers made in anticipation of a better deal today. At a minimum, all firms in this situation must consider taking the following action:

- Conduct new kinds of market research that challenge conventional wisdom about how buyers are making their decisions. Lou Gerstner of IBM did this by devoting considerable time and effort to personal meetings with customers in order to learn more about their needs.

- Acknowledge the presence of the new alternatives in discussions with buyers, and find ways to learn about the tradeoff between your products and those offered by the new business from your buyer's point of view. Many individual investors did not adopt new advisory services right away because of the inconvenience of switching and because of uncertainty about the structure of the new services. Traditional brokerages put themselves at a disadvantage by assuming that investors delayed out of loyalty to their old brokers.

- Be aware of any investments that your buyers must make to purchase from the new industry, and carefully track your buyers' investment behavior. Interpret initial purchases by buyers in the new industry as an important sign of changes in their long-term interests. For example, the cost of MP3 players initially slowed their adoption and mitigated the threat to the traditional music recording industry. The accelerated rate of adoption of the players that occurred after an initial testing phase was a signal of an impending inflection point in the Intermediation of the recording industry.

- Repeat the analysis all the way down the vertical chain from your distributors to the end-consumer. The first signs of the threat to your activities may lie downstream. For instance, the threat from online music downloads initially had a larger impact on music retailers than on the recording industry. By looking downstream, you have a better chance of seeing the threat early.

The goal of all this analysis is twofold. First, it is crucial to track how buyers' preferences are changing so that you can make better decisions about when and whether to scale back activities to satisfy buyer needs. By acknowledging that your buyers are in the process of switching to a new product, you may be able to gain their support in simplifying product features and in lowering prices incrementally. For example, a propeller-engine manufacturer, confronted with the threat from jet engines, can work with regional airlines to refocus development effort in propeller engines to smaller planes, lighter loads, and shorter routes.

Second, you may find opportunities to develop new products that ease the transition for buyers or that will continue to appeal to a segment of buyers for whom salient features of the new products are not attractive. For example, financial institutions that send many documents by overnight letter may be among the first to switch to securely encrypted Internet delivery of the documents. The overnight letter companies—aware of this threat—may find opportunity in selling analytical algorithms for evaluating the consequences of missed deliveries, fraudulent claims of nondelivery, and back-up paper delivery. This analysis is essential to predict better when and how buyers will discontinue purchasing and to offer new products that appeal to buyers during the transition.

*2. Take the perspective of the industry's suppliers, and constantly evaluate and reevaluate their best alternatives to dealing with the industry. Adjust the demands that you make on suppliers over time to reflect their abilities and long-term interests.*

The second prerequisite to surviving and earning profits under Architectural change is to take the perspective of the industry's suppliers and understand how their best options are changing. Part 1 of this book described how suppliers often initially respond to Architectural change by aggressively pursuing partnerships with the industry. An "us versus them" mentally can emerge, with suppliers offering irresistible deals that are intended to defend the industry structure against the onslaught of the new approach. Think of the concessions made by unionized workers serving the commercial rail-transport industry when confronted with the Architectural threat from long-haul trucking. The workers, concerned about a widespread loss of jobs, offered concessions that changed the economic structure of the rail business and temporarily stymied the threat. Coal miners responded similarly when their employers were confronted with an Architectural threat.

It is tempting to conclude that collaboration between suppliers and the industry represents a long-term solution to the Architectural challenge. Indeed, in some situations and in some segments of the market, this kind of cooperation may have staying power. But in the vast majority of cases, such collaboration is not sustainable because it puts unbearable ' strain on the supplier or creates only a one-shot improvement that cannot stand up against the steep learning curve of the new approach or both.

Understanding the robustness of supplier choices requires a detailed analysis that takes into account the supplier's point of view. Suppliers may have become so committed to your industry that they have few attractive outside alternatives. As a consequence, they may try to persuade you to fight to the death—theirs as well as yours—to defend the standing industry structure. In almost all cases, this choice leads to substantial excess costs that are difficult to justify. It's important not to be lulled into this position by suppliers that are even more threatened than you are by the Architectural challenge.

In most cases, however, suppliers have options other than continuing to deal with you and your competitors. With some major historical exceptions, railroad workers and miners have found alternative employment. As the Architectural threat becomes clearer, a supplier may seize the opportunity to migrate to the new approach (for example, talented aerospace engineers may leave the propeller-engine manufacturing business for the jet-engine business). When suppliers are locked into dealing with you by their prior commitments, or when there is substantial risk associated with the new approach, they may delay the transition.

Regardless of the strategy pursued by individual suppliers, you cannot survive and achieve acceptable performance without understanding how incentives are changing. The prospect of a better outside alternative may cause key suppliers to underinvest in working with you. Employees may neglect to keep their skills current and raw-material vendors may stop investing to find new sources of supply.

Your options for responding are varied and include:

- Working collaboratively with suppliers to ease their transition away from the industry. For example, offset printing companies confronted with Architectural threats due to digitization have offered workers the chance to retrain and acquire the skills necessary to operate digital presses.

- Developing new products and services that are less dependent on the proprietary input of key suppliers. Several investment brokerage firms have offered simple trading options that are not bundled with advisory services, which makes the firms less dependent on individual brokers.

- Simplifying the demands that you make on suppliers. Some brokerages have also relaxed the aggressive targets for new-account acquisition that they had imposed on brokers, thereby saving bonus costs and freeing the brokers to use their time in ways that are better aligned with the opportunities in their local areas.

- Subcontracting to guarantee supplier commitment and lower costs. For instance, many news bureaus have dealt with the Architectural threat originating with new modes of communication by subcontracting with low-cost specialists for news feeds. These contracts have allowed them to stop maintaining expensive offices in certain remote cities.

In choosing among these alternatives, avoid a naïve approach to supplier analysis that assumes that business will be conducted on the same terms as historically. Your survival and performance depend on understanding how suppliers weigh continuing to invest in your relationship against their next-best alternatives. Under Architectural change, these alternatives are moving targets.

*3. Be precise and analytical in identifying how segment boundaries are changing over time. Begin to centralize decisions about the allocation of resources across segments of the business. Be prepared to defend your position in attractive segments while conceding position in unattractive segments.*

Architectural change requires a greater degree of centralized decision making about the allocation of resources than non-Architectural change. Let me explain the reason for this: Under Architectural change, the threat of obsolescence arises at different rates in different segments of the business.

Consider the landline handset business, which has been under an Architectural threat attributable to wireless telephony. There are many segments of the landline handset business, but for simplicity consider two broad categories: (i) the conventional corded segment and (ii) the cordless segment. Keep in mind that both of these segments are part of the landline handset industry, which is the industry under an Architectural threat. Conventional handsets once were more popular than cordless phones because they offered better reception and were less expensive. The Architectural threat to the landline handset business has been accompanied by a shift in segmentation marked by an improvement in the reception of cordless telephones and stronger buyer preference for portability. For firms in the handset manufacturing business, achieving the optimal level of performance during the Architectural change depends on allocating resources across segments—away from the conventional segment and toward the cordless segment—to reflect the differences in opportunity.

Taking advantage of shifting preferences depends on understanding segment boundaries and how they are changing. Most executives are accustomed to thinking about buyer segmentation, with boundaries defined by observable differences in buyer characteristics tied to purchase criteria. For example, it is customary to define segments of the investment brokerage business in terms that reflect the sizes of the investment portfolios of customers: high-net-worth individuals, moderately wealthy individuals, younger and potentially wealthy clients, etc.

The goal here is to apply the same logic to suppliers as well as to buyers, and to conduct segmentation analysis at even greater levels of detail than before. In investment brokerage, this means segmenting the population of licensed brokers into categories, and refining the buyer categories to capture nuances in the criteria used by different kinds of customers in choosing whether to maintain a traditional brokerage account. Under Architectural change, you can get important information about which buyers and suppliers will sustain their relationships with you, and which relationships will be the most profitable in the future.

Earlier, I discussed how this analysis is tied to centralized decision making. To survive under an Architectural threat, a firm must move deftly to channel resources, products, and services to segments in which the potential for profitability over the long term is greatest. Often, there are tradeoffs between segments that offer short-term profit potential and those that offer long-term potential. To allocate resources where they will have the greatest long-run potential to generate return, firms often must choose not to support areas of the business that have been historically lucrative.

Pulling off this kind of resource allocation in a decentralized structure is virtually impossible. A firm can survive an Architectural challenge only if the authority to allocate talent, priority status, and financial resources is removed from the most profitable division and coordinated centrally. A new process is necessary, and it must allow for the allocation of resources to activities that seem risky and that may even threaten the core business. This new process must be forgiving of the uncertainty associated with new businesses and disciplined about the inevitability of the Architectural transformation in the established business.

*4. Interpret organizational conflict in terms that reflect market pressures.*

One of the most common responses to Architectural change is conflict across the organization about the best way to allocate resources. Genuine differences of opinion arise about the right thing to do, with conservative champions of the established industry pointing to its long history of profitability and with pioneering realists pointing to the threat from the new approach. At the same time, resentments develop regarding the redistribution of resources across the organization.

These kinds of conflicts take on a "Civil War" character. A case study: In institutional brokerage over the last ten years, many firms have implemented information systems and coordinating mechanisms that are designed to facilitate the presentation of a "single face" of the organization to the customer. The logic is simple. With the development of new kinds of services designed to expand the investment products available to institutional clients arises the possibility that different units might offer conflicting advice. To avoid direct competition between sister units, the institutional brokerages centralized information and funneled it back to the business units with the intention of facilitating coordination. Of course, providing information alone was not enough to stop the divisions from competing. Authority over an account also had to be allocated or held centrally. This last issue—how to handle control over accounts—created the Civil War problem. When authority was centralized, brokers in the individual divisions rebelled, claiming that they were being constrained by acting in the interests of buyers with whom they had relationships. When authority was decentralized to the division that held the greatest sales in the account, the deck was stacked against change, because the division with the greatest proportion of revenue was inevitably the one going through the Architectural threat.

How can an organization deal with the Civil War problem? By interpreting the problem in terms that reflect market pressures. The established divisions—those that generate the highest profitability, are the most stable historically, and are undergoing the Architectural threat—can legitimately lay claim to the organization's key relationships. Yet it is the new business—the one without established relationships and often without reasonable profitability—that carries the greatest long-term potential to deliver value and achieve superior performance. The difficulty arises from the fact that the success of the new business can accelerate the deterioration of the established business.

The best way to make progress is to acknowledge that the views held in the established divisions reflect market pressures rather than to focus on whether the individuals within them are subversive to the corporation's interests. Effective leadership is crucial for making it through Architectural change, especially when it is in the firm's best interests to maintain position in the established industry for a substantial period of time. The goal is to sustain relationships, retain talented employees, and begin to migrate activities into the business with better long-term prospects all at the same time.

*5. Take a fresh look at competitors, and adopt their perspective in evaluating strategic options. Keep in mind that former rivals may become allies in defending the industry structure. Develop the capability to ally efficiently.*

Architectural change often takes hold in mature or declining industries, where intense rivalries develop over many years. Differences across competitors in geographic footprint, product lines, supplier base, and culture reflect fundamentally different philosophies about value creation in the established industry. The prospect of an alliance or partnership between rivals seems almost inconceivable.

Yet alliances, partnerships, and even mergers are a major source of opportunity for firms under a common threat of Architectural change. You cannot understand the nature of the opportunity without knowing the stage of the Architectural challenge. The best way to envision the opportunities for cooperation is to evaluate the options of rivals: what it will take to stay relevant; how they can diversify; whether they are losing buyers and suppliers quickly.

Established competitors may share an interest in adopting new practices for defending against the threat to the industry structure. Consider the role of Ace Hardware in keeping independent hardware stores competitive under the threat from the home improvement warehouses. Ace consolidates the purchasing power of the independent stores to negotiate deals from suppliers and keep the independents viable. Or look at the role of Autobytel.com in keeping independent auto dealers viable against the threat from consolidated dealerships such as AutoNation. The idea is that the competitiveness of the established industry—and the welfare of consumers—may be enhanced by cooperative agreements that preserve markets.

Ultimately, the viability of an industry undergoing Architectural change may depend on mergers between rivals that would not be viable independently. This process has already begun among auto dealerships just as it occurred in the independent service-station business a decade earlier. By working together, old rivals can keep their industry competitive by rationalizing capacity, improving bargaining strength, adjusting market boundaries, and meeting the needs of a loyal cadre of buyers. (Box 5-2 deals with the general question of how networks, partnerships, and alliances figure into industry evolution.)

## Prerequisites Under Foundational Change

You'll recall that Foundational change takes hold when the core assets in a business come under a threat of obsolescence and is associated with Creative and Radical change. As a consequence of Foundational change, competition between the rivals in an industry can heat up dramatically. Companies scramble to build defenses against imitation as the foundation for stability in the industry comes under constant pressure.

The performance of a business in an industry undergoing Foundational change rests on preserving core assets and organizational advantages as long as the firm's standing within the industry is tenable and profitable, and then on unwinding the firm's commitment as quickly as possible. Chapter 6 discusses the tradeoffs that firms face as they navigate this territory. The fundamental principles that apply to all industries undergoing Foundational change are summarized in table 5-2 and fall into five categories.

*1. Evaluate and reevaluate—at least annually—how quickly assets are depreciating. Understand the incentives you face to sustain your commitment to the industry when assets become obsolete at different rates.*

As soon as you recognize a Foundational threat, evaluate how quickly your assets are depreciating under the threat of obsolescence. The centerpiece of this analysis should be a precise assessment of each

## box 5-2    Networks, Partnerships, and Alliances

Over the last decade, the field of strategy has emphasized networks, partnerships, and alliances as crucial to superior performance. In this book, these elements of strategy have received considerable attention. Network effects are central to the emergence of a dominant design, and the development of a complementary activity system has been emphasized as central to advantage on a Creative evolutionary trajectory.

Networks, partnerships, and alliances may each arise under any of the trajectories in various forms. On a Progressive evolutionary trajectory, the intra-firm network of activities is central to efficiency. Alliances between leading firms are relatively rare, although partnerships between leading firms and suppliers may arise frequently (especially after shake-out begins).

In an industry on a Creative evolutionary trajectory, alliances between firms are common. Leading companies with excess capacity in their activity systems may contract for projects. Partnerships and contracts with key suppliers are crucial to project success. Companies cannot achieve leadership until they develop partnerships with downstream distributors. In short, the network of inter-firm relationships in industries on Creative trajectories is critical to firm performance.

On an Intermediating trajectory, the established industry (undergoing the Intermediating change) can become so enmeshed with the threatening industry that the two together appear as a complex network or ecosystem. Yet understanding the differences in the trajectories is central to survival and profitability. Partnerships and alliances tend to emerge and shift over time: Established firms may bond together; they may ally with old suppliers or buyers; and/or they may pursue relationships with firms in the threatening industry. It is misleading to think of innovation exclusively at the level of the eco-system because profits are accrued to particular firms, not to the system. In other words, a primary challenge for firms under Intermediation is to strike partnership deals on favorable terms.

On a Radical trajectory, firms in the established industry may develop partnerships with buyers and/or suppliers, especially early in the transition. Over time, alliances may arise between firms in the established and threatening industries, although these relationships become increasingly fragile. In the late stages of Radical transformation, new kinds of partnerships may emerge as firms find outlets for retiring their assets.

> In short, industry evolution involves networks, partnerships, and alliances at almost every turn. The central issue for understanding industry change is to evaluate *how* networks, partnerships, and alliances matter—and the answer to this question depends on the context of change.

TABLE 5-2

## Principles for Competing Under Foundational Change

| Principle | Implications |
|---|---|
| 1. Spend the resources necessary to determine how quickly assets are depreciating | • Commission studies if necessary to obtain accurate information on the longevity of the firm's assets.<br>• Understand how differences in the depreciation rates of core assets lock the firm into renewing its commitment to the business.<br>• Invest to make assets less specialized. |
| 2. Identify the segments in which you can protect your position, and in which it will erode quickly | • Direct your most valuable assets to the segments with the potential to deliver the best performance.<br>• Embed your most valuable assets in an underlying system of support activities.<br>• Modularize less valuable assets so that they can eventually be sold or retired.<br>• Decentralize decisions to optimize the value created from specialized assets. |
| 3. Guard intellectual property intensively | • Develop a knowledge-management system to track intellectual property and to protect it rigorously.<br>• Learn what patents, copyrights, or trademarks can be used to protect your property.<br>• Track employee access to proprietary knowledge and prosecute employees who use it illegally. |
| 4. Be willing to disappoint some buyers and suppliers | • Do not rely on feedback about vital new initiatives from traditional buyers or suppliers who may not understand them.<br>• Be comfortable with criticism and willing to disappoint buyers and suppliers if necessary to avoid excessive commitments. |
| 5. Make sure that you have the capital you need | • Make sure that investors understand the volatility associated with the threat of obsolescence.<br>• Schedule asset retirements and asset rejuvenation in alignment with investor requirements and available capital. |

asset's potential to generate value under different scenarios. When assets depreciate at different rates, you face a challenge of lock-in that must be managed carefully. Think of the pharmaceutical industry, where the major firms offer several blockbuster drugs, each carrying a different patent expiration date. Even if the patent on a firm's leading blockbuster drug expires, the firm has a strong incentive to reinvest in its brand capital and selling infrastructure because of the other blockbusters in its system and the potential for more hit products out of its development pipeline. By the time the patents expire on the next round of drugs, more have developed from the pipeline.

In some situations, the lock-in created by the overlapping depreciation rates in core assets works to the firm's advantage by securing its competitive position. Think of industries in the early stages of Creative change, in which the system of core activities itself can generate a nondepreciating core asset such as the brand capital of the pharmaceutical firms. In other situations, however, the lock-in created by differences in depreciation rates on core assets works to a firm's disadvantage by creating incentives to throw good money after bad as profits deteriorate. Take the case of industries in the advanced stages of Radical change, like general merchandise department stores. The incentive is to keep stores open because of the robustness of a firm's brand name and distribution systems, but this may well lead to disaster.

In every industry undergoing Foundational change, it is impossible to make good decisions about strategic tradeoffs without knowing how each commitment to sustain a core asset locks the firm into position.

> *2. Figure out where you can protect your position and where it will erode quickly. Embed your most valuable assets, capabilities, and resources in an underlying system of support activities, and modularize your vulnerable assets to allow you to minimize the impact of obsolescence. Foundational change creates demands for decentralized decisions.*

Under Foundational change, differences in the intensities of the threats to various core assets create a significant managerial challenge. The best way to manage valuable assets is to embed them in a system of supporting activities designed to create value from the asset. Motion-picture producers do this when they introduce finished films into networks of relationships with theatrical exhibitors, and general merchandise exhibitors do this when they associate their brands with new soft-goods or hard-goods initiatives. While the assets do not generate value—either because they are in development or because they have outlasted their use—it is important to modularize the assets by cordoning them off from the rest of the system. Keep the obsolescence of a core asset from having a greater impact than necessary.

Foundational change requires centralized decisions about which core assets to develop, and then decentralized decisions about how to deploy resources within each modularized project. Decentralization provides the best chance of generating a good return on risky investments because, by definition, each core asset is idiosyncratic, and decentralization allows decision makers to tailor investments to the requirements of each project. The goal is to diversify risk by *varying* the way each project is managed.

Effective management under Foundational change requires that executives occasionally pull the plug on projects—especially big projects without the potential to generate substantial returns. Because these decisions are most effectively decentralized, the executive management team must have confidence in their project managers. Success depends on giving the right people the latitude and authority to take big risks with the potential to generate a big return. It also depends on learning across failed projects—and giving the reins to project managers without perfect track records precisely because they may have the seasoning to make better decisions in the future. It takes stamina and courage to put a project manager with a recent failure back in the saddle. Getting the balance right is critical: Project managers must have an incentive to avoid unnecessary risks, pursue big returns at reasonable risk, and learn from failed projects.

### 3. Guard intellectual property intensively.

Over the last few years, many companies have invested in knowledge-management systems that are designed to facilitate the internal transfer of intellectual property without leaking it to outsiders. Knowledge-management systems are likely to have maximal impact in industries going through Foundational change where core assets are under fire.

Research in economics and management strategy has shown that the least vulnerable core assets tend to be intangible and the most vulnerable tend to be physical. Intangible or "intellectual property" assets include brand capital, patents, and product concepts. Knowledge-management systems are particularly important in industries undergoing Foundational change because they allow firms to maximize the value of their sustainable assets.

Guarding intellectual property through knowledge-management systems and other practices is tantamount to preserving the value of the firm's intangible capital. Knowledge-management systems are effective when they don't prevent the commercialization of products and services built on the core assets. In other words, the key is in protecting the assets without preventing them from generating value. One basic principle for organizing a knowledge-management system is that it should be restrictive before products are commercialized, and more liberal about exposing core assets to exploitation across the organization after they have produced significant commercial value.

What other kinds of practices may be complementary to a knowledge-management system? Building a patenting capability for managing the patenting process to raise the number of approvals, identifying the right patent scope, and assessing the threat posed by potential imitators. Tracking employee access to proprietary knowledge and aggressively prosecuting employees that use the information illegally. Assuring that the intangible asset won't fall apart if a key employee or group of employees leaves the company. In sum, protecting intellectual property requires understanding the nature of the property in detail and building systems that are designed to protect against vulnerabilities.

*4. Don't rely on feedback from buyers or suppliers about new initiatives that they cannot appreciate until they are fully commercialized. Be comfortable with criticism and willing to disappoint buyers and suppliers if necessary to prevent entering into excessive commitments that will not be fruitful.*

Foundational change involves assessing how buyers and suppliers will react when the industry's activities are adjusted to reflect changes in the base of core assets. It's impossible for buyers and suppliers to forecast accurately how they will react because they have no experience under the adjustments, which by definition substantially affect the value created by the business.

Because Foundational change entails critical periods in which core assets are retired or introduced, firms often rely on experts to plan for the discontinuities. However, even experts cannot obtain reliable information from buyers and from suppliers about the prospective impact of the changes. For example, nobody seemed to forecast accurately the resounding success of Paramount's *Titanic*, or the dramatic failure of United Artists' *Heaven's Gate*. Even if you rely on experts, don't expect that you can learn much through buyer and supplier feedback in this situation. Find out all you can, and then rely on the judgment of experts with a track record of accurate intuition about how buyer behavior and supplier capabilities will evolve.

One of the most difficult facets of Foundational change involves the disappointment that arises when a firm pulls a popular product or severs a long-standing relationship with a supplier. Executives must be willing to accept the inevitable criticism that arises in these situations. Sustaining commitment from surviving buyers and suppliers requires clarity regarding the boundaries between core assets and the firm's plan for how sustainable core assets will be managed. Disney faces this challenge each time that it makes its classic films available in video for a limited time only. Overnight letter delivery companies will confront significant criticism when they begin to devolve their commitment to package delivery and redeploy planes into other uses. The key task is to prevent cynicism from developing about the firm's commitment to buyers and to suppliers.

*5. Make sure that investors understand the volatility associated with the new threat of obsolescence, and that you have access to the capital that you need to deal effectively with the challenges of asset retirement and rejuvenation.*

Research shows that the profits of firms in industries undergoing Foundational change are more volatile than in any other part of the economy. Core assets are "lumpy," which means that they tend to be associated with economies of scale and scope. You can't easily achieve a smooth earnings stream in an industry undergoing Foundational change because turnover in core assets creates discontinuities in product features and in supplier relationships. As products are introduced and retired, revenues become volatile. Variations in sources of supply create volatility in the cost structure of the business. Firms cannot survive over the long haul in industries undergoing Foundational change without assuring investors that profit volatility is an integral part of the business.

Yet reassuring investors about the earnings stream is insufficient. Investors—including equity shareholders, bondholders, and bankers—must support the firm with the capital necessary to pursue potentially valuable projects even if the organization has several failures under its belt. Investors must find a way to evaluate the quality and integrity of project proposals without penalizing the firm for pulling the plug on bad ideas, since fear of investor disappointment alone may drive a firm to overinvest in a marginal project or to avoid high-risk projects with the potential for high returns. You can reassure the investment community by creating measurements that reflect the efficiency of the firm in tracking the quality of investment projects.

Even when a firm finds a way to reassure investors about its project management skills, it is likely that it will eventually confront challenges in its capital budgeting processes. This is inevitable because each project carries entrepreneurial risk and relies on a champion who has a vision and is willing to make the leap of faith required to bring the project to closure. Investors are inherently skeptical about the stories they may hear about the upside potential of an investment in a core asset or the downside potential of keeping an outdated asset in place. Finding a way to get past this skepticism is a prerequisite to survival in an industry undergoing Foundational change.

## Prerequisites During Stages of Change

Part 1 of this book explained that the process of industry evolution occurs in stages. Regardless of whether the industry life-cycle model applies, there are similarities in the kinds of challenges that arise in the different stages of change. Early in the process of change, organizations almost always benefit by taking actions that create options that can be exercised later depending on how change plays out. Late in the process, high performance depends on participation in consolidating alliances and ramping down commitment to the business.

This section deals with the prerequisites for performance at the early, middle, and late stages of industry change *regardless* of which model of change applies in the specific context you are studying. The prerequisites for competing effectively through the evolutionary process are summarized in table 5-3.

*First stage: Create options that you can exercise later as uncertainties are resolved. Be sure to do this centrally.*

During the fragmentation and experimentation phases of industry evolution, firms almost always benefit by creating real options that can

**TABLE 5-3**

## Principles for Competing During the Different Stages of Change

| Principle | Implications |
|---|---|
| *First stage:* Create options that you can exercise later | • Vary experiments and debrief to obtain as much learning as possible, especially from failed experiments.<br>• Consider setting up a separate division if necessary to protect experiments from resistance that may originate within the established organization.<br>• Organize and manage experiments from a central part of the organization. |
| *Second stage:* Relentlessly benchmark against the competition | • Invest to understand how the standards for operational effectiveness are changing.<br>• Evaluate how buyers perceive the organization as distinctive from the competition.<br>• Rigorously invest to stay at parity with rivals in operational effectiveness, but not by compromising distinctiveness. |
| *Third stage:* Reconfigure processes to reflect lower revenue growth | • Modify incentive and decision-making systems to reflect lower revenue growth in the business.<br>• Reward profitability, even when it is accompanied by diminished revenue growth. |
| *Fourth stage:* Develop the ability to move productive activities and assets out of the business | • Avoid reinvesting—even in very small amounts—in the business if your strategic decision is to ramp down commitment.<br>• Develop the option to exit, but hold this option closely. |

be exercised later—after uncertainty is resolved about the pace and timing of industry change.

Consider the fragmentation phase of Progressive or Creative change. During this period, entrepreneurs strive to find the dominant model for organizing activities in the business. Firms achieve competitive advantage—that is, a return on invested capital that is above the industry average—when they find ways to test the market and experiment at lower costs or with higher hit rates. Survival is constantly threatened as experiments fail, and only a handful of firms ultimately survive into shakeout.

How can a firm use real options analysis to improve its chances for survival? By varying its experiments and by debriefing carefully on each experiment to get the benefit of as much learning as possible. A case study: Sam Walton's early innovations included experimenting with store location and then with distribution systems. Variation across his Ben Franklin stores had value because it allowed Walton to learn on a small scale about the tradeoffs associated with location choices, merchandising strategies, pricing algorithms, and purchasing relationships. Wal-Mart stores today capitalize on this experience.

The benefits of learning across experiments are even easier to see in industries on Creative evolutionary paths. Imagine the process of discovery as a firm experiments to produce movies or to acquire rights for oil drilling. Small-scale commitments provide a foundation for learning and open up options that can be pursued subsequently. You review a script that you believe has promise but that is too expensive for you to produce immediately. By buying the script, you create options that you can pursue later.

Next, consider the experimentation phase of an Architectural challenge. You'll recall that business may proceed as usual when Architectural change first takes hold. It may seem as though nothing major is happening. Chapter 2 described the current challenge that secure encryption technology presents to overnight letter delivery. Or consider the threat of video-on-demand technology to the storefront home video rental business. Both of these threats create a major Architectural threat that can be forecasted well in advance.

What should you do during the forecast period? Many organizations are fully committed to the challenge and engage in careful study to analyze trends. Large firms, particularly manufacturers and service organizations, often set up new divisions to experiment with the new approach. These efforts carry the potential to improve the firm's chances of succeeding in the new environment, and yet surprisingly often this potential is not actualized. Why? The experiments are either poorly designed—the new divisions do not have access to the strategically important resources of the corporation—or they are viewed as successes only if they ultimately generate commercially viable products that yield significant revenue. Much of the learning in the experiment is typically lost. To prevent this from happening, you can view the experiments as yielding real options for the future. Even if a new division fails to generate revenue, it may offer significant insights about the stumbling blocks that confront competitors and about better ways to experiment in the future. The key to value creation from this kind of effort is in capturing the learning.

*Second stage: Relentlessly benchmark against the competition, and learn how to balance distinctive positioning with sustained operational effectiveness.*

In the second phase of industry evolution—the shakeout or convergence stage—successful firms relentlessly benchmark against the competition to understand how the standards for operational effectiveness in the business are changing.[1] Regardless of whether change is Architectural, the competitive stakes intensify during the second phase of industry evolution. Survival depends on updating products quickly to retain proximity with rivals, who may be introducing unprecedented new features and services. Survival also depends on managing the cost structure of the business effectively even as new products are introduced. In almost all cases, cost management requires working with suppliers to create joint gains rather than only rationalizing activities within the business. Thus, organizations become embroiled in an iterative process of adjustment to meet buyer demands and to press suppliers for greater efficiencies.

To stay competitive, you must also develop a distinctive position that reflects your organization's unique approach to value creation. Distinctiveness depends on achieving especially low costs or differentiation on quality.[2] During this stage, the pressure to benchmark against the competition may be so intense that you can lose sight of this crucial facet of strategy. It is easy to lose sight of distinctiveness—or to take for granted that buyers and suppliers still see you as distinctive—when you are constantly introducing new products to meet the competition and when you are working to develop new relationships with suppliers.

Distinctiveness is important despite the difficulties of achieving it because it allows you to shape and define the standards of operational effectiveness as the industry evolves. Studies on operational effectiveness show that the standards for competing effectively in a business often originate in a leading firm's competitive advantage and then "leak" into the mainstream as the practices become customary. For instance, disposable diapers were once differentiated on the quality of their fluff pulp, but today high-quality fluff pulp is standard in disposable diapers. For another example, plug-and-play installation of hard-drive devices into computing hardware used to be a differentiating feature, but today it's considered a minimum standard for product viability. The standards for operational effectiveness eventually incorporate product features, technology, and other practices that once served as the foundation for a competitor's advantage.

By retaining distinctiveness and pursuing competitive advantage even during the stage of industry shakeout or industry convergence, the firm has an influence on how the standards for operational effectiveness evolve. Furthermore, the standards change in ways that play to your firm's capabilities. You are in a much better position to meet the minimum standards for competing effectively in disposable diapers if you were once differentiated on fluff pulp quality. The task becomes one of retaining cost proximity to remain operationally effective while building further sources of differentiation. And while this task certainly is a challenge, it is not the same kind of major challenge confronting a firm that must adopt fluff-pulp technology cost effectively.

Thus, survival over the long run depends on both retaining operational effectiveness and on developing a distinctive competitive position during the intensely competitive shakeout or convergence phase of industry change.

*Third stage: Deal with the implications of lower rates of revenue growth for the corporate culture and organizational systems.*

During the third stage of industry evolution, revenue growth drops. Firms that have motivated their employees to perform excellently through the promises of promotion and greater responsibility cannot deliver indefinitely. New incentives and systems are needed to motivate excellence as the priority in the business shifts from revenue growth to cost management.

Maturity and co-existence offer substantial opportunities to achieve high levels of return, but only for firms that do not dissipate resources unnecessarily. Firms that survive into this stage of industry evolution have often built momentum on rapid rates of growth in the prior stages of change. Incentive systems are oriented around revenue generation rather than cost management, and the culture of the business emphasizes expansion to pursue new revenue opportunities.

Surviving over the long run requires developing an approach to value creation that does not depend on sustaining historical rates of growth in the business. The stakes are high. If a firm at this stage continues to attack the competition relentlessly in an effort to win marginal business, then it is likely to be met with both competitive retribution and erosion in its own distinctiveness. In the brewing industry, Anheuser-Busch successfully avoided this kind of problem by carefully managing the way that its capacity was distributed geographically, and by deepening relationships with its distributors. Schlitz and Pabst, the industry's second- and third-ranked firms in the decades after the end of Prohibition, ultimately could not adapt as effectively to changes in the terms of competition.

Some firms, such as Microsoft, deal with the challenge by diversifying into other high-growth businesses in which their cultural emphasis on revenue generation retains its relevance. While diversification provides a useful solution for channeling resources outside the business, the issue of how to compete in the maturing industry stays on the table. Microsoft and other companies in maturing businesses cannot succeed over the long run without developing practices that account for new standards of operational effectiveness based in cost management instead of revenue generation. The same sort of challenge arises during co-existence, when opportunities for generating new revenue become limited by the success of the new approach.

The prerequisites for successful performance that develop during the third stage of industry change are subtle. The consequences of failure to meet these prerequisites may be deferred into the final stage of industry evolution, but when they do occur, they are dramatic. Your organization cannot simply deliver superior performance during the advanced stages of industry evolution with a culture and organizational systems that are designed to motivate and reward revenue growth. Firms that have succeeded in the third stage of industry evolution have adopted new incentives for managing costs, budgeted for lower rates of revenue growth, and promoted executives based on their abilities to motivate the workforce without relying principally on financial rewards for performance.

*Fourth stage: Develop the flexibility to move productive activities and assets out of the business.*

As the blast-furnace steel industry moved into the advanced stages of Foundational change in the 1990s, rumors circulated that several leading firms in the business planned to reinvest in the old technology. The sentiment was laudable: The executives in these corporations wanted to revitalize the core assets and reconstitute their competitive positions. Unfortunately, the rules of industry change offered them virtually no hope of succeeding.

In the most advanced stages of industry evolution, you cannot survive without the ability to move productive activities and assets out of the business. Now this may seem like a foregone conclusion, but many firms get caught in wars of attrition in which they recommit at a late stage in an effort to protect some of the core activities or core assets that are locked in place. The blast-furnace steel manufacturers were confronted with a very difficult choice between (i) investing a relatively small amount to keep blast furnaces running or (ii) investing a lot of money to shut down the furnaces. The problem here is that shutting down the furnaces was too costly. A company must find a way to keep the costs of exiting the business relatively low, even if it means taking the risk that the firm will be forced to exit in a war of attrition. (In wars of attrition, the surviving firm rarely recoups all the costs of fighting the war, which makes earlier exit relatively attractive.) When the costs of exiting cannot be managed, then success requires making decisions about reinvestment that account for the high costs of exiting in the future. In steel, this means understanding that a decision to invest a relatively small amount today to keep the furnaces only postpones the inevitable decision to incur high exit costs later.

Surviving through the final stage of industry evolution depends on holding the option to get out of the industry. Of course there is an irony here: if you hold the option to get out, you may be forced to exercise it. But if you can retain the flexibility for exit later, you may also be able to stay in the business. In other words, by developing the flexibility to move productive activities and assets in and out of the business, you can recommit to the business when it offers profit opportunities (i.e., when a competitor exits, for example), and you can scale back your commitment when competition is too intense.

In practice, flexibility of this type generally depends on diversification into related businesses in which old activities and assets retain their value, and in which the organization can easily direct and redirect talent. Managing a diversified organization under this kind of pressure carries its own challenges. Chapter 7 will describe proven mechanisms that corporations have used to deal with them.

## Summary and Implications

This chapter has dealt with the major prerequisites for competing effectively under Architectural and Foundational change and at the major stages of the evolutionary process. To survive, as well as to achieve an adequate return on investment, firms must meet these prerequisites, whether dealing with buyers and suppliers, forming alliances, or adjusting to the emergence of related industries. In short, the principles laid out in this chapter reflect the most basic consequences of industry evolution.

To achieve truly superior performance—that is, to take advantage of the trajectory of industry change—you must go further and make hard choices about how your organization will choose between attractive alternatives, and accept the consequences of each choice as a constraint on future options. The next chapter will deal precisely with this challenge. You may have already noticed that some of the fundamental prerequisites described in this chapter lead you in different directions. For example, under Radical transformation, you face pressures to centralize against the Architectural challenge and to decentralize against the Foundational challenge. Of course, the prerequisites described in this chapter define only a baseline for survival. In the end, survival depends on having both centralized and decentralized decision-making processes in place. But the tension between the two demands of Radical change just described reflects the kinds of strategic tradeoffs that accompany industry evolution. The ability to correctly set priorities is crucial to superior performance. Chapter 6 describes the tradeoffs that arise under each trajectory and at each stage of the evolutionary process.

# 6

# Creating a Business-Unit Strategy that Exploits the Opportunities in Industry Evolution

I F YOU FOLLOWED THE detailed process outlined in part 1, then you invested considerable effort to identify which trajectory you are on as well as the stage of change in your industry. Chapter 5 delivered part of the payoff by identifying how the rules of industry evolution constrain strategy by setting boundaries on what will work in a particular context. This chapter goes a step further by discussing how firms capitalize on the opportunities created by industry evolution. It is set at the business-unit level rather than at the corporate level and assumes that you are operating a business unit that participates in a single industry.

This chapter focuses on the various options you have regarding how you compete during each phase of industry evolution. The risks and benefits of each choice are extensively analyzed, and the payoff is a strategy that maximizes profitability and flexibility when an industry changes.

## Fundamental Strategic Choices

Every firm within an industry faces two related strategic choices, each of which is fundamental: (i) whether to lead or follow industry change; and (ii) whether to sustain its established competitive position or to attempt a repositioning.

Leading industry change is about driving the standards for operational effectiveness across the industry. It involves beating your rivals by setting the terms of competition in ways that work to your own

---

**box 6-1   Moving the Barriers on the Highway**

Chapter 1 offered the idea that the rules of industry change are like barriers on a highway. To continue the analogy: While moving the barriers is possible, the effort required is almost always too great to be worthwhile if your primary purpose is to make progress on the highway. Furthermore, it's dangerous to be standing in the road. Similarly, under industry change, the investment necessary to redirect a threat of obsolescence to an industry's core activities or core assets is extraordinary, and almost always too great to be worthwhile. Engaging in a program designed to have such a significant impact on the direction of the industry as a whole makes the firm vulnerable to competitors that can take advantage of the firm's commitment to gain an edge. It may even put the firm's survival at stake.

Sometimes—but rarely—there are exceptional circumstances that making it worthwhile to alter the course of industry change. Occasionally a firm has so much influence over industry structure that the costs of managing the threat of obsolescence (i.e., moving the barriers) are mitigated and, at the same time, the benefits of managing the threat are enhanced. Microsoft staved off threats to the PC desktop applications software market for many years by creating a powerful, complementary operating system platform. DeBeers has shaped the terms of change in the diamond-mining business, and until the early 1980s, AT&T had significant control over landline telephone service in the United States.

---

benefit. eBay is currently leading industry change in the online auctions business, where it has exemplified the dominant model in the industry through its transaction security, ease of use, user-generated evaluations, and prompt notifications of auction results. Of course, the risk of trying to lead industry change is that you'll fail by incurring excessive costs, raising buyer expectations, ceding profits to suppliers, and provoking the competition unnecessarily. There is a fine line between leading change and trying to alter the direction of industry change (see box 6-1).

Following industry change is a better choice for firms that can profit from the experience of firms that moved earlier. JetBlue, with short-haul routes, low prices, and a point-to-point system, is a relatively late entrant in the deregulated commercial airline industry that has benefited from the precedents set by defunct People's Express and New

In each of these cases, the firms held dominant market share in their industries, and yet dominance alone is insufficient to manipulate the evolutionary trajectory. Firms with this kind of power also must have so much technical, political, social, and cultural influence that they can influence how customers and suppliers respond to the dominant models in their businesses. They must also have the foresight to anticipate potential threats that could escalate to the point where obsolescence is imminent, and be prepared to use their influence to co-opt the threat to the industry structure despite the ancillary benefits created by this step for competitors.

Even firms with the ability and incentive to move the barriers on the highway eventually find that the effort is not profitable. This point comes earlier if the firm exercises its power to block progress frequently. Of course, attempts to monopolize the business are illegal in most regions of the world. (Competition policies and anti-trust legislation have had a major impact on DeBeers, Microsoft, and AT&T.) In a broad sense, the most profitable option for firms with this power is to shape—perhaps even direct—the industry structure to avoid loss of jobs, excess capacity, and consumer disappointment. The greatest opportunity may be in modulating the pace of change through the various stages of a trajectory to manage uncertainty and avoid wasteful obsolescence.

York Air (to name just two predecessors). The drawbacks: Following change exposes a firm to lower operational effectiveness, poor positioning opportunities, a reputation for imitation, finicky investors, and ultimately lower market share than a strategy of leading industry change.

The choice between sustaining competitive position and repositioning is just as complex. Sustaining competitive position, which involves committing new capital to augment the sources of a firm's uniqueness, is a natural choice when the firm has a healthy advantage based on a lower cost structure or on greater differentiation than other firms in the industry. Anheuser-Busch is sustaining its position in the brewing industry by reinvesting in distributed manufacturing capabilities, transportation economies, brand capital, and distributor relationships. The problems with this choice arise when a competitive advantage is thin or when the positioning bucks trends in industry evolution.

Repositioning provides a firm with the opportunity to abandon practices that have become constraining and to further distinguish itself

from the competition. Over the past twenty years, Sears has repositioned several times in the department store industry, focusing in turn
on soft goods, hard goods, and branded goods. The downside is that
repositioning is expensive, makes a firm vulnerable to competitive attack, and can confuse buyers. Because repositioning often takes decades
to complete successfully, it can be tantamount to exiting and then re-
entering the industry. Getting the timing right is also difficult. You may
discover later that you repositioned too early and committed yourself to
a course of action that you regret. Or you may have repositioned too
late and foreclosed options that would have been valuable.

There are relationships between the choices to lead or follow industry change and to sustain or reposition, but these two choices are
distinctive. A firm may elect to lead industry change while sustaining its
position or it may elect to lead industry change while repositioning. It is
likewise possible to follow industry change while sustaining position or
while repositioning. The right choice depends on both industry conditions and the firm's unique characteristics. While it's impossible to
cover all the possibilities, the remainder of this chapter describes the
major tradeoffs associated with these choices under each situation of industry evolution.

## Progressive Change

You'll recall that Progressive change is the most common of all four evolutionary types. Phases of the industry life cycle tend to be long, and adhering to the dominant model is essential to performance. Companies
that achieve better profitability than their rivals find ways to upgrade
their approaches through constant refinement of the links between activities, which is necessary because competitive advantages tend to bleed
into the dominant model over time. Under Progressive industry evolution, core assets are created through experience and learning effects that
accumulate from the repetition of activities.

When firms conform to the rules of Progressive evolution, they
achieve stable profits with relatively little risk to their survival.[1] In this
environment, successful companies usually operate under simple organizational structures with a straightforward decision hierarchy, a clear
allocation of responsibilities, and aggressive cost management.

How can an organization achieve superior performance in an industry undergoing Progressive change? By developing a strategy that

takes advantage of forthcoming change in the industry structure and that leads to a sustainable, distinctive competitive position. Table 6-1 summarizes the tradeoffs at each stage of Progressive evolution.

### The Fragmentation Stage of Progressive Change

Leading during the fragmentation stage requires experimenting more intensively than rivals to unlock the dominant model. The goal of aggressive leadership is to define the standards for doing business in a way that produces ongoing benefits for the firm. eBay succeeded famously by setting up a system in which sellers developed online reputations rather than by guaranteeing the auctioned items. Because the reputations are developed cumulatively through repeated auctions, new entrants to the industry have little chance of catching up.

Following instead of leading in the course of industry evolution requires taking a measured approach of limited experimentation and extensive benchmarking to learn from competitors' successes. There are

TABLE 6-1

## Strategic Tradeoffs Under Progressive Change

|  | Leading versus following the industry's development | Sustaining position versus repositioning |
| --- | --- | --- |
| **Fragmentation** | Following is relatively attractive, except for entrepreneurial firms with a clear, concrete vision for the dominant model. | Repositioning is less expensive and less exposed to failure than at later stages, although sustaining position is less costly and risky in an absolute sense. |
| **Shakeout** | Adhering to the dominant model is imperative for survival, and as a result leading tends to be more attractive than following. | Repositioning is difficult to execute effectively but may be less unattractive than at later stages because of the cover provided by shakeout. |
| **Maturity** | Leading is attractive to firms that are disadvantaged by the dominant model; following is attractive for most firms. | Repositioning is difficult to achieve successfully and is attractive only for severely disadvantaged firms. |
| **Decline** | Following is attractive for firms that continue to earn an acceptable return on invested capital; leading is attractive for firms that will benefit from rationalization. | Repositioning is very difficult to justify, except for firms that can move from breadth to focus (or vice versa) to exploit opportunities left by exiting rivals. |

some great examples from business history regarding successful "follower" strategies. Southwest Airlines ramped up operations in the 1980s, with People Express first in its headlights and then in its rearview mirror. Dell entered the PC industry after Apple, IBM, and Compaq were well established, and yet achieved a formidable competitive position by learning from the experiences of its rivals. The goal of a follower strategy is to minimize investments, wait until the dominant model is distinguishable, and then invest rapidly for operational effectiveness. The risks of "following" lie in failing to develop the skills and relationships necessary to implement the dominant model when it does emerge.

How do you resolve this tradeoff? Fundamentally, leading change in the industry structure is justifiable only when an entrepreneur is certain that he or she has tapped into a way of doing business that will become legitimized across the industry. A high level of certainty is necessary because the risk of failure is so great and the consequences so devastating. The upside of leading change is that the discovery of the dominant model can lock the firm into a virtually incontestable position for many years: Think of Starbucks in coffee retailing, for example.

What about the tradeoff between sustaining competitive position and repositioning? The burden of proof is always on the "repositioning" option since it involves substantial risks under the best of circumstances. Yet in the fragmentation phase of Progressive change, repositioning is less risky than in almost any other situation (other than fragmentation under Creative change). In the deregulated commercial airline industry, Continental tested several models for value creation before settling on its current low-cost model for serving business and leisure travelers through its East Coast hubs.

Operational effectiveness during the fragmentation phase involves experimenting with how activities form the core of a dominant model. Firms achieve advantage on this standard of operational effectiveness by conducting low-cost experiments or capturing more information than the competition from each experiment. At this early phase of industry development, repositioning involves changing the approach to experimentation by, for example: shutting down retail operations at particular locations and opening new stores; changing merchandise strategies; developing relationships with different suppliers; and changing the incentive and compensation systems. Repositioning during fragmentation requires discipline and leadership in an industry evolving on a Progressive model, and may seem daunting. Yet repositioning at *this* stage is less difficult than repositioning at later stages of Progressive evolution.

Sustaining a competitive position during the fragmentation stage is a better choice when the organization has found a way to learn between experiments so that it is converging on an efficient and effective model.

The best choice: Following the course of change is relatively attractive except for entrepreneurial firms with a chance to establish the dominant model. Repositioning is more expensive and riskier than sustaining position in an absolute sense, but it is more attractive than repositioning at a later stage. If repositioning is necessary, this stage is likely to be the best time to take on the challenge.

### The Shakeout Stage of Progressive Change

The tradeoffs under shakeout are quite different than under fragmentation. As soon as the dominant model emerges, operational effectiveness is essential for survival, and yet the process of constructing a robust activity system cannot succeed if it is attempted at breakneck speed. Success depends on building an activity system carefully so that it is supported by extensive internal communication and coordination. For example, eBay cultivated relationships with large corporations (to sell large volumes of returned and overstocked items) during several years of the early 2000s, and thus augmented its activity systems successfully. Core assets such as eBay's brand capital and seller ratings accumulate through experience and learning. In sum, a strategy of leading industry change—carefully and methodically—is relatively attractive in this situation.

What does it mean to follow industry change effectively during shakeout? A "following" strategy is attractive when there is a lot to gain by learning from leaders' mistakes and successes. It may also make sense to follow industry change when the industry has thrown an old business into Architectural change, and when the leaders in the established industry are striving to slow progress. For a time during the 1970s, department stores updated their offerings to slow down the progress of discount retailers. Similarly, the trunk airlines in the United States slowed down the post-deregulation progress of the point-to-point carriers by adjusting the mix of value that they offered to air passengers. By following industry change rather than leading it, a firm can retain the flexibility to maximize learning before making commitments.

The choice between sustaining competitive positioning and repositioning depends on idiosyncratic elements of the firm's activities, the firm's assets, and the industry structure. Firms often have difficulty in focusing their attention on distinctive competitive positioning *at all* at this stage given the escalating demands of operational effectiveness. Retaining the discipline to make this choice deliberately is important—future circumstances may force a firm into repositioning by default. As noted in chapter 5, a firm is vulnerable in the long run if it cannot sustain distinctiveness ahead of the dominant model.

The advantage of repositioning during shakeout is that it continues to be less costly and less risky than at later stages of evolution. Because the dominant model is a moving target, there is greater opportunity to achieve low costs or differentiation than at later stages. The escalation of standards under the dominant model can provide enough of a challenge to competitors that they refrain from attacking the firm as it makes the move.

Think of what a repositioning would have meant during the shakeout period in discount retailing. At the same time as a firm was aggressively adding stores, building out distribution systems, and carefully building systems to link them, it also would have had to change its culture, develop relationships with different suppliers, and alter its presentation to customers. You can see how the challenge would have been formidable, but the growth afforded by establishing the dominant model would have provided cover for the repositioning. Even during shakeout, however, repositioning may require significant resources and time, especially if the change requires a major change in the firm's culture.

The best choice: Adhering to the dominant model is fundamental to survival at this stage, which makes the choice to lead much more attractive than the choice to follow. Repositioning is difficult to execute effectively, but is less unattractive than at later stages.

### The Maturity Stage of Progressive Change

During industry maturity, the tradeoff between leading and following industry change takes a different form because the dominant model is established.

Leading change in this context involves raising the standards for operational effectiveness incrementally. Normally this involves training buyers and suppliers to make demands of competitors that may initially be difficult for them to fulfill, but that subsequently become standard practice. Examples of this sort of behavior include offering financing to suppliers and teaching buyers how to compare products on their technical features. IBM did this admirably in the PC business during the 1980s by supporting clones to encourage adoption of the Wintel platform over the Apple standard. Leading change is more attractive when changing the dominant model alters the terms of competition favorably.

Following the course of industry change involves meeting the standards of the dominant model but not escalating them actively. Firms normally pursue this option when they have little incentive to change the terms of competition (i.e., when they already profit from an attractive industry structure and competitive advantage). For example, major brewers do not have an incentive to disrupt their industry's dominant model given the average level of profits in this business. Apple Computer faced conflicting incentives to pursue change in the PC business during the 1990s because its returns were above the norm for the industry.

Thus, firms that are satisfied with their established levels of performance will be inclined to follow the course of change, while firms that seek to enhance their positions or to displace rivals may choose to lead the course of change.

Repositioning during maturity is quite risky under Progressive change because complex systems of activities are difficult to adjust holistically. As a rule, repositioning at this stage carries higher costs than in almost any other situation. Kmart attempted a repositioning during the maturity of the discount retailing business—investing to improve the look of its storefronts and carrying new upscale merchandise—but subsequently declared bankruptcy because the costs were so high. Repositioning (rather than sustaining competitive advantage) usually makes sense only when the firm suffers a significant disadvantage. Sustaining at this stage is often a dominant alternative. For example, the Montessori schools have sustained differentiation in the private school business by continuing to invest in signature programs and brand capital.

The best choice: For firms that are satisfied with their performance, following industry change and sustaining position are attractive. For firms that are dissatisfied with their performance, leading and repositioning are attractive.

## The Declining Stage of Progressive Change

What does it mean to lead change under industry decline? Operational effectiveness at this stage involves changing the dominant model to strip out costs, simplify product offerings, demand more of suppliers, and update the bases of segmentation. This is a formidable challenge when an industry evolves Progressively because it requires abandoning deeply rooted activities. An incentive to lead usually arises only for market-share leaders, as in electronics component manufacturing, where the largest firms in the business are setting new standards for efficiency despite the drop in volume.

A "following" strategy is more attractive for firms that face the prospect of declining profits as industry change progresses. Even if they are losing money, organizations can have an incentive to follow rather than lead industry change if it's expensive to get out of the business and if the industry's further decline means that losses will be even greater. This is an agonizing situation to be in. You stay in the business even though you are losing money and try to slow its decline because exiting costs even more. More commonly, firms "follow" in decline because they are profitable and because they forecast that further decline will damage their performance.

In this phase of the industry's development, leading and following the course of industry change each have their advantages. Leading the decline may be attractive for large firms that are operating efficiently and that see opportunities for consolidation among rivals, while following in the decline may be a better choice for small firms with satisfactory profitability under the established industry structure.

It is difficult to imagine circumstances under which a firm could justify repositioning from low costs to differentiation (or vice versa) in the declining phase of Progressive evolution because the activity systems at the heart of a firm's approach are entrenched. As you know, any change in an industry undergoing Progressive change is costly, and change is particularly costly when the industry offers little opportunity for profitable growth.

The only type of repositioning that may be tenable during this period is an adjustment from focus on a niche to a broader approach. Consider the strategy of Southwest Airlines, which moved from a regional focus into a national position relatively late in the industry's development.

The best choice: Ultimately, the tradeoff between sustaining a competitive position and repositioning depends on the situation facing a particular firm, but in most instances, sustaining the existing strategy carries powerful advantages during the declining stage of Progressive change.

## Creative Change

Creative change involves turnover in core assets and volatility in both revenues and profitability. Unlike Radical and Intermediating environments, change is not Architectural and relationships are not jeopardized directly. The phases of the industry life cycle under Creative change vary in length; a long period of fragmentation is usually followed by a relatively rapid shakeout and then a long period of maturity, which is often followed in turn by rapid decline. Under Creative change, threats to survival are greatest during the dramatic shakeout and decline. Superior performance for companies in Creative industries depends on generating new assets while maintaining a system of complementary activities for commercializing new products and services.

In a Creative evolutionary environment, superior performance begins with building a system of complementary activities and a portfolio of asset-development projects. Competitive advantage (i.e., achieving better performance than the average) depends on either lowering the costs of project management and product delivery or differentiating by enhancing the value of commercialized assets. *Sustaining* the advantage requires balancing commitment to a strategy with adaptation to new opportunities. You can achieve this with stable supporting activities and with risk-taking in project-management efforts.

The following discussion highlights some of the major challenges that arise under each stage of Creative change. Table 6-2 summarizes the tradeoffs associated with each stage of Creative evolution.

### *The Fragmentation Stage of Creative Change*

You'll recall that the fragmentation stage involves three sub-stages of experimentation that lead to the development of:

1. A breakthrough product based on a new kind of asset

2. Capability for repeatedly creating new core assets

3. A system of supporting core activities

TABLE 6-2

## Strategic Tradeoffs Under Creative Change

|  | Leading versus following the industry's development | Sustaining position versus repositioning |
|---|---|---|
| **Fragmentation** | Leading can lead to discovery of the dominant model, which yields unparalleled returns; following is less risky and allows for more flexibility. | Repositioning is less costly at this stage than later stages; sustaining is more attractive for firms with even minor advantages. |
| **Shakeout** | Leading is best for the few firms that can execute effectively in both creative development and commercialization; for most firms, following is necessary to stay on the dominant model. | Sustaining advantage is best for firms that can learn from their own experience and achieve profits in the process; repositioning is attractive for firms that struggle to learn from rivals. |
| **Maturity** | Large firms have an incentive to lead through incremental improvements to the dominant model; small firms without supporting activities have the greatest incentive to follow. | Repositioning is difficult to justify except for firms with very poor performance. |
| **Decline** | Leading through alliances, subcontracting and spin-offs is attractive when a firm is too large to earn an adequate return on investment; following is attractive for firms that earn satisfactory returns. | Sustaining position is attractive when it is not too costly; repositioning is difficult to justify if it involves fixed commitments to the industry. |

Leading the industry at this stage of Creative change involves discovering an effective way to accomplish these three tasks. Because of their variety and complexity, leadership can take a number of forms. Sometimes a firm distinguishes itself with a major hit product. In other cases, a firm excels by developing project-management capability. In still other cases, a firm develops an unusually efficient system of supporting activities. Each of these ways of leading carries the potential to enhance the firm's reputation and to raise the competitive standards in the industry.

A firm can set the norms for operational effectiveness during the fragmentation phase of Creative evolution by excelling in any of these dimensions, but sustained leadership during the fragmentation phase occurs only when a firm achieves a breakthrough on balancing the three competing demands for successful experimentation all at the same time.

In other words, a *strategy* of leadership involves finding a way to excel in all three dimensions of experimentation simultaneously.

Fulfilling this ambition requires a multifaceted culture that encourages risk taking and entrepreneurial venturing in project management and that simultaneously nurtures a system of supporting activities. For example, Microsoft developed a number of hit applications products during the 1980s while simultaneously cultivating project management capabilities and a series of supporting distribution and marketing activities.

Competitive success at this stage requires both the rigor to cancel failing projects and the flexibility to give managers enough free rein to hit a home run. The upside of a choice to lead industry change is that the firm may find a way to shape the terms of competition in ways that play to its strengths.

Adopting a "follower" strategy is usually less expensive than leading industry change. By following, a company can learn from the precedents set by its rivals and thereby lower the costs of achieving a balanced approach to the business. During the fragmentation stage of the PC application industry's evolution, Lotus Development (in spreadsheets) and Corel (in word processing) each created hit products, but neither was the first firm to offer a product in its category. Both firms were careful not to overinvest in risky follow-on PC applications that were outside their spheres of competence. Of course, the difficulty in following the course of industry change is that the creative capability that becomes built into the dominant model—either the ability to generate a hit product or the ability to manage a portfolio of projects—may be quite difficult to duplicate. Thus, a "following" strategy carries the risk of being left behind on achieving operational efficiency in crucial project-management skills. The best choice—either leading or following the course of industry change—depends on your firm's ambitions, tolerance for risk, and ability to finance large-scale projects.

The second strategic choice that a firm must make to achieve superior performance at this stage is the familiar question of whether to sustain position or to reposition. Competitive advantage involves either experimenting more cost effectively than rivals or structuring experiments so that they deliver more information. Again, given the variety of activities that occur in this stage of Creative change, a firm faces several different kinds of opportunity. It is possible to excel by nurturing creative talent or by commercializing products successfully, for instance.

The decision to reposition—which involves major risks—generally involves dismantling activities and restructuring to emphasize either cost leadership or differentiation in at least one major experimental activity. Trying to hit a home run on a single project may put the firm's survival at stake; building a portfolio involves achieving scale before the dominant model in the business is established; constructing a set of supporting activities may leave the firm with more capacity than is required to operate effectively. Despite all these risks, a repositioning is more likely to succeed at this early stage than in the advanced stages of Creative evolution.

Sustaining position at this stage is attractive for any firm that has excelled on any of the three critical dimensions. If a firm has discovered a way to conduct experiments more cost effectively or to get more information from them—even if the experiments are not successful—then it has achieved competitive advantage. Sustaining position may give the firm a better chance at attracting venture investment and at establishing the dominant model in the business.

The best choice: Leading exposes the firm to the benefits of discovering and establishing the dominant model, but "following" may be less risky and can provide the firm with greater long-term flexibility. Repositioning is less costly than at later stages, but even a sliver of an advantage usually can be sustained and compounded to deliver significant profitability.

### The Shakeout Stage of Creative Change

During the shakeout phase, firms go out of business if they cannot meet the industry's standards for operational effectiveness in all three categories: hit-product development, portfolio management, and supporting activities. The dominant model becomes established, the volume of sales ramps up, and firms cannot survive if they continue to operate in ways that are simply inefficient or lack legitimacy given the industry's new standards.

Leading change at this stage of evolution means acting as a pioneer in establishing new standards. The firm must build scale at the same time as it teaches buyers how to compare products and encourages suppliers to build physical and intangible infrastructure. The choice to lead is sensible for firms that benefit more than their rivals from the surge of volume that occurs during shakeout. The companies that are most likely to be in this position are market share leaders that have also been at the forefront of industry development during the fragmentation stage. Consider what happened in the development of hand-held electronic organizers such as the Newton and the Palm Pilot. The first wave of products that were introduced around 1990 did not take off because of a lack of standardization. Buyers waited to purchase until they were confident that products would have staying power, and software developers held back until they were sure that they were writing for the winning standard. The industry's volumes rose dramatically after standards were established. The firms that benefited from this surge in volume were those that led the process of standardization.

The real risk to a strategy of leading industry change during shakeout is that you may not create essential capabilities in one of the three fundamental areas of the business. For example, a movie studio that is particularly effective at managing relationships with exhibitors may develop a culture that tends to favor feedback from the exhibitors over the instincts of key creative talent dedicated to particular projects. The resulting "customer-oriented" culture may blunt the emergence of project-management capabilities. Or a studio with unusually strong special-effects capabilities may become so focused on supporting a portfolio of ambitious adventure movies that it neglects its marketing activities. In shakeout—more than at any other stage of industry change—balanced excellence across all three dimensions of the dominant model is necessary for survival.

A strategy of following the course of industry change tends to be more attractive for firms that can commit quickly in the wake of successful leaders and subsequently adopt the dominant model at lower cost. This strategy is risky for firms that are in danger of being left behind—that is, of never achieving the scale or complexity necessary to compete effectively. It tends to be most attractive for large firms that are diversifying into the industry after succeeding in other, related businesses. By adopting a "fast follower" stance, the firm spares the expenses associated with multiple revisions in approach.

Sustaining a competitive position during shakeout is most attractive when the firm is truly distinctive in its strategy through lower costs or greater differentiation, or specialized focus on an unusually attractive segment. In an industry on a Creative path, this may mean that the firm has figured out a way—perhaps through learning across modularized products—to generate bigger hits or more high-yield projects than its rivals. These advantages tend to leak gradually into the dominant model and become standard practice in the industry. Sustaining advantage requires capitalizing on the firm's experience to further lower costs or enhance quality. Schlumberger, the legendary oil-services company, became famous for systematically reaping the benefits of learning across projects to upgrade and enhance its approach to project management.

Repositioning tends to be attractive to firms that find themselves constantly trying to catch up to their rivals. If you find that you are surprised by your competitors' breakthroughs and that you must cancel projects and scramble to stay competitive, repositioning may be a better choice than sustaining your competitive position. The downside of repositioning during shakeout is that it compounds the risks of throwing the dice on each new project launch, and may put a firm's survival in jeopardy.

The best choice: Leading is attractive for the few firms that may have learned how to balance creativity with disciplined execution; for most firms, however, following on at least some dimensions is necessary to assure conformity to the dominant model. Sustaining advantage is attractive when firms can create proprietary capabilities from their own experience, and repositioning is attractive for firms that struggle to learn either from their own experience or from their rivals.

### The Maturity Stage of Creative Change

During maturity, the option of leading change in the industry structure is open only to those firms that have achieved operational effectiveness through the shakeout period. By this phase, the industry's dominant model is locked into place. Profitable competitors have protected themselves from the fits and starts of project commercialization with a system of supporting activities. Think of today's breakfast-cereal and baseball industries, where a complex infrastructure of activities allows firms to bring new products and new talent to market quickly. Competition tends to revolve around exciting products and services generated by both leaders and by smaller independent firms that strive for breakthroughs.

Continuing to lead the industry involves a commitment to raise standards for generating value. The greatest potential for incremental change—that is, the kind of predictable, systematic change that can be planned—is in the system of supporting activities. Kellogg in breakfast cereal and the Yankees in baseball are pioneers in achieving incremental efficiencies as well as in project management, and thereby raise the standards for competing effectively in their industries.

A strategy of following the course of change may be the only choice available to smaller firms with one or perhaps a few hit products, but without systems in place for commercializing new products repeatedly. Firms in this situation must seek partners each time that they want to bring something new to the market. Consider what happened at Snapple, which was acquired by Quaker Oats in 1994 (and divested in 1997). Snapple had hit products during the 1980s and 1990s (in particular, a popular iced tea drink), but analysts viewed its profitability as limited by the absence of supporting distribution systems, which Quaker intended to provide.[2]

The gray area exists for firms that are at the cusp of market share leadership. In pharmaceuticals, the choice between leading and following in the industry's development arose for companies such as Genentech in the 1980s and Millennium Pharmaceuticals in the 2000s—each with more than one patented drug and a high-potential pipeline. Organizations in this position have to decide whether to build the infrastructure required to operate on the dominant model or whether to contract for supporting activities when necessary. The tradeoff arises because of the expense and commitment of infrastructure development. Continuing as a follower is attractive when contracting is inexpensive and the pipeline isn't too full.

What are the benefits, risks, and costs of sustaining competitive positioning versus repositioning during industry maturity? The choice to sustain position is most attractive for firms that have beat the standards of the dominant model and lead the industry—or a segment of the industry—in costs or quality or both. Repositioning makes the most sense when the firm is struggling to retain operational effectiveness. Several residential contractors in the Boston area that had specialized in building premium high-end homes repositioned during an economic downturn to building low-cost housing. The repositioning was difficult because of the skills required to bid successfully for state contracts and of the systems required to execute the contracts without sacrificing quality. In most mature industries undergoing Creative change, repositioning makes the firm vulnerable to poor performance.

The best choice: Large firms usually have an incentive to lead the course of industry change, while small firms without a system of supporting activities have an incentive to follow. Sustaining advantage dominates repositioning except for those firms with very poor performance.

### The Declining Stage of Creative Change

During the decline stage, leading change typically involves finding ways to ratchet back new-project development without compromising creativity. One of the most fertile areas for profit enhancement is in alliances across competitors to share systems of supporting activities. Firms may subcontract services to one another or spin off their supporting activities into separate companies that can serve multiple firms within the industry. In short, leading change requires enhancing the odds of generating a hit from each project while scaling back support activities.

General Motors has pursued leadership during the decline stage of Creative evolution by restructuring its activities to become more efficient. John Smith, CEO during the 1990s, was celebrated for his efforts to implement "badge engineering," which dropped the number of separate car platforms from twelve to five. Badge engineering lowered the costs of development by reducing the number of design projects. Furthermore, under Smith, the design costs per platform declined to an estimated $1.5 billion from $2.5 billion as the company became more efficient at project management. At the same time, General Motors cut back its manufacturing infrastructure by closing 20 assembly and 53 component plants, which provoked a major backlash by the United Auto Workers Union, which struck during the summer of 1998. During the 1990s, the number of separate dealer franchises had also declined significantly. Leading industry change in this way was expensive for General Motors in the short term but bolstered GM's stature as the industry's leader by making the economic structure of the business viable.

Following industry change involves preserving the industry structure as long as possible. This alternative is attractive when the organization operates in a segment of the business where new products continue to be valued highly. For example, Volkswagen invested in new products and infrastructure during the 1990s, reinvigorating its commitment despite the industry consolidation. A strategy of following industry change is more appealing than a strategy of leading it for organizations that are achieving their profitability goals.

The choice between sustaining position and repositioning during the decline stage of Creative evolution is complex because it involves abrupt shifts in underlying infrastructure and in the norms for contracting. Sustaining position tends to be more attractive for firms with better performance than the industry average, and is usually associated with the selection of a "follower" posture on industry change. Volkswagen is reinvesting to sustain its advantage, but the tradeoff is that the reinvestments also lock the firm into a declining industry.

Repositioning is risky and may throw the firm's survival in the business into jeopardy. At the decline stage, repositioning is rarely worth the risk, although there are a few noteworthy examples of successes in late-stage repositioning. For example, in baseball, the Oakland Athletics repositioned to a low-cost position by assessing the value of players to the team and by making tactical choices based on disciplined statistical analysis.[3] The move was less risky than in most cases of industry decline because baseball teams are protected by an antitrust exemption.

The best choice: Leading is attractive when the firm's commitment can be scaled back through alliances, subcontracting, and spin-offs. Following and sustaining position are attractive for firms that are especially profitable. Repositioning is difficult to justify when it involves reinvestment in fixed infrastructure.

## Intermediating Change

Managing through Intermediation is among the most challenging tasks in business because core assets retain their value while core activities are threatened (see box 6-2). Because Intermediation occurs *relatively* quickly (i.e., often over a period of about a decade rather than several decades), companies have difficulty in dealing with the implications. The sheer complexity of Intermediating change creates disagreement, political struggles, and conflicting information within an established organization. The incentives to diversify into the new industry that creates the Architectural threat may be great and are discussed in chapter 7. Here, the discussion focuses on the challenge of managing the firm's position within the established industry as it goes through Intermediating transformation.

In the early years of the twenty-first century, Intermediation is often associated with digital technologies that improve information flows and make new kinds of transactions possible. How can you identify

---

**box 6-2    Managing a Profitability Challenge is Usually Harder Than Managing a Survival Challenge**

Although it may seem counterintuitive, a threat to profitability can be harder to manage than a threat to survival. The reason is that when survival is at stake, the motivation to change is profound. For investors, a worst-case scenario involves a failure to innovate effectively and the abandonment of assets through bankruptcy. As a result, there is a sense of urgency to innovate. By contrast, when profitability is at stake, an organization may make only incremental changes for years in an effort to recover competitive position. Regardless of whether the effort succeeds, the organization may ultimately lose even more money than if it had exited quickly through bankruptcy or merger. By aligning strategy with the trajectory of industry change, a company can avoid becoming trapped in a vicious circle in which it escalates its commitment to an untenable approach.

---

Intermediation early enough to maximize your options for dealing with it? How have firms avoided underestimating the structural challenges associated with improved information flows? Are there ways of migrating assets out of the business rationally to preserve profitability as long as possible?

Superior performance under Intermediation depends on striking the right balance between moving core assets out of the old business (where they are under threat) and into new uses where they carry the potential to create more value. The balance is difficult to achieve because short-term profitability is often greater in the established industry. The rest of this section discusses some approaches that have proven effective in situations of Intermediating change. Table 6-3 summarizes the tradeoffs at each stage of Intermediation.

### The Emergence Stage of Intermediating Change

Leading during the emergence stage of Intermediating change involves moving early to deal with the implications for the established industry. You'll recall that during the emergence stage the economic impact of the new approach is minor. Leading requires recognizing the significance of the impending change and experimenting with different

TABLE 6-3

## Strategic Tradeoffs Under Intermediating Change

| | Leading versus following the industry's development | Sustaining position versus repositioning |
|---|---|---|
| **Emergence** | Leading is attractive when the potential for learning is high enough to swamp the costs of alienating some buyers and suppliers; following is best for firms with unusually loyal buyers and suppliers. | Sustaining position is best for firms that can easily move core assets out of the business; repositioning is more attractive for firms that will lose buyers and suppliers early. |
| **Convergence** | Leading is appealing when the industry can continue to create value through incremental improvements; following is attractive when the new industry is in trouble and the established industry is still profitable. | Sustaining is attractive when it does not require much investment; repositioning is best when it also allows core assets to be redeployed outside the industry. |
| **Co-Existence** | Following is usually a better choice than leading change; leading is sometimes attractive to diversified firms with positions in the new industry. | Sustaining position is attractive only when the investments can be recouped quickly—that is, only when the firm's advantage is unusually distinctive; repositioning is usually more attractive. |
| **Dominance** | Leading is attractive only under very usual circumstances, such as the expectation of a major exit wave. | Repositioning is usually imperative for preserving the value of core assets through redeployment outside the industry; sustaining position is justifiable only for firms that can avoid capital outlays. |

kinds of transactions to identify where their assets carry the potential to create value over the long run.

The principal risks of leading the experimentation are in alienating buyers and suppliers and in accelerating the threat itself. Alienation can occur because buyers and suppliers have bought into the logic that the established industry has put forward, namely that the best way to get value is by continuing with business as usual. For example, individual investors were at first alienated by online trading because they had been trained by brokerages to invest only after thoughtful analysis and consultation. As soon as the traditional brokerages within the established industry lent legitimacy to the new approach by experimenting with it, investors' resistance began to break down, and the process of

Intermediation accelerated. Acceleration can also occur even when there isn't resistance among traditional buyers or suppliers. The deregulation of the electricity distribution business was accelerated because of the initial successes of established firms that experimented with new kinds of contracts.

Leading industry change is appropriate when an organization can enhance its performance by acting as a pioneer as the process unfolds, i.e., by influencing the terms of competition in the new business. State and federal legislators and regulators are currently considering modifying the standards and restrictions on financial advisers. By experimenting early, an established firm may be able to guide this process, enhance the firm's reputation, and provide the firm with better access to important partners.

A choice to follow rather than lead industry change is more attractive for firms with profitable positions in the established business. Under this choice, experimenting to generate new options must be minimized if it disrupts profitable relationships. Some established brokerage firms are testing the waters in a limited way by offering advisory services independently of traditional integrated contracts, but the goal is to reach new customers rather than to convert existing customers to adviser-only relationships. Overall, following is more attractive than leading when there is little to learn through aggressive experimentation (perhaps because the form of the new approach is clear) and when there is a lot to lose by driving forward the Intermediation.

Sustaining the firm's competitive position is especially attractive when it involves reinvesting in assets that will retain their value as the Intermediation progresses. For the traditional brokerage firms, this involves advertising, maintaining a team of research analysts, and investing in information technology to enhance communication and store proprietary information. Reinvesting aggressively to sustain a distinctive position carries the significant disadvantage of committing the company to the old industry structure, but this disadvantage is softened when the assets that are developed through the reinvestment will retain their value after transactions are reorganized. For example, some brokerages may have brand capital that can be deployed in other businesses, and some may have proprietary information about customer needs that can be used in other businesses such as banking.

At this early stage of Intermediation, sustaining position is usually more attractive than repositioning given that the core assets carry the potential to create value over the long run. In other words, the burden of proof is on repositioning (just as it is under non-Architectural change) and yet the standards for proof are somewhat lower than under non-Architectural change because of the consequences of over-committing to the established industry structure.

Repositioning during the emergence stage of Intermediation is most attractive when the firm occupies a position that will be an early casualty of the Intermediation, when there is little chance of learning in partnership with existing buyers and suppliers, and when the company's core assets are likely to be most valuable if redeployed early. These conditions are met when the firm's buyers and suppliers have made compromises and are dealing with the firm because they are trapped by old promises and investments. For encyclopedia publishers that had enjoined buyers to sign contracts for large numbers of volumes, a repositioning strategy was attractive at the onset of Intermediation because there was little chance of losing the locked-in buyers. Repositioning in the *established* business can provide the organization with the chance to test its assumptions about how to create value.

The best choice: Leading is attractive for firms that can afford to alienate some buyers and suppliers. Following is attractive when a firm's buyers and suppliers are likely to be unusually loyal. Sustaining advantage is attractive when the reinvestment keeps the value of core assets high but does not prevent them from being migrated outside the business. Repositioning is the better alternative for firms that will lose buyers and suppliers early.

### The Convergence Stage of Intermediating Change

During the convergence stage of Intermediation, the advantages of the new approach become clearer. Buyers begin to experiment with new ways of transacting, although they often continue to buy from established firms to hedge their bets. Suppliers may recommit to the established industry in a bid for survival at the same time as they begin to explore outside alternatives.

Leading the course of change in this environment requires finding ways to organize the business so that it becomes more efficient and can compete with the new approach. AutoNation was quite effective in implementing this strategy when the auto dealership industry went through the convergence stage. AutoNation consolidated more than

400 independent new-car franchises to offer buyers access to more inventory, better financing, and equitable pricing, while also consolidating bargaining strength to put greater pressure on suppliers. The strategy built on old assets such as the physical storefronts and local brand awareness of established dealers to create a formidable impediment to intermediaries that sought to cherry-pick the most profitable activities of the dealers and organize them independently. (AutoNation also entered into the emerging industry and became a formidable competitor on the new approach, as described in chapter 3.) Leading change during the convergence phase involves creating new standards that influence the way the whole industry deals with the challenge of Intermediation. The goal is to raise the bar for effective competition and thereby rationalize capacity in the established industry while simultaneously defending it against encroachment by the new approach.

Following in the course of industry change is a better choice for firms that are already profitable on the established model and that see little opportunity for acceptable performance as the Intermediation progresses. In music recording and publishing, there are few clear ways that the industry's leaders can benefit from the free distribution of songs through electronic media. For these firms, "following" in the course of change is a dominant strategy. The Recording Industry Association of American (RIAA), the industry's trade association, has become a central institution for filing copyright-infringement lawsuits on behalf of the publishers and studios. This development demonstrates how powerful the threat of obsolescence has been in unifying the publishers and studios in defense of their industry structure. Prior to the threat, the same firms that are cooperating to protect their mutual interests had competed tooth and nail for talent and consumer attention.

A choice to follow in the course of industry change also may be attractive to firms when the transformation is slow, the established industry is profitable, and the new approach is confusing and occasionally disappointing. If there is enough diversity in the customer and supplier bases, then the threat of substitution from the new industry may be much stronger in some segments of the industry than in others. If the firm occupies a position in which threat of substitution is less significant, then the firm may have an augmented incentive to try to delay the change.

Sustaining competitive position during the convergence phase of Intermediation involves retaining distinctiveness as well as operational effectiveness by operating at low costs or with greater differentiation than the standard for the business. This may be expensive as Intermediation progresses through this stage. Consider RCA Records, which historically adopted a strategy of signing artists when they were not well known and then working with the artists over many years—often a decade or more—to develop their talents. Should RCA Records sustain its competitive position in the convergence phase of Intermediation? Given the conditions of change in the business, writing long-term contracts with artists is much less attractive than it used to be. Repositioning the firm to sign popular artists increases the company's up-front costs of contracting but it also frees up artist-development capabilities. For RCA Records, the alternative of repositioning is more attractive if the company sees a way to redeploy its artist-development skills in other businesses where they promise to retain their economic relevance over a longer horizon.

Ultimately, the tradeoff between sustaining position and repositioning depends on the firm's opportunities for redeploying core assets in other businesses. The risks of repositioning may be mitigated if the organization can also take valuable core assets out of the business and commit them to other industries. Sustaining competitive position is most attractive when the organization envisions that reinvestment will deliver superior performance over the short run either by delaying the Intermediation or by appealing to a cadre of loyal buyers and suppliers.

The best choice: Leading is appealing when change keeps the established industry competitive with the new industry. Following is more attractive when the new industry is floundering. Sustaining position is attractive when it does not require much investment, but repositioning is attractive when core assets can be committed to new uses inexpensively.

### The Co-Existence Stage of Intermediating Change

The co-existence stage of Intermediation is a period in which the old and new approaches each create value in an uneasy balance. The long-term viability of the new approach to the business is no longer debatable, although there may be strong disagreement about whether it will ultimately take over and dominate the established industry. An illusion may arise at this stage that the two businesses are actually part of the same industry and that they can co-exist indefinitely.

A choice to lead industry change at this phase of the industry's development involves pressing forward to set new standards for delivering value while unwinding old commitments to the business. During co-existence, it is difficult for market share leaders to justify this choice because of the advanced threat of obsolescence to core activities. The exceptions arise for firms like AutoNation that have achieved leadership in both the emerging and established industries and that stand to gain the most by the escalation of requirements for operational effectiveness in the traditional business.

A choice to follow the course of industry change tends to be more attractive for the industry's market share leaders. The period of co-existence may be the last in which the old model generates profits for established firms. By lengthening the co-existence phase, the industry's survivors may be able to earn an acceptable return on invested capital for years. Personal financial advisers in the United States have enjoyed a renaissance over the past few years because changes in tax law and investment losses have compelled many individuals to consult professional advisers instead of preparing their returns by themselves. In such situations, following in the course of industry change yields better performance than escalating the standards for operational effectiveness across the industry as a whole.

Sustaining competitive position during the co-existence phase of Intermediation means reinvesting in the sources of the firm's distinctiveness. This choice is attractive when reinvestment does not lock the firm into the business for a period that is longer than the industry will remain attractive. For example, reinvestment by H&R Block in brand capital through a seasonal advertising campaign is certainly justifiable given the long time horizon before personal tax-preparation services become dominated by electronic services.

At this phase of Intermediation, repositioning may be a viable choice for surviving firms because of the opportunities created by the consolidation and exit of rivals. The difficulty with this approach is that many remaining firms may reposition to serve customers that continue to demonstrate a high willingness to pay, and a war of attrition may occur. The tradeoff between sustaining position and repositioning depends on whether the prospect of such a war is significant enough to outweigh the benefits of preserving core activities for as long as possible.

The best choice: Following is usually a better choice than leading change, except for firms that have diversified into the new industry. Repositioning is attractive when it allows the firm to generate profits from core activities without hindering the redeployment of core assets.

Sustaining position is attractive only when the reinvestments can yield a significant return before the industry turns unprofitable.

## The Dominance Stage of Intermediating Change

By the time an industry moves into the dominance stage of Intermediating change, the choice to lead the decline is attractive only to those firms that anticipate an early exit by rivals and that have found ways to combat the threat of obsolescence through an unusual approach to the business. The stringency of these conditions reflects the fact that leading change requires persuading buyers and suppliers to compare the value of the industry's products and services against those of the industry that has created the threat of obsolescence.

Following in the course of industry change is more attractive when the established industry continues to generate an acceptable return on investment despite the changes that have been made to remove core assets from the business. For example, some local newspapers continue to carry classified job listings, although they no longer employ a sales force dedicated to the business. If the listings continue to attract some advertisers despite the newspaper's lack of commitment, then the newspaper may be able to publish them profitably for some time. The risk is in disappointing advertisers that continue to place ads under the mistaken assumption that the organization has continued its commitment.

Sustaining competitive position at this stage is difficult to justify. The most compelling arguments for reinvesting in the firm's competitive position arise when the value delivered by the established and emergent industries are similar in a significant segment of the business. For example, the business of hand-building wooden sailboats is now in the dominant stage of an Intermediating change. The industry that created the threat of obsolescence is vertically integrated and focuses on achieving massive operational efficiencies through large-scale production. Yet there is a core group of buyers who attach great value to the hand-built wooden boats, and a core croup of dedicated craftsman willing to work at low wages to make them. For a firm that operates to serve these core groups of buyers and suppliers, reinvesting to sustain competitive position may be justifiable.

In this case, the dominance phase may last for a long time and generate acceptable profits for a group of surviving firms that has pared

down the asset structure and configured activities to serve only the remaining customers.

Repositioning is attractive only in those rare cases where additional
investment carries the potential to revive the company's overall ability
to generate value in its core segment. In the hand-built wooden sailboat
business, this occurs when the craftsmen who have traditionally valued
simplicity find themselves installing accessories for the leisure sailors
willing to pay for their products.

The best choice: Leading is attractive only to firms that anticipate a
massive wave of exit or that hold an unusually strong competitive position. The burden of proof at this stage of the industry's development is
on sustaining rather than on repositioning; the priority is to move valuable core assets out of the industry and into other uses.


## Radical Change

Under Radical change, survival depends on a strategy for becoming
more efficient or for migrating core assets and activities out of the industry. You'll recall that Radical change occurs only infrequently. Ironically, because Radical change is so unforgiving, the managerial challenge for established firms may be straightforward compared to the
challenge under Intermediating change, where greater ambiguity arises
regarding the best course of action.

Many established companies confronted with advanced Radical
transformation abandon ship and enter the new industry, but very few
companies pull off the transition successfully because this move requires
reconfiguring a broad range of activities, developing new buyer relationships, and working with new suppliers. IBM is the only major mainframe
manufacturer that leads in the personal computing business and it is
often held up as the one of the only *Fortune* 100 firms that has succeeded
at diversification into an industry that threatened its core business. The
reason for the widespread failure at diversification of this type is that the
new industry evolves by a different set of rules that almost always conflict directly with those of the core business. This fact leaves firms in industries undergoing advanced Radical transformation with few options.
Chapter 7 discusses in detail the challenge of adapting into a new environment. Here, the discussion focuses on the transition in the established industry where the Radical transformation is under way.

How do companies earn superior profits through Radical transformation? What distinguishes firms that have survived the longest from those that have not? How have executives dealt with the threat of Radical transformation? This section outlines several approaches that have been particularly effective. Table 6-4 summarizes the tradeoffs and compares them across the stages of Radical change.

### The Emergence Stage of Radical Change

Leading at the emergence stage of Radical transformation entails accelerating change instead of defending the structure of the established business. Yet there are circumstances when accelerating change is

**TABLE 6-4**

## Strategic Tradeoffs Under Radical Change

| | Leading versus following the industry's development | Sustaining position versus repositioning |
|---|---|---|
| **Emergence** | Leading is better when it allows a firm to remain competitive without investing; usually, following is more attractive. | Repositioning is less risky than it was before the Radical change began, but sustaining position is usually more profitable for firms that held any sort of prior competitive advantage. |
| **Convergence** | Following continues to be relatively attractive; leading is better only for firms that can benefit by the exit of rivals or by gaining position in other businesses. | The tradeoffs between sustaining and repositioning depend on the firm's distinctiveness; the priority is preventing price competition. |
| **Co-Existence** | Leading is attractive when the industry is unprofitable and consolidating; following appeals to firms with uncontested positions and good profitability. | Repositioning is usually necessary to avoid over-investing in the business; sustaining position is attractive when it requires little additional investment. |
| **Dominance** | Leading is more attractive for firms with interests in the new industry where the standards for the business originate; following is better for firms that are harvesting. | Repositioning is almost always necessary; sustaining position is justifiable only for firms that are unusually distinctive and profitable without much fixed investment. |

an attractive alternative: in particular, when defending the industry structure requires making investments that cannot deliver a reasonable return and that redouble the firm's commitment to the old industry. In most cases, however, defending industry structure is more attractive than accelerating the emergence of a Radical transformation. For example, in overnight letter delivery, firms spend hundreds of millions of dollars at hub airports to build systems for receiving, sorting, and sending mail on a fast turnaround despite the emerging threat from secure encryption technology for Internet mail. It is conceivable that an overnight letter firm that operates at full capacity might eventually decide to stop investing and to choose the alternative of acknowledging and even accelerating the Radical transformation. If this occurred, an overnight letter company might go as far as to encourage its customers to send documents via the Internet. Yet it is hard to conceive of circumstances where this choice would be optimal—even under significant capacity constraints.

Much more common is the situation where following in the course of industry change is attractive. Firms in the overnight letter delivery business as well as others that are early on a Radical path may continue to reap a significant return on invested capital in the business. Profitability may increase as the firm is freed from commitments to reinvest in assets.

What about sustaining competitive position or repositioning? It is difficult to justify repositioning because the time required to achieve a payoff may be limited (keep in mind that the restructuring may take years to effect, so that a return on the investment may be difficult to achieve even if the industry remains profitable for some time).

You'll recall that the competitive environment in the earliest stage of Radical change may not seem at all different than before the Architectural change began. The terms of competition may be similar and the firm's competitive advantage may not come under pressure immediately. The major difference is in the prospect of a future return on the investments that are made today. While the burden of proof is on repositioning (as it is under non-Architectural change), the paradox of the emergent stage of Radical change is that repositioning may become *relatively* more attractive because a firm gives up less when it departs from its former approach to the business.

For example, an independent trucker that had carried only nonrefrigerated goods may find it worthwhile to expand into the refrigerated segment because the profits in the non-refrigerated segment are dropping. The problem is that independent refrigerated carriage is also under a threat of obsolescence from large, integrated carriers; but if the threat takes longer to influence the refrigerated segment, the repositioning may be justifiable.

The best choice: Leading is better than following only under unusual circumstances (i.e., when it helps a firm to avoid costly investments). Following is much more attractive under normal circumstances. The limited time horizon for the industry lowers the risk of repositioning, and yet sustaining position almost always leads to better performance for firms that were profitable before the Radical change began.

### The Convergence Stage of Radical Change

During the convergence stage of Radical change, the viability of the new approach becomes clear. Buyers and suppliers begin to weigh the pros and cons of the new model, although they may also be conservative and delay abandoning the old approach. For example, many of us now have both wireless and landline telephones instead of only landline telephones. We probably would agree that landline telephones will become less prevalent over time, and yet we continue to pay for landline service because it is reliable and convenient.

Choices by landline telephone companies to become more efficient represent strategic decisions to lead the industry's transformation. This decision is defensible when it leads to rationalization of the industry structure through exit by rivals, or when the efficiency improvements allow the firm to influence the pace and character of the transition.

The choice to follow continues to be attractive for many firms in the established industry during the convergence phase. This choice entails defending the established business against the new competition. In landline telephony, firms have invested in new features such as caller identification that have quickly become standards across the landline business but that are difficult to implement for wireless carriers. The goal is to defend the industry against obsolescence. As a result, the "follower" strategy is often more attractive than one of leading the transformation.

Sustaining competitive position at this phase requires reinvesting in activities and assets that lower costs or enhance differentiation. Because assets begin to depreciate more quickly than they have historically, and because activities lose their robustness in generating value, this alternative becomes less attractive over time.

The principal positioning challenge during the convergence phase is in achieving enough distinctiveness to avoid becoming embroiled in price wars as excess capacity develops. In landline telephony, the leading firms in the industry have had difficulty in retaining enough distinctiveness to avoid price wars. In general, rationalizing capacity to avoid this problem may require partnerships and even mergers among former rivals.

The best choice: Following continues to be relatively attractive for the majority of firms. Leading is the best strategy only for a firm that can influence the transition to its advantage because rivals will exit or because the firm will benefit in other businesses. The tradeoffs between sustaining advantage and repositioning are driven by the opportunity to remain distinctive without escalating commitment to the industry.

### The Co-Existence Stage of Radical Change

The co-existence stage of Radical change may be a long period in which established firms remain competitive with the emerging industry. The choice to lead at this stage is attractive for firms that anticipate that rivals will be forced to exit by the transformation, but it is a risky proposition under the best of circumstances.

Much more common is the decision to follow industry change and to benefit by serving a core group of buyers and suppliers that remain loyal to the established industry. For example, surviving shipbuilders that once served a wide range of private carriers find that their principal customers have become governments and government agencies. Following in the course of change involves accepting this outcome and striving for profits despite the Architectural challenge.

As growth in the established industry diminishes, the tradeoff between leading and following in the process of Radical change may change. A small firm that has diversified successfully into the new industry may profitably accelerate the transformation. For example, energy generation companies that do not dominate the traditional industry but that do have a stake in the emerging nuclear business may be advocates of change. Yet for the majority of firms in the business, it is difficult to imagine attractive conditions for leading the industry toward a greater threat of obsolescence; the "follower" strategy continues to dominate during this stage of the industry's transformation.

By the convergence phase of Radical change, the burden of proof is on any firm that chooses to sustain position instead of to reposition.

Surviving firms must find ways to avoid price competition and yet often distinctiveness is achieved through exit by rivals rather than active reinvestment by survivors. Look what has happened to news bureaus, which used to maintain offices in countries around the world. It was once true that CBS was differentiated and that a number of private agencies pursued low-cost strategies. As new modes of communication threw the business into Architectural change, the surviving firms have retained their distinctiveness partly as a result of exits by others. Repositioning in this situation may be necessary, but the predominant goal must be to avoid sinking too much fixed investment into a business with limited potential to generate a long-term return on the invested capital.

The best choice: Leading is attractive when consolidation is under way through mergers, partnerships, and bankruptcies. Following is a better choice for firms that have an uncontested position in a segment of loyal buyers and suppliers. Repositioning is a better choice than sustaining for most firms. Exceptions occur for firms with self-reinforcing positions that can be sustained with little investment.

### The Dominance Stage of Radical Change

During the dominance stage of Radical change, the terms of competition in the established industry are set in reference to the dominant model in the new industry. The threat of obsolescence to both core activities and core assets has advanced to the point where firms in the established industry operate at a lower scale than historically. Consider what has happened to typewriter manufacturers, theaters, and music retailers.

For firms that survive into this stage of the transformation, leading the course of change may once again become relatively attractive. Leading involves establishing a new set of standards for operational effectiveness that are pegged to the new industry, and is attractive for firms that can control the standards to their advantage. For example, theater companies around the United States have established a precedent of attracting television and movie stars onstage to perform in live productions. This allows the theaters to draw an audience that is familiar with the stars through films, and sets a high bar for rivals that compete for audience attention.

Following in the course of industry change involves accepting the new standards for operational effectiveness rather than trying to define them. This approach tends to appeal to firms that are harvesting their positions rather than actively seeking to remain viable for the long run. (There are many theater companies in the United States that are hanging on to the traditional model for running shows despite the implications for profitability.) Ultimately, the tradeoff between leading and following industry change depends on how changes in the new industry will influence the standards for competing successfully in the established business. If the new business will continue to depress profitability (i.e., if the pressure on theater profitability from films is unlikely to get worse), then following rather than leading the change may be more attractive.

Investing to sustain competitive position during the dominance phase of Radical change is difficult to justify for most companies. At this stage, most firms are saddled with excess capacity and must focus on rationalizing their cost structures without compromising the delivery of value. Consider what has happened to music retailers such as Tower Records and Sam Goody. The terms of competition in music retailing are no longer set independently of electronic distribution. For retailers that have survived, repositioning opportunistically to achieve a return on investment is a better strategy than pouring more money into a business with a limited future. Exceptions to this rule occur when the new approach is distinctive enough to allow companies in the established industry to operate profitably at historical levels of scale and scope. For example, some Broadway producers have been able to sustain their positions despite the pressure on the industry structure because they are so widely known and appreciated. In these situations, the surviving firms may find that measured reinvestment to sustain position generates enough return to be justifiable.

The best choice: Leading is more attractive for firms with interests in the new industry and following is best for firms that are harvesting position. The choice between sustaining position and repositioning depends entirely on the details of the required investment and the time to payback.

## The Payoff

Effective business-unit strategy depends on insights about the trajectory of change, the stage of change, the industry structure, and the firm's competitive position. Identifying the right course of action for a particular organization requires a deep understanding of the context in which the firm operates.

For all the hard work required to integrate an understanding of industry change into your strategy, the payoff is considerable. First, there is greater awareness throughout the organization about how to make tradeoffs with respect to industry evolution.[4] What would you salvage if it there were a fire and you had time to gather only one armload before you left the building? The customer list? The factory blueprints? A product prototype? Tradeoffs arise when there is more than one right answer to a question, and a choice must be made between attractive alternatives. *Consistency* in following a strategy allows employees to develop intuition about how to react in high-stress situations.

A second payoff to a carefully developed, comprehensive business-unit strategy is better resource allocation. Executives in an organization are responsible for making general management decisions about how to allocate resources among opportunities at a single point in time, and how to make choices that trade current profitability for future performance. An effective strategy that integrates an understanding of industry evolution offers principles for reacting quickly and flexibly to unforeseen opportunities.

Yet another payoff to a clear business-unit strategy is realism about how to deal with unforeseen opportunities and problems as they occur. The key is in understanding the kinds of contingencies that can arise, even when the outcome of the contingencies is unknown. It's possible to anticipate a recession, competitive aggression, or a change in buyer needs without knowing exactly when these events may occur. The reaction of the leadership team to unmet profit targets represents a moment of truth in an organization. When a strategy has been developed realistically to account for the possibility of poor results, then the organization is better equipped to turn away from unrealized opportunity and toward real opportunity without becoming burdened by internal politics.

The payoffs of formulating business-unit strategy are considerable, and yet they are only part of the story. The next chapter deals with decisions about industries in which the firm will participate. Integrating insights about industry evolution and its implications for both business-unit and corporate strategy is essential for the organization's survival and for its long-term financial performance.

# 7

## Diversifying Across Businesses to Capitalize on Industry Evolution

INDUSTRY EVOLUTION RAISES profound questions about whether a firm should diversify across businesses to maximize the value of its activities and assets:

- Can the firm achieve better performance by participating in industries on different evolutionary trajectories?

- When should a company enter an industry that is throwing one of its divisions into Architectural transformation?

- How can a company take activities and assets developed in one business and use them effectively to gain an advantage in another business?

- When none of a firm's industries have attractive prospects, does unrelated diversification make sense?

These questions cannot be answered successfully without considering the context of change in each of the relevant businesses. Industry evolution in the different divisions of a corporation is fundamental to the effectiveness of diversification.

This chapter discusses some of the diversification strategies that companies have pursued to improve profitability by capitalizing on the insights described in this book. Mitsubishi operates in a range of industries on Creative evolutionary paths with loose connections between businesses, while General Motors operates in a range of Creative industries with tight connections across divisions.

The purpose of this chapter is to provide you with an overview of the issues and a set of effective practices for setting a corporate strategy that accounts for industry change. Again, it is impossible to be comprehensive but insights can be gleaned from the track records of successful diversifiers. The approach rests on the fact that all diversified firms face a universal set of questions about which activities and assets to share across divisions, and the degree of sharing that will occur.

The first section of the chapter deals with prerequisites for effective corporate strategy under industry evolution and the second covers common strategic tradeoffs that influence a firm's decision to diversify.

## Prerequisites for Effective Corporate Strategy

The burden of proof for justifying joint ownership of divisions is firmly on the parent corporation. Membership in a diversified firm saddles the divisions with an extra layer of overhead and removes them from access to the capital markets. The benefits of coordination under the corporate umbrella must be great enough to outweigh these costs.

Diversified firms are constantly under pressure to show that the diversification generates more value than could be created by the business units run as independent corporations. As a result, it is usually impossible to justify diversification for a one-time transfer of activities or assets (including a transfer between a declining business and an emerging business). Diversification makes sense only when you've got activities and assets to share regularly, or when you anticipate the need for the repeated transfer of activities and assets between divisions.

The following discussion highlights several prerequisites for effective corporate strategy in light of industry change.

*1. Anticipate constant testing on whether ownership is justifiable as the industries of the different divisions evolve.*

Diversification is stable when:

- the relationships between divisions cannot be organized more efficiently through partnerships, alliances, or arms-length contracts, and

- the corporation's profitability is higher than if the divisions were managed independently or as affiliates of different companies.

When either of these conditions is violated, then pressure builds to divest one or more of the organization's divisions. If the pressure isn't relieved, then the executive team may be challenged by the board of directors to improve its corporate strategy, or may even face a takeover bid.

There are several important implications for corporate strategies motivated by industry evolution. First, diversification is especially challenging when the firm participates in businesses that are diverse in their evolutionary trajectories. This is because the opportunities for coordination are constantly changing under diversity across divisions. The pressure is exacerbated when some of the divisions face Architectural or Foundational change, where a threat of obsolescence creates an incentive to retire activities or assets.

Second, when diversification is designed to facilitate coordination between business units that are evolving on different schedules—that is, that are out of sync in their phase of change—then the pressure grows with time. The inflection points that occur between phases of change create enormous pressure on divisions to pursue new and different objectives in activity and asset utilization. Whenever these changes occur in a diversified corporation, there is incentive to change the corporate systems and coordinating mechanisms. When the needs of divisions arise at varying times and with differing intensities, the pressure is compounded and the diversification may become hard to defend.

Does this mean that diversification is justifiable only when the subsidiary businesses all participate in industries on the same evolutionary trajectory and are in exactly the same phase of change? No. Diversification may be justifiable even when the divisions are on dissimilar trajectories or at dissimilar phases. However, corporate strategy is more effective when it is set to *anticipate* the pressures that will arise as industry evolution progresses in each division. The firm will be more profitable and more effective in promoting coordination across divisions if corporate activities and assets are constructed in ways that reflect future pressures on the diversified organization.

*2. Decide if the firm will deal with industry evolution through divestitures, acquisitions, alliances, or long-term contracts.*

Some corporations are committed to divestitures, acquisitions, or alliances. During the 1990s, Chevron divested more businesses (completing fifty-one separate deals) than any other *Fortune* 100 company as reported by SDC.[1] Against the significant pressures of industry evolution facing the organization in its individual divisions (which, for Chevron, included Kleenup Weedkillers, Guatemalan Import facilities, and Petal

Gas Storage), a strategy of widespread acquisitions was not feasible. LTV Steel engaged in seventeen deals as reported by SDC—including acquisitions, divestitures, and alliances—fewer than any other *Fortune* 100 company of the 1990s. Over the same period, IBM engaged in 566 separate revenue-generating alliances as reported by SDC, although it also conducted a significant number of acquisitions and divestitures. Thus, IBM's strategy emphasized alliances but also accommodated other forms of corporate control. By contrast, Apple Computer booked 152 different revenue-generating alliances but just four acquisitions and two divestitures.

Apple is known for its de novo growth. Industry evolution should be a centerpiece in the firm's strategic priorities for acquisitions, alliances, and divestitures. All else being equal, de novo growth is particularly important to superior performance in Progressive industries. Under this form of change, growth through acquisition, contraction by divestiture, or management by alliance may compromise business-unit strategy.

In general, divestitures may be the only option for exiting an industry that has advanced into a final evolutionary stage. Alliances may be especially attractive as the company manages transitions through the shakeout, convergence, or co-existence phases of evolution in its industries.

*3. Clarify how core activities and core assets will be shared by divisions on different evolutionary trajectories.*

Many diversified companies use complex coordinating systems that involve both the sharing and the transferring of core activities and core assets. As other authors have argued, this kind of complexity tends to escalate, and can eventually lead to a loss of clarity in a company's corporate strategy.[2] Great corporate strategies are built on the principle that business units should not be saddled with unnecessary overhead. Headquarters functions and requirements should support only the sharing and transferring necessary to improve corporate performance.

There are strong implications of the nature of change in participating business units' industries for coordinating systems. Because of the torque created by the abrupt and dramatic changes in each division's requirements as the threat of obsolescence develops, the sharing of core activities is difficult to manage when one or more of the involved business units undergoes Architectural change. Frustrations arise as managers across divisions struggle to make adjustments that do not compromise their positions while continuing to fulfill commitments to sister divisions.

Similarly, it is difficult to share core assets across businesses undergoing Foundational change. Each division is constrained from retiring assets when they are useful in other parts of the company. Extensive coordination is needed to assure that the assets are available to the divisions for which they have the greatest value.

Transferring core activities and core assets may be difficult when a business is *not* undergoing an Architectural or Foundational threat. Transferring is different than sharing because it involves ceding control over activities and assets to other divisions. This process is hampered when there is no compelling reason for the division that developed the activities and assets to turn over control. Under Progressive evolution, the process of disengaging the activities and assets from the system for transfer is likely to damage their potential for value creation.

The bottom line is that effective corporate strategy depends on a clear understanding of the logic behind the firm's diversification across business units. Decisions about corporate capabilities, divestitures, and acquisitions all depend in a sensitive way on the firm's fundamental approach to value creation through inter-business coordination.

*4. Develop clear lines of authority for resolving disputes between divisions on different evolutionary trajectories.*

In the formulation of corporate strategy, fundamental issues tend to arise regarding:

- Who decides how to resolve contention about divisional access to valuable assets and activities

- Who decides and pays for the development of new activities and assets that will be shared

- Whether the organization will develop *corporate* activities and assets that generate value by enhancing coordination and communication between business units

It must be clear who within the firm has authority to make important decisions about resource development and allocation. Tension arises between executives in business units and at corporate headquarters. Often, the largest business units, or those that have the most at stake, seek control of essential activities and assets. The problem with decentralization is that transfer-pricing schemes rarely reflect all the benefits and costs of coordination, and political and organizational conflict can become quite significant. Yet centralizing the activities and assets at corporate headquarters also has its disadvantages, particularly when decisions about investment and reinvestment are sensitive to the details of developments in each of the business units.

Perhaps the greatest risk regarding the allocation of decision-making authority is lack of clarity about who has it. Business units in the earliest stages of Progressive and Creative evolution may require the investment of substantial capital to build resources and create the activities necessary to adhere to the dominant model. By contrast, business units in the final stages of Radical and Intermediating transition may be sources of activities and assets that can be shared with other units. In still other instances, a corporation may operate several business units at similar stages of evolution that share activities or assets.

A prerequisite for effective corporate strategy is a system that reflects the character and stage of industry evolution of each business unit and that is adaptable enough to change with the circumstances in each unit. Consider Merrill Lynch, which participates in a range of industries including personal financial advising, investment brokerage, and corporate finance. Financial advising is at the convergence stage of Radical transformation; investment brokerage is undergoing Intermediation; and corporate finance is a mature Creative business. Decision-making authority on managing accounts, training new employees, and maintaining brand capital (to name just a few activities with value across divisions) has historically been shared between the corporation and the individual units. As the corporation confronts massive, jarring, and asynchronous changes in several business units simultaneously, the company must make quick and appropriate decisions about who should have ultimate authority over these activities. The risk is that the company will leave important coordination opportunities on the table, and ultimately be confronted with questions about whether the firm should continue to operate as a diversified firm that participates in these diverse industries.

*5. Identify the right level of commitment to particular buyers and suppliers when activities are shared across divisions on different evolutionary trajectories.*

Sharing activities is particularly difficult when the firm participates in a range of industries that evolve on different trajectories. Sharing is only sustainable when the cultures, organizational processes, and systems of different divisions are compatible. If you plan to share activities across businesses over the long run, then make sure that your businesses are all in industries that are evolving on the same type of model.

In general, a tradeoff can arise between specializing activities for particular business units and generalizing activities so that they can be shared easily. All else being equal, specialization tends to allow a firm to enhance the value that it creates for the buyers in a particular business unit. Generalization of activities across business units amortizes their costs across divisions, and can make the corporation as a whole more efficient. There are other subtle benefits and costs to specialization and generalization. Specialization can make it difficult for the business unit to adapt to changes in the industry structure and competitive environment, while generalization may facilitate competitive imitation (because the transparency of activities to the firm's own divisions spills outside the company).

Diversified companies manage the tradeoffs in different ways. For many years, Coca-Cola's corporate strategy was oriented around supporting the soft-drink concentrate production business.[3] It would have been unthinkable to organize the core advertising and merchandising activities broadly enough to cover other products.

The benefit of this activity specialization for Coca-Cola was unparalleled effectiveness in the marketing of soft drinks. The company's signature trademark is generally acknowledged as the most widely recognized corporate symbol in the world. Coca-Cola continues to post high profitability yet the legacy of its soft-drink concentrate business created marketing and organizational challenges as the company broadened to other beverages such as orange juice and bottled water.

Other great companies manage activities differently. From the 1960s into the 1990s, Philips Electronics of the Netherlands committed to developing laser optics technology in its R&D labs.[4] The technology was applicable to the consumer electronics, medical devices, and security systems businesses, all of which were accessible to Philips through various divisions. The corporate strategy, which was celebrated by C. K. Prahalad and Gary Hamel in "The Core Competence of the Corporation," rested on the idea that Philips would benefit by sharing its generalized optics capabilities across businesses.[5] The Philips example demonstrates how a corporation can preserve its distinctiveness and fend off imitation while generalizing activities. In this instance, the technology was too complex to imitate easily, and the firm focused on sharing activities that incorporated tacit knowledge that would be difficult to imitate.

To capitalize on the trajectories of change in its industries, a company should have clear priorities regarding the specialization of activities. Generalizing activities is not as costly when the phase of industry evolution is advanced in the firm's businesses, simply because the firm is less vulnerable to imitation. Similarly, firms that participate in more than one Progressive industry may be less vulnerable to imitation through the generalization of activities as long as the sharing of activities does not compromise operational efficiencies in the different divisions. By contrast, firms that participate in industries that are in their early phases may have much greater difficulty in sharing activities without vulnerability to imitation.

Thus, there are tradeoffs between keeping activities general for use across the corporation and specializing activities for particular divisions. Industry change in each of the divisions can influence the future value of specialized activities, and in turn affect the corporate strategy.

*6. Identify the right level of commitment to particular buyers and suppliers when assets are shared across divisions on different evolutionary trajectories.*

Specialization within particular business units commits the firm to the idiosyncratic needs of buyers and of suppliers, and can set the foundation for superior profitability in the business. However, companies that generalize their assets across businesses may lower their total costs. Generalized assets for use across business units are less customized for the needs of particular buyers and suppliers, but also tend to create less value for them.

Take Citigroup as an example. The assets of Citigroup are specialized across business units. The company's capabilities in commercial banking have distinctive historical roots at Citibank, and differ in character from the capabilities in the investment banking divisions, for example, that became part of the firm with its acquisition of Smith Barney. Some of Citibank's most noted resources include localized brand capital in major banking markets, sophisticated systems for working-capital management, distributed local expertise in credit assessment, and credit-card operations. Smith Barney's resources include its retail brokerage presence and expertise in trading. Each of these assets developed out of activities in particular divisions. As a result, the company holds a commanding competitive position in many of its business with long-term customer relationships built around tailored solutions.

In contrast, Disney has mastered the art of keeping its assets generalized enough to share across its own business units without exposing the firm to imitation. The company's legendary characters—Bambi, Snow White, Mickey Mouse, and Simba the Lion King, to name a few—are featured in films, theme parks attractions, and Disney merchandise. By developing characters that represent a set of core values, the company has reinforced its brand identity and carefully defended its competitive positions.

The costs and benefits of generalizing assets are tied directly to the evolutionary trajectories of the businesses in which the firm participates. For example, when assets are generalized in industries undergoing Foundational change, then the firm may never gain the kind of edge necessary to achieve competitive advantage in its business units.

## Strategic Choices Under Diversification

Ultimately, a corporate strategy generates value by facilitating relationships between member businesses. These relationships may be direct, such as the Disney Corporation's development of theme park attractions based on film characters, or indirect, such as the accumulation of Disney brand capital through the film business that pays off in higher theme park attendance per advertising dollar.

There are several benefits when a corporate strategy accounts for differences across divisions in industry change. First, an organization can be more effective at making decisions about headquarters projects. Differences across businesses in the trajectory of industry evolution can gradually create pressure to change centralized headquarters activities. The most effective policies for managing divisions may change. Even the culture may evolve. Anticipating these challenges makes the organization more efficient and adaptable.

The second payoff is better resource allocation. The demands of industry evolution and of changing competitive position create different opportunities across businesses, yet many organizations use a rigid capital expenditure system and apply it the same way to each business unit. By developing a corporate strategy that accounts for variation in industry trajectories, a company can invest more effectively.

Finally, a clear corporate strategy leads to better responses across the company to unforeseen contingencies within specific divisions. An organization can respond quickly when unanticipated opportunity arises to buy or sell a business or to build competitive position quickly. Understanding the objectives of corporate strategy also allows executives to interpret and respond quickly to bad news, such as a competitive blow or an adverse change in industry structure. In each of these cases, clear corporate strategy serves as the foundation for a quick and accurate redirection of activities and assets between divisions.

The rest of this chapter lays out the issues that firms face in three distinctive situations where industry evolution is particularly important to corporate strategy: (i) diversifying to address problems in a core business; (ii) gaining advantage in related businesses; and (iii) leading the emergence of a new industry. While these are not all of the situations in which industry evolution is essential to corporate strategy, they are among the most prevalent and important.

### Diversifying to Address Problems in a Core Business

One common motivation for diversification is trouble in a core business. Companies diversify to limit their dependence on an industry that offers little chance for superior performance. Participating in a new industry improves the chances of preserving the company's heritage and of achieving satisfactory profits. The following section describes some of the most common tactics used to make this move.

#### Dealing with an Architectural Challenge by Diversifying Into an Emerging Industry That Is the Source of the Threat

Established organizations often enter an emerging industry—one that is the source of threat to a core business—through de novo experimentation, acquisition, or even full-scale commitment to transfer the established business, although these options are not mutually exclusive.

TESTING THE WATERS IN THE NEW INDUSTRY THROUGH EXPERIMEN-TATION. Established companies often use skunk works to explore new industries. Corporate-backed venture funds that are designed to provide the sponsoring firm with points of entry into emerging industries effectively provide the company with several skunk works simultaneously. These approaches allow the firm to modularize their diversification into separate divisions so that their failure does not have serious consequences for the corporation as a whole.

The *Boston Globe* set up a wholly owned subsidiary in 1994 called "Boston Globe Electronic Publishing" (BGEP) to experiment with new electronic media such as the Internet for distributing news.[6] The subsidiary, which soon launched the Boston.com Web site, operated on a number of principles that reflected a balance in its charter between experimenting with the new approach and maintaining the integrity of the *Globe's* position as the paper of record in New England.[7] To this end, the company relied on the *Globe* and on wire services for content and did not employ reporters on its own. But BGEP marketed online job listings, auto listings, and other advertisements. The paper received high marks from analysts and users both for the quality of its Web site and for its foresight. And yet the challenges facing the *Globe* and its parent, the New York Times Company, in dealing with the Intermediation of the newspaper industry were only partly addressed by BGEP. While BGEP represented a diversification into the new industry, it left open the question of what would happen to the core operations of the *Globe* in the face of the threat.

In general, companies that test the waters in a new industry through experimentation in a separate division defer the hard work of adapting the core business to the Architectural threat.[8] Sotheby's profitability dropped dramatically despite attracting significant traffic to the sothebys.com site in 2000.[9] Companies like Lucent and Xerox that have sponsored successful new businesses through venture funds have struggled to implement a strategy that integrates the insights into the core business. Testing the waters may help to address the challenge but is not a complete solution.

ENTERING THE EMERGING INDUSTRY THROUGH ACQUISITION. Some companies have managed the risks of entering an industry by acquiring an entrepreneurial firm with a successful track record in the new industry. The advantage of acquisition is that the acquirer can wait until after the dominant model for the new business emerges, and lower the risk of buying into a failing approach. Disney acquired a significant stake in Infoseek, AOL bought Netscape, and @Home bought Excite in a spate of deals that occurred after a dominant model emerged in the portal industry. The advantage for the acquirers was in entering the industry with an edge by acquiring proven firms that clearly had achieved operational effectiveness. But the challenge was to integrate the acquired businesses with the core activities of the acquiring firms. This problem is especially challenging because the core business is usually so much more profitable than the acquired businesses.

FULL-SCALE COMMITMENT TO TRANSFER ACTIVITIES OUT OF THE ES-TABLISHED BUSINESS AND INTO A NEW BUSINESS. In 1999, Merrill Lynch introduced "Integrated Choice," a set of products that dealt with the threat to full-service brokerage (which was a core business for the firm) from discount brokerage. As a market leader in the traditional industry (full-service brokerage), Merrill was particularly vulnerable. Integrated Choice was offered to all of the company's clients and allowed each one to select a method for paying for transactions and advisory services. A client could continue to maintain a traditional full-service account or could elect to move to a discounted trading account. The move at Merrill Lynch involved substantial risks, but it also represented a bold step for confronting the hard work of adapting to the threat at full scale.

In general, the risks of a full-scale commitment to transfer activities out of one industry (in this case, full-service brokerage) and into the in-dustry that is the source of the threat (in this case, discount brokerage) are substantial. Poor productivity, morale problems, severance costs, financ-ing requirements, customer-relationship costs, supply-chain problems, and many other transitional costs may arise. The company is almost sure to experience a decline in performance, and in some cases survival is at stake. Yet an organization that takes on the transition through a bold, sys-tematic, and carefully conceived transitional strategy has the potential to lead in the new business. The risks are enormous, but the payoff can be substantial. And, of course, the organization is taking on the hard work of confronting the basic problems in the core business—work that is only deferred into the future when the company depends on a skunk works or an acquisition to set its position in the new business.

### Dealing With an Architectural Challenge by Leapfrogging Across Generations

Occasionally, a company diversifies successfully by leapfrogging across technical generations through direct investment or acquisition. Some electric utilities, particularly outside the United States, have de-veloped corporate strategies designed for diversification from fossil fuel sources into renewable sources such as solar and hydro without emphasizing nuclear technologies. (The electricity-generation industry is undergoing Architectural transformation in geographic areas where traditional marketing and distribution activities have been displaced because of deregulation.)

When leapfrogging works, it can allow a company to preserve its established position unimpeded by concerns about migrating activities and assets to a new environment until there is little chance of sustaining superior performance in the old business. Ideally, the company builds position in the new business just as the dominant model develops. Getting the timing right is very difficult.

### Diversifying to Improve Performance When the Core Business Undergoes Foundational Change

Firms have diversified successfully to improve their performance in industries undergoing Foundational change, where core assets are threatened. The goal is to make the company more productive through better asset management. Some proven methods are discussed below.

DEVELOPING ASSETS IN ONE DIVISION FOR USE IN ANOTHER DIVISION. Several large companies in the North American and European railroad industries have used their brand capital and skills to develop new consulting divisions devoted to logistics management. Diversification has also been effective in electric utilities, which have set up energy-management consultancies based on established capabilities in the generation business. These organizations in industries undergoing Radical transformation have diversified to increase the productivity of assets in related businesses.

In general, a diversification strategy *designed* to transfer assets from one division into another involves substantial risks. In many cases, the assets were acquired or developed because they were essential to value creation in the original division. Wresting them lose for transfer may damage the profitability of the originating division, but if the Foundational transformation has progressed far enough, this may be a small price to pay in exchange for the chance to generate a long-lived return in the new business.

SPREADING RISK AND STIMULATING CREATIVE COMPETITION.  In some industries undergoing Foundational change, project failure can be catastrophic for a firm because the scale of each project is so large. A commercial construction company that builds a skyscraper can be forced out of business if a major accident occurs on the site, if the building does not conform closely enough to specifications, or if major delays arise. As a result, the contractor may incorporate a subsidiary for managing each of its large projects. The goal is to protect uninvolved assets from exposure to catastrophic risk.

Another, related motivation for diversification is to stimulate competition between divisions in the development of new capabilities. Here again, the goal is to spread risk across multiple projects. When it introduced its high-end luxury line, Toyota organized Lexus as a separate division even though the Camry, positioned at the high end of the Toyota line, was designed for buyers that were targeted by the new Lexus division. Competition between the two divisions of Toyota stimulated creativity and allowed for multiple entries by the corporation into the lucrative middle and upper middle segments of the business.

DEVELOPING COMPLEMENTARY ACTIVITIES. Companies in industries undergoing Foundational change cannot achieve satisfactory profitability without an effective network of complementary activities. One of the most dramatic examples of diversification to rejuvenate the activity system occurred when General Motors created Saturn in the 1980s. Small-car manufacturing at the time was on a Creative trajectory. For large, diversified car companies, achieving significant share in the small-car market was crucial to long-term performance because customers tend to be loyal over the course of their lives to the manufacturer of their first cars.

During the 1970s and 1980s, General Motors had offered small cars like the Chevette, the Vega, and the Geo Prizm, and had lost significant share to Toyota and Honda. Experience with the Prizm was particularly poignant. The car was built at NUMMI, a joint venture with Toyota. The car, sold by Chevrolet, shared the same fundamental design and was built at the same plant as the Corolla. While customers flocked to Toyota dealerships for its small car, they seemed uninterested in the Prizm, even though it was significantly less expensive that the Corolla.[10]

The idea for the Saturn Corporation dates back to the early 1980s, when a group of engineers at General Motors envisioned a new small car designed from scratch. Over the next ten years, GM teams dedicated to the Saturn project would design and build a prototype of one of the finest small cars ever built.[11] There is no question that the Saturn small car compared favorably with the Toyota Corolla and the Honda Civic when it was first introduced, a major reason for Saturn's success.[12]

Yet Saturn's greatest achievements were organizational and not entirely related to the design of the car. The company had been conceived in cooperation between General Motors and the United Auto Workers to improve relationships between the corporation and its employees. Many of the innovations at Saturn had to do with breaking through barriers to trust that had become deeply entrenched over decades of adversarial relations. Retailers were also crucial to the company's success. In 1993, Saturn operated 340 dealerships, compared with about a thousand each for Toyota and Honda and upwards of five thousand each for American companies.[13] Because the Saturn retailers were not plagued with excess capacity, a spirit of collaboration and partnership between Saturn and its dealers developed. The net result was a powerful system of complementary activities that accounted in large part for the early successes of Saturn.

Saturn is a remarkable example of how diversification can be used to generate a new supporting infrastructure in a Creative evolutionary environment. In general, firms in industries that are undergoing Creative or Radical change can often enhance the productivity of their core assets through diversification that focuses on the efficiency of the complementary activity system in the business.

### Diversifying to Exit an Industry in Decline

The dog racing industry is in decline; a recent article reports that attendance peaked in 1991 and has dropped ever since.[14] Companies in this industry have diversified to use their assets in new businesses; for instance, greyhound tracks have been converted for car racing. Such has been the case for other industries facing decline as well—for example, fishing boats have been converted into tourist vessels.

Diversifying out of an industry in decline is often easier to manage than situations in which the core business is under a threat of obsolescence. Under Architectural and Foundational change, the temptation is to diversify into the industry that is causing the threat to the core business. Ultimately this can create significant conflicts as the older, profitable businesses resist the transfer of activities and assets into the new industry. When the core business is in decline, there is less resistance and conflict of interest to overcome by diversifying.

### Gaining Advantage in Related Businesses

A second and powerful motivation to diversify is to share activities or assets so that the company can enhance its position in all of its businesses. Performance improves only if the gains from sharing are large enough to outweigh the costs of generalizing activities and assets. In particular, success depends on making sure that capabilities aren't destroyed in the process of making them accessible across divisions. Researchers in the field of strategy have shown that this can be difficult because core activities and assets are often intangible (such as culture, brand, and knowledge capital) and hard to generalize.[15]

Diversification to gain advantage across divisions is even more difficult when the industries are evolving on different evolutionary trajectories. Imagine trying to share activities between a division in a Progressive industry and a division in a Creative industry. The demands for operational efficiency in the Progressive industry compel the company to manage costs with discipline and to make changes incrementally and deliberately. In the Creative environment, the organization must respond quickly and flexibly to breakthroughs in new-product development. Cultural differences alone can create enormous friction across organizational boundaries.

Difficulties also arise when corporate strategy rests on the sharing of activities or assets between a division undergoing Architectural transformation and a division in a Progressive or Creative environment. Consider a corporation that shares a sales force across Intermediating and Progressive industries. This would occur, for example, when a newspaper sells both online and offline advertising and classified space. An integrated sales force (that sells both types of ads) may provoke criticism from the newspaper division for dropping rates and accelerating the demise of advertising revenue and at the same time provoke criticism from the Internet division for adhering to the old model and remaining inflexible. The tensions worsen as the Architectural transformation continues.

The difficulty of sharing activities and assets across industries on different evolutionary paths arises from the balancing act required to stay specialized enough within divisions to sustain value creation. Even under the best of circumstances, this balance requires careful management. When industries evolve on different trajectories, the challenges become compounded because the requirements for success in each division do not change in tandem. One division may require the greater specialization of activities at the same time as another allows greater generalization.

When industries do evolve on similar trajectories, the sharing of activities and of assets across divisions can act as a powerful mechanism for achieving superior performance. The following examples provide background on how companies have diversified successfully to take advantage of this opportunity.

### Diversifying Across Industries That Evolve by the Same Rules to Share Core Activities

Sharing activities is particularly effective when a company diversifies across businesses that evolve on similar evolutionary paths. There are many examples of companies that have shared activities between industries on Progressive trajectories. You already have read about how Wal-Mart shares distribution activities across its discount stores and Sam's Club warehouses. Amazon.com used its capabilities for selling books to develop an effective position in toy retailing. Panera Bread applies its business methods and processes in company-owned stores and in the restaurant franchising industry.

The key to success in these situations is to diversify across industries that are similar enough in their requirements to soften compromises in the generalization of activities across systems. Compromises occur when the divisions have grown so different in their core requirements that their common activities become generic. The announcement in 2001 of AT&T's restructuring into four separate businesses—wireless, broadband, business services, and consumer services—was motivated in part by this problem. The divisions had been unified previously in an effort to share activities, but industry change had led to major differences in core requirements. The divestitures announced in 2001 were intended in part to remove the pressure to compromise in the design of shared activities.

The reason for the prevalence of diversification across Progressive industries is that the threat of imitation is relatively low as long as the company remains on the dominant model in each of the industries in which it participates. But for a diversification strategy to work, the businesses have to be similar enough to share core activities without compromise.

Sharing activities across industries on Creative evolutionary paths is also relatively common. Remember that activities are different from assets in that they are regularly repeated and have no lingering value once they cease. Centralized selling, marketing, and licensing activities are commonly shared within firms that are diversified across Creative industries. Sharing of assets can be more difficult because of their rapid depreciation.

In industries that are undergoing Intermediation, shared activities are often designed to preserve and deploy valuable assets owned by divisions. Several media giants that participate in the recording industry, magazine publishing, and news generation businesses have developed centralized functions dedicated to experimenting with new business models using assets from a range of divisions.

Companies in industries undergoing Radical transformation also may benefit from diversification. Restructuring specialists make their names by developing capabilities for trimming down businesses as the transformation progresses. By developing centralized expertise at unwinding a firm's activities and at selling off assets, a company holds a corporate advantage that can be shared across divisions.

### Diversifying to Share Core Assets

It's also possible to gain advantage through diversification across businesses that share assets. When the character of industry evolution is the same across business units, then sharing assets is as straightforward as sharing activities. United Technologies participates in the jet-engine and helicopter-manufacturing businesses, sharing a reputation for excellence in aircraft components.

Since assets can often be shared more flexibly than activities, firms sometimes diversify successfully across businesses that are not on the same evolutionary trajectory—but the diversity in industry evolution must be limited for this corporate strategy to remain stable. An example makes this clearer. QUALCOMM licenses its computer-mediated discourse analysis (CMDA) technology through one division and builds CDMA components for wireless phones in another division.[16] The core assets—the patents on CDMA technology—are centerpieces of the company's strategy. But the licensing business evolves on a Creative trajectory while the component manufacturing business is on an Intermediating path with a threat from software. The sharing of assets generates value across divisions because there is no compromise in operational effectiveness in each constituent industry.

In general, the sharing of assets across industries that evolve in different ways is robust when no division depreciates the assets at a high rate. When one division runs down assets that are important to the competitive position of another division, cooperation breaks down. While this principle holds in a general sense, it applies particularly when a firm is diversified across industries that undergo Foundational change and those that do not. In short, it is very difficult to develop a stable corporate strategy for sharing assets across one division in a Progressive or Intermediating environment and another division in a Creative or Radical environment. The *transfer* of assets across this boundary may create value, but *sharing* assets is very difficult to accomplish.

### Integrating Vertically Across Businesses to Gain Access to Core Assets or Core Activities

Vertical integration occurs when a company enters the industry of its buyers or suppliers. Many companies integrate vertically to gain access to raw materials or to create bargaining power, such as Coors when it entered into the can-manufacturing business. The evidence suggests that it is difficult to raise overall performance for a sustained period through vertical integration when activities and assets are shared across industries that are truly distinctive. Vertical integration is sustainable when activities and assets are transferred rather than shared.

You'll recall that diversification creates advantage only when it allows for better coordination than is available through partnerships and alliances. Modern companies have difficulty meeting this test for long periods if their strategies depend on sharing across vertical boundaries. For example, consider what it takes to share activities and assets between a manufacturing business and a distribution business. Activities such as research and development must be relevant to the distribution division as well as the manufacturing division to be truly shared. Selling activities are only truly shared when the company offers manufactured goods both F.O.B. (freight on board) and delivered directly to the customer's doorstep, with intensive attention to the character of the distribution process. Marketing assets are shared when brand capital is developed both upstream and downstream.

The difficulty has to do with the fact that true boundaries between industries are shaped by differences in the dominant models at each level of the supply chain. Pharmaceutical manufacturing evolves on a Creative model, but the prescription benefits management industry evolves Progressively. The investment management industry evolves on

a Creative model, while investment brokerage is undergoing Intermediation after a long history of Progressive evolution.

Because industry boundaries in a vertical chain reflect differences in
dominant models, a transferring strategy through diversification may
be more practical than a sharing strategy. Of course, even transferring
strategies can be difficult to implement because they create conflicts of
interest between divisions.

What are the exceptions to the rule? When can a company create
advantage through vertical integration that involves sharing activities
and assets across divisions? First, when the company is protected from
conflict of interest because of a lack of competition in the downstream
or upstream industry. Coca-Cola and Pepsi have integrated forward to
purchase bottlers with little conflict of interest because of the geographic exclusivity afforded to bottlers under prior contracts.

Second, vertical integration through sharing can yield benefits
across the corporation when one division participates in an industry at
an early stage of development. In some situations, the company can use
its position in the established industry to provide advantage to the division in the emerging industry. With success, the tables turn, with
growth in the new division benefiting the established business. Time's
diversification into the cable television business during the 1970s had
these characteristics.

### Leading the Emergence of a New Industry

Companies also diversify from established businesses into emerging
industries with the intention of becoming leaders in the field. The evidence suggests that diversification of this type can provide powerful
benefits to the fledgling business.[17]

There are two reasons for this. The first is that large corporations
can protect new businesses from the pressure of the capital markets to
generate returns. For this effect to take hold, however, there has to be
some reason why the capital markets are inefficient at judging the character of the entrepreneurial effort. One of the most compelling reasons
for capital-market inefficiency arises when the new division has developed a product or process that would be imitated quickly if it were revealed to the public through disclosures to the investment community.
By offering managerial expertise and funding, a diversified corporation
can protect the new division against the appropriation of its ideas. Of

course, there is a dark side to this rationale. Diversified corporations must maintain the discipline to pull the plug on fledgling divisions with untenable business models.

The second mechanism can be more robust and pervasive. Diversified companies often can develop new businesses that are related or that eventually become related to other divisions. The corporate strategy in these situations involves gradually changing the nature of the sharing and transfer. In the beginning, the established divisions may lend resources to the emerging business. This sharing of activities and assets may be followed by a transfer from declining businesses into the newly developed business. By stimulating the inception of the new industry, the corporation creates a foundation for future diversification.

The following sections describe the issues that arise when firms establish related and unrelated new businesses.

### Defining a New, Related Business

In October 1998, Nippon Telegraph and Telephone (NTT) issued an initial public offering of stock in its DoCoMo subsidiary, although it retained 67 percent ownership of the shares. DoCoMo, viewed as a "sort of exile" by NTT engineers just a few years earlier,[18] offered a wireless telephone network that had integrated Internet access, and had become the crown jewel of NTT, contributing 50 percent of the NTT group's profit at the time of the IPO.[19] As the core operating companies at NTT confronted a decline in landline usage beginning in 1997, subscriptions to DoCoMo's wireless services escalated dramatically, largely because of excitement surrounding i-mode, which was popular among teenagers, business people, and consumers. By the summer of 2001, DoCoMo attracted over half of the new subscribers to telephone service in Japan,[20] and for the 2002 fiscal year, NTT reported that DoCoMo contributed over 44 percent of the company's revenue and 100 percent of recurring profit.[21] NTT's diversification into wireless telephone service with integrated Internet access had proven to be critical for the corporation as a whole.

DoCoMo's success can be traced to the brand, marketing, and engineering talent of its corporate parent, NTT. Other examples: Turner Broadcasting founded CNN, the first twenty-four-hours news cable network, in 1980, when less than 10 percent of U.S. households had access to cable television service. Adobe Systems led the emergence of the electronic documents industry through diversification from its applications software interface business. Despite these successes, there are also prominent examples of companies with early access to burgeoning industries that failed to achieve leadership, such as Xerox in personal computing and Polaroid in digital imaging.[22]

What kinds of factors improve a company's success at nurturing the development of a new business through diversification? It is impossible to generalize comprehensively but the examples suggest some broad patterns.

First, the three firms cited earlier that have been successful—NTT, Turner Broadcasting, and Adobe—entered businesses that were initially highly complementary to their core divisions (for NTT, wireless telephones provided a channel for long-distance service). The new businesses were also tightly related, and drew extensively on the distinctive capabilities of the parent businesses. NTT's telecommunications engineers, TBS's dedication to the broad distribution of programming, and Adobe's relationships with applications developers were unparalleled in their industries before the diversification took place.

Second, new activities and assets with value for the corporation as a whole were quickly created within the emerging businesses. A key insight here is that the established divisions were not required to change fundamentally to benefit from the new businesses. NTT's success at wireless did generate more traffic for the long-distance company, CNN generated demand for cable service, and Adobe's PDF enhanced demand for graphics-enhanced printers.

Third, there was no imperative to use the new business as a receptacle for resources and activities from troubled divisions. The established businesses were not in industries undergoing Architectural transformation when the new divisions were established. As a result, the new businesses developed without the pressures and constraints that arise when executives are concerned about the viability of established divisions.

Finally, the emerging industries had the same evolutionary character as the established divisions of the parent company. As a result, the culture of the new business, the inherent project-development risks, and the organizational systems were compatible across divisions.

### Defining a New, Unrelated Business

There are situations in which companies diversify far afield from their original industries. Nokia, a leader in mobility and networking telecommunications, traces its roots to paper pulping and rubber works in Finland. The Tata Group of India manufactures cars, operates hotels, offers mutual funds, markets food products, and has announced plans for further diversification into service industries.

When can companies gain advantage through unrelated diversification? By finding underlying relatedness despite appearances to the contrary. Nokia's corporate history traces the company's current emphasis on mobile communications products to its early emphasis on paper communications and to the technological competences of its early rubber business. (These links are difficult to measure in modern terms, and yet there is credibility to Nokia's claim.) Researchers have shown that Tata's reputation and extensive engineering capabilities are particularly valuable because it operates in regions where it is difficult to contract on a large scale for specialized services.

One of the most pervasive principles of strategy is that diversification of any sort—related or unrelated—requires the development of a corporate culture and resource-allocation process that influences every division. When diversification involves participation in industries that differ substantially in their evolutionary trajectory and in the phase of development, corporate functions are strained.


## Conclusion: Corporate Strategy That Accounts for Industry Change

Many organizations build corporate strategy from the top down instead of from the bottom up. Decisions are made to enter or acquire new businesses based on their potential to create value for established divisions rather than from a holistic view of the industry. And in many cases these decisions are made on shallow understanding of the needs of buyers and of suppliers in the core business.

Corporate strategy is much more likely to succeed when it is grounded in a detailed understanding of competitive conditions in each business unit, including awareness of industry evolution. How should a company react if Architectural change proceeds more slowly than projected in an established division? What are the stakes for the corporation if an entrepreneurial unit cannot adhere to the dominant model in its industry? Corporate strategy is effective when it is conceived in light of the contingencies that may subsequently emerge in execution.

An effective corporate strategy deals with the risks of compromising the strategy of a specific business unit to benefit the sister divisions on the understanding that too much compromise may raise questions from investors about whether the division would be better operated independently. Stable corporate strategy arises when every division benefits from the incorporation. Achieving this kind of stability is difficult when the character and pace of industry evolution differs across businesses (although there are some exceptions). The reason is that the sharing of activities and of assets becomes difficult to balance when the demands of different divisions are changing asynchronously due to fundamental changes in their industries.

An effective corporate strategy should be internally consistent and should deal clearly with industry evolution and the sustainability of competitive position in each major business unit. The great news is that companies that excel at using diversification to deal effectively with industry change tend to perform significantly better in every division that is affected.[23]

# 8

## Epilogue

CONSULTANTS, STRATEGISTS, BANKERS, and board members often challenge executive management about its plans for dealing with industry change. Many companies—especially large public companies—have merged with rivals, diversified into distribution, and even entered into unrelated businesses to contend with the implications of industry evolution. Companies have set up venture funds only to lose talented executives and significant capital. Even more common have been initiatives to develop entrepreneurial capability and information architecture to defend against the threats associated with change. Many executives complain that simply sustaining position in an industry requires greater and greater investment over time, and that their organizations are constantly fighting against encroachment on performance. The accumulation of disappointments can exhaust the executive team and make it increasingly difficult for functional specialists to respond effectively to opportunities with high potential.

This book provides you with tools for avoiding this cycle of unprofitable investment, disappointment, and unacceptable performance. A basic premise is that investments cannot deliver an acceptable return—that is, innovation cannot succeed—if your plans for the business break the rules for change in your industry. Industries evolve on one of four trajectories: Progressive, Creative, Intermediating, or Radical. There is no middle ground. It is not possible that an industry lies somewhere on a spectrum in between two types, or that an industry belongs to more than one category. Furthermore, each type of change evolves over periods of many years, typically spanning decades.

This book also provides you with tools for identifying opportunities that truly carry the potential to deliver superior performance over the long run. Understanding the trajectory and stage of industry change provides you with the confidence to pursue particular initiatives with full commitment—and without the kind of hedging that makes a firm vulnerable to competitive incursion. By identifying the trajectory of industry change, you can better assess the implications for investment, culture, organization structure, information architecture, and leadership. Your options for responding to change are significantly greater early in the process than later.

There are acid tests for determining which of the four trajectories applies in an industry. You'll recall that Architectural change occurs only when core activities in an industry are threatened with obsolescence and Foundational change occurs when core assets are threatened with obsolescence. By examining whether Architectural and Foundational change are occurring, you can home in on the nature of the trajectory in your business. If a threat of obsolescence exists and is affecting value creation, it is relevant to your future and should be at center stage as you set strategy.

## Operating Within the Bounds of Change

Evaluating the trajectory of change allows you to avoid the most fundamental of errors about how investments in innovation can pay off. The most serious strategic errors involve misdiagnosis of the trajectory in a business. These misdiagnoses are common under each of the four evolutionary trajectories.

Many of the most noted retail dot-coms—for example, Petstore.com, e-Toys, and PlanetRX—got into trouble because they attempted to change the structure of industries on Progressive paths. Instead of playing by established rules for serving customers in their industries, the companies tried to convince buyers to change their preferences. Several dot-coms operated under the idea that their business models would be so compelling that they could actually change the trajectory of industry evolution to their advantage. The plans were to drive industries into Intermediating transformation. Nearly all failed miserably.

Serious strategic errors made by firms in Creative industries often can be traced to the misconception that change is Radical or Progressive. The mistaken perception that the industry is undergoing Radical transformation arises when firms underestimate the relevance of their activities to value creation. This is easy to do when assets are threatened with obsolescence. For example, consider the fate of a pharmaceutical company with expiring patents and a poor track record of innovation in new-drug discovery. The firm may be tempted to conclude that Radical transformation in the industry is under way. The mistake in this logic is in assuming that the poor record of new-drug discovery is a sign that research and development activities across the *industry* will not be relevant to future value creation; they fail to realize that the real problem is ineffective competitive positioning. The mistaken perception that change is Progressive occurs when a firm underestimates the importance of new core assets to value creation. A film production studio makes this error when it assumes that its profitability depends on its library of hits rather than the generation of new films.

Strategic errors occur under Intermediation when executives fail to understand that core activities are threatened. This misperception is common in firms that historically had been on a Progressive trajectory, where the rules of competition require measured, incremental, conservative responses to changes in the environment. Under Intermediation, it is easy to underestimate the threat of obsolescence to core activities because core assets continue to create value. It's tempting to assume that you can quickly transform activities down the road because your capabilities are relevant to buyers and suppliers under both the old and new models. This kind of assumption can lead to disastrous consequences, leaving a firm last in line to develop a strategy for redeploying its assets in a new business.

Strategic errors occur under Radical transformation when companies underestimate the nature of the threat to their assets and activities. There is no question but that early diagnosis is a critical element of success as firms deal with Radical change. Creating a sense of urgency in the organization is a fundamental challenge as the company confronts the obsolescence of its approach. For firms that do recognize the threat associated with Radical transformation, the greatest danger may arise from a lack of leadership. Many great companies have been permanently damaged when their executive teams refused to confront the challenges of Radical transformation simply because the consequences were so daunting.

Avoiding these errors is an antidote to "innovation fatigue," which takes hold after repeated failures to achieve a targeted return on investment in strategic initiatives. Chapter 5 laid out the prerequisites for conforming to the bounds of change within business units, and Chapter 7 discussed the prerequisites for effective corporate strategy. A few of the core themes are discussed below.

### *Architectural Change*

When your industry is changing Architecturally—that is, when you are on an Intermediating or Radical trajectory—staying within the bounds of change depends on getting better information about your buyers and suppliers than you have historically needed. In this situation, buyers are considering new alternatives to your products and services, but may delay purchasing them out of uncertainty, loyalty, or fixed commitments that lock them into dealing with you. As the alternatives improve, buyers may test them, be disappointed, and temporarily renew their commitment to you. If your direct buyers are manufacturers, distributors, or retailers, their businesses may be threatened along with yours, and they may seek to deepen their relationships with you to coordinate a defense against the alternative approach. The same kind of pattern may emerge among suppliers, which may seek to achieve greater efficiencies through defensive alliances with you or your competitors.

As the Architectural threat builds, the defection of buyers and suppliers from your industry is inevitable. The best response depends on the circumstances. If you are in a large and relatively secure segment where buyers are particularly loyal, then the major effect of the change may be the repositioning of rivals that have excess capacity. A detailed analysis of competitors *by segment* is fundamental for understanding the implications of change for the performance of your business unit.

As a business adapts to the shifting economics in each segment of the industry, conflicts within the organization are almost inevitable. Disagreement about the legitimacy of the new approach may give way to frustration about how to coordinate an effective response. Competition within the business for resources commonly occurs as relationships with key buyers are strained. One of the most important and difficult management challenges in this context is in dealing with the tensions that may form within the organization. This book shows that it is imperative to interpret the conflict in terms that reflect market pressures. When managers are held personally accountable for flagging sales and increasing costs, then they have a disincentive to reveal the problems in their businesses. A successful and strategic response requires a clear assessment of how buyer needs, supplier capabilities, and competitive conditions are changing.

### Foundational Change

The prerequisites for effective strategy under Foundational change involve managing the business unit's balance sheet even more vigilantly than normal. Rules of thumb about the rate of depreciation on core assets should be abandoned because the threat of obsolescence accelerates the rate on nearly every asset. Performance depends on understanding which assets are depreciating most quickly, and on finding ways to protect their value cost-effectively.

The process of evaluating the rate of depreciation on assets is complicated by the fact that buyers and suppliers often cannot provide good feedback about their preferences until new products and services are fully commercialized. Chapter 5 illustrated this point by asking you to imagine in advance whether you would be willing to see a movie that will be released in the future. Even if you knew the plot and the actors, you would likely have difficulty assessing your future preferences without seeing the reviews, hearing the post-release buzz, and knowing what will be on your mind when the movie is released. Now imagine instead that you were an executive at a movie studio trying to project the value of your library of current films. Assessing their value depends on forecasting buyer willingness to pay for the new releases in the pipeline even before the buyers themselves have any information about what is forthcoming. And yet to succeed in an industry undergoing Foundational change, accuracy in forecasts such as these is essential.

The forecasts are necessary because they can guide decisions about how to protect the assets you already have. For example, you may decide to accelerate the release of a film to video to harvest its value if you foresee that a blockbuster sequel is in the works. You might sponsor a pilot for a television show based on a successful film or hold the release of a film if it will compete with another that you are offering around the same time. If you've had a number of flops in a row, you might want to take steps to ameliorate the difficulties that the flops created for theatrical exhibitors. The objective is to make investments to protect the system of activities for commercializing products and services based on core assets while their value is robust.

Foundational change also has organizational implications: modularizing and decentralizing decision-making authority so that assets can be created and then retired independently of one another. This insulates the organization as a whole from failure in a specific project or area of the business. In practice, firms accomplish this by outsourcing, allying, and venturing with independent firms as well as by creating separate organizational units that are each dedicated to particular assets.

### Diversification of Change

Corporations often deal with the evolution of particular businesses by diversifying to share and transfer both activities and assets. Chapter 7 offered a number of prerequisites for effective corporate strategy, which cover the following major points:

- Be realistic about the pressures on corporate ownership that will emerge as the corporation's industries evolve.

- Identify a vision for how each business unit will benefit from membership in the corporation.

- Develop clear lines of authority in decision-making about resource allocation.

These principles are important to any effective corporate strategy, but they are especially important when industry evolution motivates diversification. Consider the kinds of pressures on corporate ownership that can arise. If a firm participates in a business that is undergoing Architectural change and then diversifies into a related business to salvage key relationships or assets, then the value of the partnership may eventually dwindle and the capital markets may create pressure for divestiture. Or if a firm participates in multiple industries that are each undergoing Progressive change, then the diversification may be challenged on the grounds that the activity systems are largely distinctive. Anticipating the implications of industry evolution for coordination through diversification rather than through arms-length arrangements can allow you to avoid costly mistakes and to anticipate impediments.

Chapter 7 discussed the "torque" that can develop in corporate strategy as separate divisions evolve by different rules. Even seemingly small differences in the stage of change can create tension in the cultures and the resource-allocation processes of organizations. Imagine a division in the maturity stage of Progressive evolution—in which measured, incremental investments in activities are appropriate—operating under the same corporate umbrella as a division in the declining stage of Progressive change—where the dismantling of activities is under way. In the mature industry, stability and careful execution are critical, while in the declining industry, the shearing off of activities may create major but necessary disruptions. Clarity about the vision for corporate diversification is essential for holding together an organization under this kind of strain.

Similarly, clear lines of decision-making authority are a prerequisite for effective corporate strategy under industry evolution. The *only* justification for joint ownership of divisions is in the sharing and/or transfer of activities and/or assets. As a result, there are inevitable questions about where within the organization decisions will be made about how the sharing or transferring will take place. Questions also arise about whether and how to invest in activities or assets. Industry evolution can make old processes for resolving these questions ineffective. Clarity about decision-making authority both within processes and about changing in the processes is crucial for preserving corporate value.

## Making Better Strategic Decisions

Chapter 1 promised that strategic decision-making would become easier and would lead to better performance for firms that take advantage of industry change. That chapter began with a list of questions that executives regularly confront, and that can be very difficult to address ad hoc. By framing seemingly unrelated decisions in context of broad change in the environment, the implications become clearer. Not only are decisions easier to make, but they become part of a cohesive strategy that leads to better performance over the long run.

The following revisits the issues raised in the questions of chapter 1 and shows how each question can be answered more effectively in context of a strategy for dealing with industry change.

### Reacting to New Technology

In the electricity-generation industry, new technologies such as hydroelectric and nuclear power have broad implications for change in the business. Evaluating the impact using the concepts of this book clarifies their economic implications. Nuclear technology, for example, promises to make petroleum-fueled turbine generators obsolete, and thereby creates Foundational change. In regions where core activities such as downstream marketing and distribution relationships are not threatened, the threat is not Architectural: Electricity is sold the same way as previously. As a result, the industry structure is changing Creatively.

This insight provides you with the confidence to invest and reinvest in core activities despite the underlying change in the business. It suggests that nuclear technology may be important to the organization's long-term economic survival. At the same time, the existing core assets in the business may not all become completely obsolete as a result of the new approach. Even if you are committed not to adopt nuclear technology, an awareness of the tradeoffs is essential to effective decision making.

The broad lesson is that your reaction to new technology should be filtered through a careful assessment of its implications for the core activities and core assets in your industry. The threat of a new technology does not necessarily mean that your business cannot benefit from the new approach. The challenge is in assessing the extent of the threat to the core activities and core assets in your business, and then committing fully to a viable position.

### Innovating Cost-Effectively

Many large companies have sponsored entrepreneurial ventures in an effort to innovate without jeopardizing the integrity of the core business. The goal is to pursue modularized projects that are isolated organizationally and that each can be shut down relatively easily. Unfortunately for many of the sponsoring corporations, the cost has outweighed the benefits. This pattern is not reserved for entrepreneurial venture funds. Executives in firms of all sizes and characteristics have been frustrated with their companies' lack of productivity in generating a return on investments in innovative capabilities.

The ideas in this book affirm that innovation *can* yield a significant return on investment, but only if they are aligned with the course of change in your business. For example, modularized innovation through venture funds is simply inappropriate for dealing with the opportunities in industries on Progressive trajectories. Even under Intermediating and Radical change, the potential for achieving significant returns through venture funds is limited. Initiatives such as venture funds carry the greatest potential in industries undergoing Creative evolution.

## *Improving the Hit Rate on New-Product Introductions*

New-product development is a risky proposition, and yet it is essential for sustaining profitability in almost all businesses. The range of new products introduced to markets encompasses everything from Procter & Gamble's new Swiffer products (mops, dusters, and mitts for household cleaning) to Iridium's satellite-based communications services to Kinko's computer rental service. Executives in all of these businesses face questions about when the market is ready to accept new products, when a product is ahead of its time, and when more development is necessary before commercialization can succeed.

The answers to these questions depend fundamentally on the stage of change in the industry structure. Early in the process of Progressive and Creative change, experimentation is an essential element of strategy for firms that intend to become leaders in the business. Later in the process, new-product development continues to be important but must take on a different character to generate superior performance. Under Progressive change, new products *cannot* succeed if they disrupt the system of underlying core activities, but under Creative change, unusual new products are the centerpiece of successful strategy. New products in industries undergoing Intermediating and Radical change are likely to be most effective when they are part of a program for retiring core activities and assets. The message: Whether to pursue new products, and how to time their introduction, depends in a basic way on both the trajectory and stage of industry evolution.

## *Reacting to and Rejecting Feedback*

When should you solicit buyer and supplier feedback? When should you rely on it as basic to your decision processes? When should you actively reject feedback from buyers and from suppliers? The answers to these questions again depend on the trajectory and stage of change in your industries.

Perhaps one of the more controversial messages here is that your existing buyers and suppliers cannot provide reliable feedback in many situations. For example, under Creative change, it may be difficult for buyers to envision in advance how they will benefit from a product that you have in development. Under Intermediating change, your suppliers have incentives to tighten their relationships with you to defend against a threat of obsolescence—and if you succumb to their pressure you may be lashing your organization to a sinking ship. In yet other cases, such as the maturity stage of Progressive change, buyer feedback is essential to successful strategy.

### Rushing Versus Refining

The dot-coms of the late 1990s have been criticized for the ways in which they rushed their services and products to market, often without the systems in place to fulfill and deliver on orders. The compulsion to rush for many of these companies was a sense that competitive pressure was so intense that speed was essential to market presence. Of course, there are also companies that are known for testing and retesting products before introducing them to market, and then losing ground to competitors because of the associated delays.

The right choice—whether to rush or refine products before bringing them to market—depends on the stage of industry change. During a shakeout, speed to market may be necessary to adhere to the dominant model for organizing activities in the business. For almost all of the dot-coms, this pressure was an illusion based on the flurry of entry associated with widespread access to the World Wide Web. In fact, most of the dot-coms were new entrants into industries that were evolving on a range of different trajectories. Some of the most famous dot-coms, such as e-Toys, had even entered industries that were well into maturity, and as a result, their rush to market did not conform to the rules of change.

### Using Alliances Effectively

The mid-1990s and early 2000s were characterized by a wave of interest in alliances and partnerships as mechanisms for delivering value and coping with industry change. While many alliances do not involve much economic activity, some have been viewed as crucial to the survival and performance of firms. For example, consider the success of Fuji Xerox in promoting the development, distribution, and sale of small copiers, which by many accounts surpassed the capabilities of both of its parents in this business. Other alliances have served as a precursor to acquisitions, while yet others have led to long-term contracts between a firm and its buyers.

There is no sense in which pursuing alliances is a comprehensive strategy for dealing with change. Alliances are simply organizational arrangements that tie firms together. A strategy requires evaluating which *kinds* of partnerships in the first place—if any at all—are likely to lead to superior performance. As a result, a firm's policies for accepting, rejecting, and pursuing alliance proposals should be part of a broader plan for dealing with industry change and with the implications for its competitive position.

Consider the role of alliances under the following situations of industry change. The role for coordination between direct competitors under Progressive change is relatively limited because of the nature of rivalry and the terms of competition, and yet alliances between firms and their suppliers may serve as powerful sources of advantage (as Wal-Mart and Procter & Gamble have demonstrated). Under Creative change, alliances between competitors may allow companies to improve the utilization of their underlying systems of activities. For example, in the music recording industry of the 1980s (which was undergoing Creative change prior to the current Intermediation), firms regularly subcontracted with one another for CD-pressing capacity. Under Intermediating change, alliances between a firm and its competitors, suppliers, or buyers may be essential to strategic positioning to defend the structure of the business, although the alliances almost always break down under continuing evolution. Similarly, alliances between competitors under Radical transformation may allow for the efficient rationalization of capacity.

While there is no general rule for how alliances can be used to improve performance, there are many situations in which alliances can be powerful mechanisms for effecting a transition through the course of change.

### Leading Effectively

Management textbooks often suggest that successful entrepreneurs don't have the organizational acumen to lead their firms into maturity. The drive, ambition, and scrappiness that lead to success in the experimental stages of an industry's development will damage a larger organization. Questions also arise about the appropriate leader in a firm going through an Architectural transition. Should the same management team that built a business lead during its dismemberment? Can executives with the skills to motivate an organization during a period of stability be effective during the turbulence of decline or Architectural change?

The techniques in this book suggest that the answers to these questions depend on the trajectory and stage of industry evolution as well as the strategy that the business will employ to deal with impending change. Walt Disney led his firm from its inception during the fragmentation stage of the film-production industry into maturity with enormous success. The skills required to lead a business in an industry undergoing Creative change may be relatively similar during the fragmentation, shakeout, and maturity stages: Disney's ability to identify high-potential projects was as important to the company in maturity as in fragmentation. Similarly, the skills required to lead a business through the early stages of Radical transformation may be similar to those that were important prior to the Architectural change, simply because the execution may not change much until later in the process.

Questions about the appropriate leadership team should be answered in tandem with the expression of a strategy for dealing with industry change. Leading the implementation of a strategy depends on more than just the skills to envision how the company can generate profits—a leader also must have the presence and talent to evoke commitment across the organization. Answering questions about the right person to lead change requires a comprehensive assessment of the strategic requirements as well as of the capabilities of the individual candidates for the role.

### Tolerating Poor Performance

Organizations with poor performance often invest too much in pursuit of a business idea that cannot pay off given the conditions of the industry. The executive team hangs on in the hope that buyer preferences will change, supplier capabilities will improve, and competition will abate. And yet occasionally, an organization with a history of poor performance does go through a spectacular turnaround and finally recoups years of investments.

When should a firm tolerate poor performance and continue to invest in a business idea that has not yet met forecasts? The framework in this book suggests that the prospects for a turnaround in performance are substantially greater in the earliest stages of Progressive and Creative change than in almost any other situation. Intermediating change can create the illusion of potential in the business, but achieving a deferred return on this kind of trajectory is difficult at best. Pulling the plug on an approach with poor potential is difficult but necessary in these situations. Radical change often delivers excellent short-term results in its early stages, but the prospects for long-term profitability are dim except in unusual circumstances.

Understanding industry evolution and its implications for strategy can provide you with a foundation for ensuring the firm's survival over the long run. It also can improve the efficiency of your decisions and provide you with the background necessary to forecast performance more effectively. But the real payoff to understanding industry evolution is in generating strategic options ahead of the competition. Achieving and sustaining superior performance depends on preparing the organization for forthcoming change and capitalizing on its implications.

# Notes

## Preface

1. The theory on industry evolution has not developed fully.

2. Michael E. Porter described the importance of the course to the development of his analytical frameworks in "An Interview with Michael Porter," by Nicholas Argyres and Anita M. McGahan, *Academy of Management Executive* (May 2002): 41–53.

## Chapter 1

1. An early version of some of the ideas expressed in this book appears in "How Industries Evolve," *Business Strategy Review* (Autumn 2000): 1–16.

2. Alternative definitions of innovation involving technology development and deployment do not cover all the issues associated with the commitment of resources today to achieve better performance in the future. As defined here, "innovation" is not an abstract industry-level phenomenon but rather reflects specific decisions made within an organization to invest for the future. This approach avoids the confusion that is sometimes created when the term is used more loosely to discuss scientific advances regardless of whether the advances lead to profitable new ventures.

3. In some situations, tradeoffs arise between these goals. Richard Foster and Sarah Kaplan offer evidence on this tradeoff in *Creative Destruction: Why Companies That Are Built to Last Underperform the Market—And How to Successfully Transform Them* (NY: Doubleday/Currency, 2001).

4. The term "Creative" reflects the discussion in Richard E. Caves, *Creative Industries: Contracts between Art and Commerce* (Cambridge: Harvard University Press, 2000).

5. It may be tempting to try to make progress by moving an industry off a trajectory of change, but like moving the barriers on a highway, the effort required is almost always too great to be worthwhile, and failure can be devastating.

6. A threat of obsolescence to core assets occurs when a new approach accelerates the rate of depreciation. In Progressive industries, this threat is absent.

7. Competitive advantage requires distinctiveness within the broad parameters established by the dominant model.

8. Anita M. McGahan, David B. Yoffie, and Les Vadasz, "Creating Value and Setting Standards: The Lessons of Consumer Electronics for Personal Digital Assistants," in *Competing in the Age of Digital Convergence*, ed. Yoffie (Boston: Harvard Business School Press Press, 1996): 227–264.

9. The five forces were defined by Michael E. Porter in his seminal book *Competitive Strategy: Techniques for Analyzing Industries and Competitors* (New York: Free Press, 1980).

## Chapter 2

1. As noted in figure 1-2, this approach reflects the definition of value creation in Adam M. Brandenburger and Harborne Stuart, "Value-Based Business Strategy," Journal of Economics and Management Strategy 5:1 (spring 1996), 5–24.

2. Tangible assets are balance-sheet items. An analysis of an industry's trajectory may be made even more rigorous by exploiting the affinities between core activities and core assets and the industry's financial profile.

3. The fact that activities and assets fall into a hierarchy creates opportunity for further analysis to identify the ways in which assets and activities are related.

4. Previous authors have used the term "Architectural change" to describe disruptions in industry structure. See Rebecca M. Henderson and Kim B. Clark, "Architectural innovation: the reconfiguration of existing product technologies and the failure of established firms," *Administrative Science Quarterly* 35, no. 1 (2002): 9–30; *and Michael L. Tushman and Charles A. O'Reilly III, Winning Through Innovation: A Practical Guide to Leading Organizational Change and Renewal* (Boston: Harvard Business School Press, 2002). The definition of Architectural transformation here is somewhat more restrictive than that used in most prior studies.

5. In "What is Strategy?," *Harvard Business Review* (November–December 1996): 61–78, Michael E. Porter shows how activity maps can be used to identify linkages.

6. This figure reflects new-car dealerships in the United States as reported online by the National Automobile Dealers Association.

7. After this final transition back to a stable Progressive or Creative trajectory, the industry may appear to be a segment within a new industry. This may well be an illusion, however. Unless the established industry operates on the dominant model of the new industry, it remains separate.

## Chapter 3

1. Many of these ideas were formalized by William Abernathy and James Utterback in "Patterns of Industrial Innovation," *Technology Review* (June–July 1978): 41–47, following an extensive product-life-cycle literature in the marketing field. The S-Curve model was further developed by Richard Foster in *Innovation: The Attacker's Advantage* (New York: Summit Books, 1986).

2. Please keep in mind that general merchandise retailing and discount retailing were distinct businesses that followed different evolutionary paths. Today, general merchandise retailing is in the dominance stage of Radical change, and discount retailing is in the mature stage of Progressive change.

3. The form of the traditional contract is described in "RCA Records: The Digital Revolution" by Cate Reavis, Caren-Isabel Knoop, and Jeffrey Rayport, Harvard Business School case 9-800-014 (Revised October 25, 1999).

4. *Shattuck v. Klotzbach*, Massachusetts Supreme Court. No. 01-1109A, December 11, 2001.

5. Clayton M. Christensen, in *The Innovator's Dilemma: When New Technologies Cause Great Firms to Fail* (Boston: Harvard Business School Publishing, 1997), emphasizes that the technical performance of firms in the emergent segment is not as great as in the mass market. The idea is that the overall performance on established criteria of a new technology such as encryption software is not as high initially as an old technology such as overnight letter delivery. This insight rests on the idea that technical performance should be defined broadly enough to include all the attributes of the technology, including its costs. By this definition the lower technological performance is evident in the fact that only a segment of the market adopts the new approach. The explanation offered here rests on a somewhat more restrictive definition of technical performance, in which the cost of the new technology is independent of other attributes used to assess its overall effectiveness.

### Chapter 4

1. See Louis V. Gerstner, Jr., *Who Says Elephants Can't Dance?* (New York: HarperBusiness, 2002).

2. Adam M. Brandenburger and Harborne Stuart suggest this method in "Value-Based Business Strategy," *Journal of Economics and Management Strategy* (Spring 1996): 5–24.

3. See Brandenburger and Stuart, "Value-Based Business Strategy," for a discussion of value creation.

4. You'll recall from chapter 1 that this exercise, which is developed from suggestions by Brandenburger and Stuart's "Value-Based Business Strategy," involves imagining how the value created by an industry would change if an activity were immediately disallowed.

5. When supporting activities but not core activities are threatened, the industry may be moving into a period of decline in its life cycle. For example, the brewing industry is likely to see a slowdown in industry volume over the next few years because of the economic recession; from the Beer Institute, "State of the Industry: Industry Growth Pauses," Annual Report 2000–2001, p. 1. Because there is no threat from a new approach, there is no Architectural transformation. The industry may simply be entering a period of decline.

6. Brandenburger and Stuart "Value-Based Business Strategy."

7. Information on the S&L crisis is available online at <www.fdic.gov/bank/historical/history> (accessed 22 February 2004), and especially in "History of the Eighties—Lessons for the Future, Volume 1: An Examination of the Banking Crises of the 1980s and early 1990s." The figures reported in this and the subsequent paragraph on S&Ls are drawn from chapter 4 of this history, "The Savings and Loan Crisis and its Relationship to Banking."

8. Matthew Sandoval and Stephen P. Bradley, "NTT Docomo: The Future of the Wireless Internet?" Harvard Business School case 9-701-013 (Revised October 17, 2000).

9. Dale O. Coxe and Anita M. McGahan, "African Communications Group," Harvard Business School case 9-796-128 (Revised March 4, 1996).

10. This insight about buyers is central in Clayton M. Christensen's book *The Innovator's Dilemma: When Technologies Cause Great Firms to Fail* (Boston: Harvard Business School Publishing, 1997). Here the role of suppliers receives more emphasis. Thus, the definition for Architectural change is more restrictive than the definition of disruptive change in Christensen's work.

11. Christensen, *The Innovator's Dilemma*, explains this.

12. Ibid.

13. In an excellent book on the role of assets in strategy, *Commitment* (NY: Free Press, 1991), Pankaj Ghemawat showed that assets are strategically important when they are specialized, durable, and hard to trade. This "resource-based view" of strategy focuses on the strategic importance of assets.

14. For the Cape Cod ice cream shops, the deeds on storefronts are core assets.

15. As noted earlier in figure 1-1, assets may be tangible or intangible.

16. The numbers reported here on the consumption and group of soft drinks and bottled water come from Exhibit 1 of Sharon Foley and David B. Yoffie, "Cola Wars Continue: Coke vs. Pepsi in the 1990s," Harvard Business School case 9-794-055 (revised March 31, 2000).

17. Bottled water also did not pose an Architectural threat in the first place, since bottled water did not threaten to make obsolete the relationships of the soft-drink concentrate manufacturers with their suppliers and buyers. I use this example only to make clear why growth in the new industry must be above a threshold high enough to lead to convergence.


## Chapter 5

1. You'll recall that the distinction between operational effectiveness and distinctive positioning is defined in Michael E. Porter's "What is Strategy?" *Harvard Business Review*, November–December 1996, 61–78.

2. For a discussion please see Michael E. Porter, *Competitive Advantage: Creating and Sustaining Superior Performance* (New York: Free Press, 1985).


## Chapter 6

1. *Money* magazine published a list in November 2002 of companies that had generated the best return to shareholders over the past thirty years. Southwest Airlines and Wal-Mart Stores topped the list, which suggests that the risk-return profile in Progressive industries can be quite favorable.

2. In 1995, Snapple's revenue declined and it posted a significant loss. After a contentious fight, Quaker Oats divested Snapple to Triarc in 1997. Quaker Oats was acquired by PepsiCo in 2000. The story points to the importance of executing a strategy effectively.

3. Michael Lewis's *Moneyball: The Art of Winning an Unfair Game* (New York: W.W. Norton & Company, Inc., 2003) chronicles the story.

4. This is the central idea in Michael E. Porter's "What is Strategy?" *Harvard Business Review*, November–December 1996, 61–78.

## Chapter 7

1. Anita M. McGahan and Belen Villalonga, "Does Governance Form Matter? Evidence from Stock-Market Reactions to Acquisitions and Alliances," Boston University and Harvard Business School manuscript (2002). The statistics in this paragraph on the numbers of divestitures, acquisitions, and alliances among members of the *Fortune* 100 are all drawn from this analysis, which draws on the SDC database published by Thomson Financial. The remaining statistics in this paragraph are also from this source. Please note that the SDC database includes only deals that were completed and material in their impact.

2. Michael E. Porter makes this argument in "From Competitive Advantage to Corporate Strategy," *Harvard Business Review*, May-June 1987, 2-21.

3. Sharon Foley and David B. Yoffie, "Cola Wars Continue: Coke vs. Pepsi in the 1990s," Harvard Business School case 9-794-055 (revised March 31, 2000).

4. C. K. Prahalad and Gary Hamel, "The Core Competence of the Corporation," *Harvard Business Review*, May–June 1990, 79-90; Anita M. McGahan, "Philips' Compact Disc Introduction (A)," Harvard Business School case 7-972-035 (revised November 26, 1993).

5. Prahalad and Hamel, "The Core Competence of the Corporation."

6. Jon K. Rust and Thomas Eisenmann, "Boston.com," Harvard Business School case 9-800-165 (revised August 30, 2000).

7. Ibid.

8. Michael L. Tushman and Charles A. O'Reilly III discuss this problem in *Winning Through Innovation: A Practical Guide to Leading Organizational Change and Renewal* (Boston: Harvard Business School Press, 2002).

9. The company lost $189.7 million on revenues of $397.8 million in 2000. See <www.hoovers.com> (accessed February 10, 2002).

10. See Jack O'Toole, *Forming the Future: Lessons from the Saturn Corporation* (Cambridge: Blackwell, 1996) for a detailed discussion.

11. The Saturn Web site, <www.saturn.com> (accessed January 24, 2002), reports that engineers came up with the idea in 1982.

12. Saturn won a wide range of accolades in the early 1990s for its cars, including the highest rating for a small car from *Consumer Reports* as reported in Greg Keller and Anita M. McGahan, "Saturn: A Different Kind of Car Company," Harvard Business School case 7-795-010 (revised November 21, 1994).

13. Ibid.

14. Leann Zalasky, "Greyhounds: From Racetrack to Recliner," *River Country* 1, no. 7 (July 2002): 31.

15. See Sidney G. Winter, "Knowledge and Competence as Strategic Assets," in D. Teece, ed., *The Competitive Challenge: Strategies for Industrial Innovation and Renewal* (Cambridge: Ballinger Publishing, 1987).

16. Qualcomm Annual Report, 2001.

17. Anita M. McGahan, "Competition, Strategy, and Business Performance: 1981–1997," *California Management Review* 41, no. 3 (spring 1999): 74–101.

18. Matthew Sandoval and Stephen P. Bradley, "NTT DoCoMo: The Future of the Wireless Internet?" Harvard Business School case 9-701-013. (revised October 17, 2000).

19. Ibid.

20. NTT DoCoMo Web site, "Corporate Highlights." <www.nttdocomo.com> (accessed October 16, 2003).

21. "NTT Announces Financial Results for Fiscal Year Ended March 31, 2002," NTT Press Release, May 14, 2002.

22. See Henry Chesbrough, "Graceful Exits and Foregone Opportunities: Xerox's Management of its Technology Spinoff Organizations" *Business History Review* (2001): 803–837, and Mary Tripsas and Giovanni Gavetti, "Capabilities, Cognition and Inertia: Evidence from Digital Imaging" *Strategic Management Review* (October–November 2000): 1147–1161.

23. Evidence for this appears in Anita M. McGahan, "Competition, Strategy, and Business Performance: 1981–1997," *California Management Review* 41, no. 3 (spring 1999): 74–101.

# Index

# About the Author

*Anita M. McGahan*, Everett V. Lord Distinguished Faculty Scholar and Professor and Chairman of Strategy and Policy at the Boston University School of Management, is also a Senior Institute Associate at the Institute for Strategy and Competitiveness at Harvard University. She holds a B.A. from Northwestern University, an A.M. and Ph.D. in business economics from Harvard University, and an M.B.A. from the Harvard Business School, where she was a Baker Scholar. Prior to entering academics, she spent several years at McKinsey & Company and at Morgan Stanley.

McGahan has taught courses in strategy to M.B.A. candidates, executives, and doctoral students at both Boston University and the Harvard Business School. She is the author of more than sixty articles and case studies on strategic issues of competitive advantage, industry evolution, and financial performance. In 2001, she was named by *CIO* magazine as one of five international experts on the strategic use of technology, and was elected in 2003 into the leadership cycle in the Business Policy and Strategy Division of the Academy of Management. McGahan's academic publications include studies on the brewing, consumer electronics, insurance, and pharmaceutical industries. She is coeditor of the twenty-first volume of *Advances in Strategic Management* in 2004, and is on the editorial boards of the *Strategic Management Journal*, *Academy of Management Review*, *Management Science*, and *Strategic Organization*.